W9-ATO-367

THE FUTURE OF JUST WAR

EST. 75 1938
YEARS
THE UNIVERSITY OF GEORGIA PRESS 2013

STUDIES IN SECURITY AND INTERNATIONAL AFFAIRS

THE FUTURE
OF JUST WAR

New Critical Essays

Edited by Caron E. Gentry and Amy E. Eckert

The University of Georgia Press
Athens and London

© 2014 by the University of Georgia Press

Athens, Georgia 30602

www.ugapress.org

All rights reserved

Set in Minion Pro by Graphic Composition, Inc., Bogart, Georgia.

Printed and bound by Sheridan Books, Inc.

The paper in this book meets the guidelines for
permanence and durability of the Committee on
Production Guidelines for Book Longevity of the
Council on Library Resources.

Most University of Georgia Press titles are available from popular e-book vendors.

Printed in the United States of America

17 16 15 14 13 P 5 4 3 2 1

Library of Congress Cataloging-in-Publication Data

The future of just war : new critical essays / edited by Caron E. Gentry and Amy E. Eckert.

    pages cm. — (Studies in security and international affairs)

    Includes bibliographical references and index.

    ISBN-13: 978-0-8203-3950-4 (hardback)

    ISBN-10: 0-8203-3950-4 (hardcover)

    ISBN-13: 978-0-8203-4560-4 (paperback)

    1. Just war doctrine. 2. War—Moral and ethical aspects. I. Gentry, Caron E., author,
editor of compilation. II. Eckert, Amy, author, editor of compilation.

U21.2.F874 2014

172'.42—dc23

2013020499

British Library Cataloging-in-Publication Data available

CONTENTS

Introduction   *1*
Caron E. Gentry and Amy E. Eckert

SECTION ONE. *Jus ad Bellum*

CHAPTER ONE. Epistemic Bias: Legitimate Authority and
Politically Violent Nonstate Actors   *17*
Caron E. Gentry

CHAPTER TWO. Strategizing in an Era of Conceptual Change:
Security, Sanctioned Violence, and New Military Roles   *30*
Kimberly A. Hudson and Dan Henk

CHAPTER THREE. Is Just Intervention Morally Obligatory?   *48*
Luke Glanville

CHAPTER FOUR. Private Military Companies and the
Reasonable Chance of Success   *62*
Amy E. Eckert

SECTION TWO. *Jus in Bello*

CHAPTER FIVE. Postheroic U.S. Warfare and the
Moral Justification for Killing in War   *79*
Sebastian Kaempf

CHAPTER SIX. From Smart to Autonomous Weapons:
Confounding Territoriality and Moral Agency   *98*
Brent J. Steele and Eric A. Heinze

CHAPTER SEVEN. An Alternative to Nuclear Weapons? Proportionality,
Discrimination, and the Conventional Global Strike Program   *115*
Alexa Royden

CHAPTER EIGHT. Rethinking Intention and Double Effect   *130*
Harry D. Gould

CHAPTER NINE. Just War without Civilians   *148*
Laura Sjoberg

SECTION THREE. *Jus post Bellum*

CHAPTER TEN. *Jus post Bellum*: Justice in the Aftermath of War   *167*
Robert E. Williams Jr.

Contributors   *181*

Index   *185*

INTRODUCTION

Caron E. Gentry and Amy E. Eckert

Critical scholarship questions the ontological and epistemological constructions that are taken to be "natural," a "given," or too long-standing to question.[1]
Like security studies, terrorism studies, or international relations, the Just War
tradition also contains such assumptions.[2] The Just War tradition assumes a
particular epistemic perspective: in this current global system, the state is *the*
legitimate authority able to possess right intention, justify cause, and maneuver
last resort and is the sole entity in possession of the ability to direct proportionate and discriminate violence. The presumptions in favor of the state can
quickly lead to further presumptions that the state always acts justly when it
wages war, that conventional weapons do not violate discrimination and proportionality, and that civilians, and not military forces, are at the center of a
state's consideration of moral harm. Such thinking creates operational binaries:
states are always the legitimate author and nonstate actors illegitimate;[3] the use
of conventional weapons always falls within discrimination and proportionality, and nuclear weapons do not; military leaders need to consider the moral
harm to noncombatants but not necessarily to soldiers.

These operational binaries often lead to uncritical assessments of claims
about war and justice. Epistemic assumptions and hermeneutics need to be
challenged and rescripted in light of an international system where nonstate
actors, including rebel groups, terrorist movements, criminal syndicates, and
corporations, engage in political violence, where state-to-state wars are on the
decline, and where the imperative to reconfigure sovereignty as a system of
shared responsibility for individual well-being so as to require intervention for
humanitarian purposes is becoming more accepted. Moreover, even when states
do engage in war, their methods, strategies, and weapons are often presumed to
be just even if they break the norms of war and the international system. Both
by the immediate presumption of state legitimacy and through the claim of
supreme emergency, state violations of international norms are often allowed
to "slide." Just as previous periods of political crisis have caused the tradition
to change and grow,[4] these new developments provide the prospect for similar

growth and transformation. Thus, this collection argues, within the spirit of the tradition, that as a *tradition* without a singular defining voice that has evolved over millennia the Just War tradition needs to critically engage some of the practices that have been epistemologically written out of or not-as-of-yet dealt with by *jus ad bellum*, by *jus in bello*, and in the continued emergence of *jus post bellum*. The chapters in this volume come together to point to the erosion of epistemic norms for mutuality, reciprocity, and moral agency as well to argue for the continued complication of conflating sovereignty with legitimacy.

While the chapters in this volume support the Just War tradition, they are also mindful of criticisms toward it. Prominent American pacifist Stanley Hauerwas states that "violence used in the name of justice . . . is simply a matter of the power of some over others."[5] Speaking from within the tradition, Nick Rengger has stated, "Just War is still just war."[6] Being aware that when power and force are used there are always costs has typically imbued the tradition with intention, meditation, and caution. Yet, contemporary policy invocations of Just War, such as the Bush administration's use of it to justify the wars in Afghanistan and Iraq, undermines these nuanced and careful considerations. The administration reached the decision to wage war and then deployed Just War terminology to create a moralistic justification for its political choice.[7] The Bush Doctrine, in particular, sought to capture the language of preemptive self-defense to wage war against states that supported or harbored terrorists.[8] By eliding preemptive self-defense against imminent threat and preventive war against a future threat, the Bush Doctrine and its wars threatened to dilute Just War principles by utilizing the moral language of the tradition to serve political purposes. This manipulation is not limited to policy circles; it was also found in scholarship that supported both wars, such as Jean Bethke Elshtain's *Just War against Terror*,[9] in which she argued that the hegemony of the United States necessitated intervention in Afghanistan and that the United States had fulfilled enough *jus ad bellum* criteria to do so legitimately.

Yet, there was a significant backlash to Elshtain's reasoning within academic communities[10] and later to President Bush's manipulation of *jus ad bellum* criteria, particularly "preemptive" self-defense. Thus, one potential response to this misuse of the Just War tradition is cynicism about the utility of discourse about war and morality. In contrast, *The Future of Just War* takes seriously the possibility of applying the principles of the Just War tradition to contemporary normative problems while being wary of the (mis)use of power. Specifically, the book uses emerging or evolving issues to explore the demands, limitations, and promise of the Just War tradition.

THE TRADITION AND THE MARGINS

As a tradition, Just War scholarship has been able to adapt to contemporary crises and situations. Such adaptation spurns debate and conversation—a method and means of pushing its thinking forward. With a few notable exceptions, like Eric A. Heinze and Brent J. Steele's 2009 volume and Laura Sjoberg's feminist critique of the war in Iraq,[11] the recent proliferation of Just War literature remains welded to traditional (conceivably outdated) conceptualizations of Just War; for instance, chapters in this book argue that Just War needs to be pushed to deal with substate actors within the realm of legitimate authority, the ongoing issue with private military companies, and the indiscriminate and disproportionate rapid deployment of conventional weapons under Conventional Prompt Global Strike, and reciprocity when casualty aversion has become a key operational objective. These developments challenge traditional Just War assumptions like the preference in favor of the state or the dichotomy between conventional and nuclear weapons. These underpinnings, which in many cases date back centuries, cannot be applied to contemporary challenges in the absence of new interpretation.

The need to bring interpretation and understanding back into Just War reasoning also addresses another trend that potentially marginalizes the tradition. As recent policymakers or scholars have tried to make the Just War criterion legalistic, as in Elshtain's *Just War against Terror*, they have weakened the tradition's ability to draw from and adjust to its contemporaneous setting. It is particularly troubling that some scholars have begun conflating the tradition with an epic battle of good versus evil. While it is true that the tradition is rooted in moral and normative perspectives, typically tied to Catholic theology, Just War scholars in the 1600s, particularly Alberico Gentili, recognized that no one had a full grasp on which side of a war lay the ultimate good or a blessing from God. Mutuality then applies: two enemy states may be at war, but they are at war *together*, and from this "brotherhood of death"[12] the methods and means of fighting war have been established in the tradition. As a result, *jus in bello* rules came to be as significant as *jus ad bellum* considerations.[13] This tension, though, persists. Contemporary warfare has transformed this mutuality by introducing a problematic power dynamic between those lucky enough to have advanced technology and those who do not.

It has been long held that the achievement of justice can come only through serious consideration and thought—this can be traced throughout Western thought—from Plato to present scholars, such as Tarik Kochi and Virginia Held. There are, of course, exceptions to this, and such exceptions make this book possible; these include but are not limited to Michael Gross's well-received *Moral Dilemmas of Modern War* and the Just War classic, Michael Walzer's *Just and Unjust Wars*.[14] Yet, legalism inhibits such reflection and meditation on what it means to achieve justice in the contemporary setting.

Furthermore, there is growing concern that the check-mark legalism with the addition of positivist "rationale-ity"[15] has begun to define Just War policy-making. This legalism reflects not only the aforementioned epistemological starting point but also how such thinking intersects with other binaries in International Relations. In *Sovereignty, Rights, and Justice*, Chris Brown argues that the Westphalian system has constructed states as "insiders" and nonstates as "outsiders." And while we must recognize that states do provide security and stability, it is when one does not reflect on the reification of power that one becomes perhaps too comfortable with how it may be used to create, replicate, and maintain structural and actual violence. Parallels may be drawn to Just War thinking.

Brown delineates how intervention for humanitarian purposes previous to the end of the Cold War were only staged by the West for people that were Western or held Western attributes—for instance, intervention in Lebanon to protect and aid Maronite Christians.[16] As Sebastian Kaempf mentions here and in previous publications, the Just War tradition has been brushed with more than a twinge of Western superiority. During colonialism and imperialism, Just War criteria were only applicable to wars between Europeans (white and Christian).[17] Further, in the tradition, states as insiders are granted automatic legitimacy.[18] Such insider status does not have to be a negative. As Luke Glanville argues in his chapter, sovereignty can be a starting point for intervening in humanitarian crises. Yet, we still have to engage carefully with this construction of legitimacy.

In contemporary classics, such as Walzer's *Just and Unjust Wars*, and more recent well-regarded work by Bellamy (*Just Wars*) and the more controversial Elshtain, legitimate statehood is conflated with a liberal democracy that is respectful of human rights (at least within its borders) and pits this normatively framed state against "extranormal" actors. This exiles actors who do not reflect such figurative and actual characteristics from the tradition, as argued here by Caron E. Gentry. Such a dichotomy cannot stand as interstate wars are on the decline and as civil and extranormal wars are happening with increased frequency. Questions that arise from current conflicts, both interstate wars and failed state conflicts, include how to best intervene, not just for civilians there but for military personnel, as complicated here by Kimberly A. Hudson and Dan Henk, as well as how is a better peace best secured, as discussed in Robert E. Williams Jr.'s *jus post bellum* chapter.

It seems to be somewhat forgotten that Just War thinking is meant to limit and slow the process to war. As Nick Rengger has written, Just Wars are limited as well as few and far between.[19] While this statement stems more from pessimism about human nature's (in)ability to handle power, if we hold tightly to Just War dictums and only go to war when it is just, then we will not be going to war often. Nicholas Fotion adds to this: Just War thinking "should prevent war if it is to be good for anything."[20]

Yet the issues that need to be addressed by the tradition are not just within *jus ad bellum*; epistemic problems are also embedded in the construction of *jus in bello* methodology. Many *jus in bello* norms, including command responsibility, implicitly assume the hierarchical structure associated with a state military, as well as a sharp divide between combatants and civilians. Both of these assumptions become problematic. Peter W. Singer has done an excellent job bringing attention to technology, which can be problematic with respect to the problem of distinguishing between combatants and civilians from afar.[21] Amy E. Eckert's piece in this volume incorporates private military companies (PMCS), which fall outside the hierarchical structure of state militaries and, because they are formally civilians who are performing military functions, erode the line between combatants and civilians. The reintroduction of private force as a significant factor in conflict introduces a fluidity to conflict that poses problems for *jus ad bellum* criteria, most notably the reasonable chance of success. Brent J. Steele and Eric A. Heinze further contribute to this conversation in their chapter by questioning how unmanned aerial vehicles (UAVS) challenge the autonomy, intentionality, and responsibility foundations of moral agency. Sebastian Kaempf's chapter engages this as well by challenging how risk aversion has fundamentally eroded reciprocity in *jus in bello*.

The essays in this book seek to reorient the tradition around its core concerns of preventing the unjust use of force by states and limiting the harm

inflicted on vulnerable populations such as civilian noncombatants and pris-
oners of war. Traditional Just War criteria have become weakened through
their use (or abuse) in providing moralistic justification for war. In addition,
the increasing complexity of twenty-first-century warfare poses new problems
that the tradition has yet to confront. The pursuit of these challenges involves
both a reclaiming of traditional Just War principles, such as reciprocity, as well
as the application of Just War principles to emerging issues, such as the growing
use of robotics in war or the privatization of force. The essays share a commitment to the idea that the tradition requires a rigorous application of "Just War"
principles rather than the satisfaction of a checklist of criteria to be met before
waging just "war" in the service of national interest.

THE STRUCTURING OF THE BOOK

As alluded to above, the chapters engage common themes of sovereignty and
mutuality. The first shared theme deals with the Just War tradition's conflation
of sovereignty with moral agency and legitimacy, which has become increasingly
in need of being problematized. Several chapters in the volume offer insight
into how state sovereignty is the "center of gravity" within the Just War tradition. From this center, ideas of moral and political legitimacy as well as legiti-
mating norms revolve. This can be both harmful and helpful. Both Caron E.
Gentry's and Laura Sjoberg's chapters conclude that sovereignty and legitimate
authority's historic conceptualizations have lent themselves to problematic performances of morality and power politics. Yet, sovereignty still grants a method
for acting and means of responsibility taking, which is troubled by Harry D.
Gould's deconstruction of Double Effect in his chapter. While the "Responsibility to Protect" (R2P) doctrine erodes sovereignty through the authority of
suprastate organizations and by weakening it with the acceptance of intervention for humanitarian purposes, Luke Glanville's chapter also offers how sovereignty creates a moral imperative. Finally, Robert E. Williams Jr.'s introduction to *jus post bellum* argues that a responsibility to ethically resolve war exists,
relating it to human rights and state sovereignty.

The second theme engages the important epistemic platforms upon which
the Just War tradition has been built in a conceptualization of mutuality.
The following chapters build upon one another nicely as Brent J. Steele and
Eric A. Heinze argue how unmanned aerial vehicles have fundamentally altered
responsibility and sovereignty in international affairs and the Just War tradi-

tion. From this idea of responsibility integral to mutuality, Amy E. Eckert's chapter articulates a disconnect in the tradition between the current usage of the private military industry and a reasonable chance of success. Alexa Royden's examination of Just War thinking on nuclear weapons and the understood mutual risk in deployment demonstrates how this has led to an uncritical acceptance of rapid deployment of conventional weapons, which may result in indiscriminate and disproportionate noncombatant death. Sebastian Kaempf's chapter highlights how an overcommitment to protecting soldiers' lives in U.S. military policy has betrayed notions to reciprocity and mutuality. Alternatively, Kimberly A. Hudson and Dan Henk's piece on human security actually argues that relevant emerging policies put the mental and physical health of U.S. soldiers in harm's way.

As we encourage the reader to find these themes throughout the chapters, we have still opted to structure the book in a straightforward and traditional manner through the use of the core concepts of the Just War tradition: *jus ad bellum*, *jus in bello*, and *jus post bellum*. In the *jus ad bellum* section, we begin with Caron E. Gentry's chapter on legitimate authority, followed by Kimberly A. Hudson and Dan Henk's chapter, as they both question epistemic frameworks with the tradition as opposed to the material concerns, as explored in the following chapters by Luke Glanville's examination of the duty to enter humanitarian interventions, and Amy E. Eckert's criticism of the growing reliance upon PMCs.

In "Epistemic Bias," Caron E. Gentry establishes that legitimate authority, as both procedural and moral in scope, has become tied to state sovereignty and authority. From its earliest articulations legitimate authority was diffused across a range of political and religious authorities, all of which wielded some degree of sovereign authority. However, the present-day application of legitimate authority more often than not ties this criteria to state authority solely. This has led to the operation of an epistemic bias in international affairs to more often than not treat the actions of states as legitimate and the actions of nonstate actors, such as politically violent ones, as wholly illegitimate. This is a problematic that must be undone.

Kimberly A. Hudson and Dan Henk turn mutuality inward when they examine how the change in *jus in bello* tactics places U.S. troops inadvertently in harm's way. "Strategizing in an Era of Conceptual Change: Security, Sanctioned Violence, and New Military Roles" argues that *jus in bello* rules have long sought to protect those involved in conflict, including soldiers, and to maximize the proportional goodness achieved by military activities in relation to harm done. These rules are premised on the assumption that the military's primary function is the management and protection of force. Hudson and Henk argue that this is no longer the only, or even the primary, function of state militaries, which are now dispatched for operations like peacekeeping and humanitarian assistance. These types of operations generate new requirements for combatants in accomplishing their missions. These new functions require intelligence activities including understanding social networks in a variety of cultures, building rapport across cultural difference, and pursuing cooperative activities with members of partner nation militaries, noncombatants, and international organizations.

Luke Glanville's chapter, "Is Just Intervention Morally Obligatory?," examines the notion that, in those instances where humanitarian intervention is understood to be a just response to mass atrocities, it ought to be understood not merely as a right but as a duty incumbent upon states and upon the international community more broadly. This idea can be found in the writings of some early Just War thinkers who framed the rescue of populations as a duty rather than a discretionary right. It is also a key aspect of the present-day "responsibility to protect" concept, though it is one whose meaning and implications have not yet been fully thought through. The chapter seeks to trace the historical development of this idea and offers some insights into present-day questions about who in particular might bear this duty of intervention in certain circumstances, and whether or not the duty might be enforceable.

In the following chapter, "Private Military Companies and the Reasonable Chance of Success," Amy E. Eckert takes up another, the reliance on private force. Eckert argues that the growing reliance upon the employment of private military companies by the supposed legitimate state has altered reasonable chance of success. Although the Just War tradition evolved when the use of private force was commonplace, the tradition has also evolved to reflect the state's consolidation of the legitimate right to use force. While the decision to wage war remains with the political leadership of states, the use of PMCs requires that we rethink many of the *jus ad bellum* criteria that apply to this decision, particularly the principle of reasonable chance of success. Whether a war is likely to be successful depends on a calculation of each party's relative capabilities. With the growth of the private military industry, these capabilities can increase substantially and instantaneously with the stroke of a pen. Yet the involvement of PMCs raises some important questions about this *jus ad bel-*

lum principle. Using the involvement of the PMC Executive Outcomes in Sierra Leone to get at some of the issues surrounding reasonable chance of success, this chapter asks what success really means in the context of *jus ad bellum* and how the growing role of the private sphere can change the moral reasoning surrounding this principle specifically and *jus ad bellum* more generally. Eckert argues that a critical approach to the application of *jus ad bellum* norms like the reasonable possibility of success requires that they be applied on an ongoing basis rather than in a one-time manner prior to initiating a war.

The *jus in bello* section begins with Sebastian Kaempf's chapter on risk aversion policies in warfare before moving rather seamlessly to Brent J. Steele and Eric A. Heinze's chapter on how military technology advances have changed understandings of moral legitimacy in war. Alexa Royden's chapter contrasting the rather permissible usage of highly destructive conventional weapons with nuclear weapons builds upon the previous two chapters. The following two chapters by Harry D. Gould and Laura Sjoberg, respectively, examine ideas of agency and responsibility. Gould looks at the effectiveness of personal immunity and the principle of Double Effect, whereas Sjoberg argues that the noncombatant immunity principle is dead in contemporary conflicts due to gendered assumptions and norms in war regarding women and men.

Sebastian Kaempf's chapter, "Postheroic U.S. Warfare and the Moral Justification for Killing in War," takes on the problem of impunity and risk aversion policies. This chapter conducts a theoretical investigation into the challenges that the advent of casualty-averse and posthuman American warfare poses to both the laws of war and the ethics of the use of force. It focuses primarily on the question of when it is permissible to kill (another person) in war rather than the more specific question of when it is permissible to kill noncombatants. If the fundamental principle of the morality of warfare is a right to exercise self-defense within the conditions of mutual imposition of risk, then the emergence of extreme forms of asymmetrical warfare represents a deep challenge. This challenge is posed by contemporary U.S. warfare: the United States is the first actor in the history of warfare who can kill without suffering the risk of dying in return. Such a deployment of force might be politically justified, but in this case we might no longer be able to appeal to the morality of warfare to justify this mode of combat.

Kaempf argues that reciprocity (conditions of mutual imposition of risk) is the key conceptual condition upon which the moral and legal permission for killing in war rests. He goes on to argue that it then demonstrates how reciprocity implicitly assumes a certain degree of symmetry between warring factions. In the case of contemporary U.S. warfare, conditions of asymmetry have emerged on such a historically unprecedented scale that they have started to push beyond the conditions of reciprocity. The rise of American casualty-aversion is the core driving force behind the implementation of military reforms that have started to allow the U.S. military to kill without suffering the risk of dying in return. These developments are pushing the American war machine beyond the principles underpinning the ethics and laws of war.

In their chapter, "From Smart to Autonomous Weapons: Confounding Territoriality and Moral Agency," Brent J. Steele and Eric A. Heinze interrogate how advances in military technology have affected our moral thinking about the legitimacy of war in profound ways. In this chapter, they argue that one of the most recent advances in military technology—that of unmanned and computer-guided weapons systems—effectively circumvent certain foundational principles of *jus in bello*. While UAVs and computer-based targeting systems supposedly enhance the precision of military attacks as well as minimize risks to combatants and noncombatants alike, Steele and Heinze argue the following three points. First, while these developments are hardly sui generis in terms of their implications for Just War, they substantially remove human agency from wartime decisions, thus creating a situation where there may be no identifiable agent(s) to hold morally responsible if these weapons systems fail. Second, while the notion of "intent" has always been seen as a problematic Just War precept, the use of UAVs takes this notion to the point of near absurdity, especially if humans begin to trust (as they have in certain cases with UAVs) the judgment of machines more than their own. Finally and more broadly, when used in a nonterritorial postmodern "war on terror" epoch, UAVs extend the "battle space" into a third dimension. Having advanced and defended these three assertions, the chapter concludes that while the these technologies demonstrate problems for the notion of "Just" War in terms of justice, it is nevertheless the sine qua non of twenty-first-century manifestation of *jus in bello*. In essence, Just War practitioners, and contemporary Just War defenders, find in the UAV their technological soul mate.

Alexa Royden's chapter, "An Alternative to Nuclear Weapons? Proportionality, Discrimination, and the Conventional Global Strike Program," argues that while the invention of the atom bomb forever altered the potential conduct of war, militaries became too reliant upon, if not complacent with, the deployment of conventional weapons. In part responsible for the twentieth-century resurgence in the Just War tradition, nuclear weapons, due to their sheer destructive power, are generally perceived to violate two of the central criteria associated with *jus in bello*, or justice in war: discrimination and proportionality. Nonetheless, certain scenarios persist in which the use of nuclear bombs, under very specific conditions, could prove advantageous, specifically as a means of destroying underground stockpiles of nuclear, chemical, or biological weapons. Consequently, the United States has focused significant effort and invested considerable resources in the construction of a range of advanced conventional capabilities that would alleviate reliance upon this nuclear option. The emergence of a new and seemingly uniquely destructive form of weapons had the effect of licensing the use of conventional weapons virtually without question because they did not inherently violate norms of discrimination and proportionality. Conventional weapons, unlike most weapons of mass destruction, do not suffer the inherent stigmas associated with their just use, and as a result they are often perceived as a legitimate alternative to nuclear weapons. Such an assumption, however, has received little focused attention and is open to debate. This chapter explores this debate and considers the extent to which conventional "super" bombs meet *jus in bello* criteria. By examining specific weapons, including the Daisy Cutter, the Massive Ordnance Penetrator, and the Prompt Global Strike system, it will be possible to ascertain their relative justness vis-à-vis nuclear weapons. More importantly, this chapter takes issue with the lack of stigma attached to conventional weapons that are as destructive as weapons of mass destruction.

In "Rethinking Intention and Double Effect," Harry D. Gould returns to the established notions that actions can have both foreseen and unforeseen effects as well as intended and unintended consequences and looks for the relationship between these two outcomes. It is sometimes argued that not all foreseen consequences are intended. In ascriptions of responsibility, the latter types of cases are problematic. If an agent foresees that a certain outcome will result from his or her action, we are faced with the question of whether the agent is *morally* responsible for the outcome—one of the great questions of both ethics and moral theology. The question is brought into sharp relief when the not specifically intended consequence is something that agents are normally forbidden to bring about. In the literature, this situation is normally called a "double effect," and a rule for determining when a foreseen but not specifically intended *bad* (or indeed forbidden) consequence does or does not disallow the intended act has been worked out under the label the Doctrine of Double Effect (DDE).

DDE raises a number of interesting questions for Ethics and International Relations (EIR) beyond just its immediate usage as a test for the permissibility of a proposed action; implicit in the formulations of the doctrine are a number of issues about agency and intention that speak to debates in International Relations about the agency and personality of states. Why has EIR paid so little attention to DDE? One of the doctrine's key concerns or applications has historically been the use of force, and while DDE is often *mentioned* in texts on the ethics of the use of force, there is remarkably little sustained analysis and almost no challenging of the logic of the DDE or the conclusions its use yields.

Laura Sjoberg's chapter, "Just War without Civilians," critiques the noncombatant immunity principle as shallow, outdated, infeasible, underspecified, ineffective, biased, and susceptible to manipulation. In previous work Sjoberg has argued that these flaws are the result of and reflective of the immunity principle's inseparability from gendered sex role stories about male "just warriors" and female "beautiful souls" that legitimate war, fantasize protection, and render actual protection impossible.[22] More recently, Sjoberg and Jessica Peet have recognized that these gendered narratives also provide belligerents with a warrant and a justification to victimize civilians (as a proxy for women) intentionally.[23] This chapter asks what Just War theories would look like if wars were not fought "for" women, "over" women, attacking women, or "protecting" women. It proposes revising Just War theorizing, putting aside the gendered combatant/civilian dichotomy—that is, Just War "without civilians."

Finally, Robert E. Williams Jr.'s chapter, "*Jus post Bellum*: Justice in the Aftermath of War," serves as the conclusion to the project and speaks to the emerging literature on *jus post bellum*. As one of the leading scholars on *jus post bellum*, Williams is prompted by the problems associated with the American occupation of Iraq. Although "just peace" has been a concern within the field of conflict resolution for many years, and some antecedents of contemporary thought on *jus post bellum* can be found in the writings of the classic Just War thinkers, the idea that the principles of a just peace might be developed as an extension of the Just War tradition is relatively new. This chapter surveys the development of *jus post bellum* thought and evaluates its potential for transforming the way we think about the Just War. It concludes by suggesting that *jus post bellum* is best understood as a set of principles that facilitates the transition from a belligerent rights regime to a more expansive human rights regime as war gives way to peace.

Notes

1. See, for instance, Richard Jackson, *Critical Terrorism Studies: A New Agenda* (London: Routledge, 2009); Richard Jackson, *Writing the War on Terrorism* (Manchester: Manchester University Press, 2005); Christine Sylvester, *Feminist International Relations: An Unfinished Journey* (Cambridge: Cambridge University Press, 2002).

2. See Eric A. Heinze and Brent J. Steele, eds., *Ethics, Authority, and War: Nonstate Actors and the Just War Tradition* (New York: Palgrave Macmillan, 2009); Virginia Held, *How Terrorism Is Wrong: Morality and Political Violence* (Oxford: Oxford University Press, 2008); Tarik Kochi, *The Other's War: Recognition and the Violence of Ethics* (Abingdon: Birbeck Law Press, 2009); Hilary Putnam, "The Epistemology of Unjust War," *Royal Institute of Philosophy Supplement* 58 (2006): 173–88; Laura Sjoberg, *Gender, Justice, and the Wars in Iraq* (Lanham, Md.: Lexington Books, 2006).

3. Some scholars, notably Michael Walzer, address the question of intervention by outside powers in civil wars, supporting counterintervention when another outside power has already upset the balance between the factions. Otherwise, the tradition has been largely moot on the subject of noninternational armed conflict. See also John Williams, "Space, Scale and Just War: Meeting the Challenge of Humanitarian Intervention and Trans-national Terrorism," *Review of International Studies* 34, no. 4 (2008).

4. Nicholas Rengger, "On the Just War Tradition in the 21st Century," *International Affairs* 78, no. 2 (2002): 353–63, 355; Alex J. Bellamy, *Just Wars: From Cicero to Iraq* (Cambridge: Polity, 2008); Williams, this volume.

5. Stanley Hauerwas, *The Peaceable Kingdom* (South Bend, Ind.: University of Notre Dame Press, 1983), 114.

6. Nicholas Rengger as quoted in Christopher Brown, *Sovereignty, Rights and Justice* (London: Polity, 2002), 102.

7. See Lee Jarvis, *Times of Terror: Discourse, Temporality and the War on Terror* (London: Palgrave Macmillan, 2009).

8. Bellamy, *Just Wars*; Alex J. Bellamy, "Is the War on Terror Just?," *International Relations* 19, no. 3 (2005): 275–96; Chris J. Dolan, *In War We Trust: The Bush Doctrine and the Pursuit of Just War* (Aldershot, Hants, Eng.: Ashgate, 2005), 2.

9. Jean Bethke Elshtain, *Just War against Terror: The Burden of American Power in a Violent Age* (New York: Basic Books, 2003).

10. See Cian O'Driscoll, "Jean Bethke Elshtain's Just War against Terror: A Tale of Two Cities," *International Relations* 21, no. 4 (2007): 485–92; Maja Zehfuss, "The Tragedy of Violent Justice: The Danger of Elshtain's Just War against Terror," *International Relations* 21, no. 4 (2007): 493–501; Michael Walzer, "On Fighting Terrorism Justly," *International Relations* 21, no. 4 (2007): 480–84; Nicholas Rengger, "Just War against Terror? Jean Bethke Elshtain's Burden and American Power," *International Affairs* 80, no. 1 (2004): 107–16.

11. See Heinze and Steele, *Ethics, Authority, and War*; Laura Sjoberg, "Gender, Just War, and Non-state Actors," in Heinze and Steele, *Ethics, Authority, and War*, 151–76.

12. Kaempf, this volume.

13. See Bellamy, *Is the War*; Larry May, *War Crimes and Just War* (Cambridge: Cambridge University Press, 2005).

14. Michael L. Gross, *Moral Dilemmas of Modern War: Torture, Assassination, and Blackmail in an Age of Asymmetric Conflict* (Cambridge: Cambridge University Press, 2009); Michael Walzer, *Just and Unjust Wars: A Moral Argument with Historical Illustrations* (New York: Basic Books, 1977).

15. See Putnam, "Epistemology of Unjust War," 174.

16. Chris Brown, *Sovereignty, Rights, and Justice: International Political Theory Today* (Cambridge: Polity Press, 2002), 138.

17. Sebastian Kaempf, "Double Standards in U.S. Warfare: Exploring the Historical Legacy of Civilian Protection and the Complex Nature of the Moral-Legal Nexus," *Review of International Studies* 35 (2009): 651–74.

18. See also Heinze and Steele, *Ethics, Authority, and War*.

19. Rengger, "Just War against Terror."

20. Nicholas Fotion, *Just War and Ethics* (New York: Continuum, 2007), 30.

21. Peter W. Singer, *Wired For War: The Robotics Revolution and Conflict in the 21st Century* (New York: Penguin, 2009).

22. Sjoberg, *Gender, Justice, and the Wars in Iraq*.

23. Laura Sjoberg and Jessica Peet, "A(nother) Dark Side of the Protection Racket," *International Feminist Journal of Politics* 13 (2011): 163–82.

Jus ad Bellum

CHAPTER ONE

Epistemic Bias

Legitimate Authority and
Politically Violent Nonstate Actors

Caron E. Gentry

FROM THE EARLIEST Western articulations to current understandings of legitimate authority, *jus ad bellum* criterion has been granted to a political entity with the most sovereign power, while said entity has also been imbued with a perceived moral competency. Within both the classical and contemporary writings on the Just War tradition, legitimate authority is often presented as having dual elements: the first element reflects a political or procedural "authority" to declare war; the second is a moral investiture of what it means to be "legitimate," "right," or "competent." Thus, this chapter traces the historical development of political authority and then examines what it means within the tradition to possess moral or ethical legitimacy.

In doing so, this chapter, much like Kimberly Hudson and Dan Henk's to follow, deals more with a priori epistemological constructions of Just War than with the tradition's material concerns. Whereas Hudson and Henk's chapter deals with rapid conceptual changes to human security, this chapter argues that constructions of legitimate authority are perhaps not moving quickly enough. Today, both political authority and moral legitimacy are reflected in Westphalia's emphasis on sovereign states as the primary actors in international affairs. Therefore, I argue, the conflation of political and moral authority results in an "epistemic injustice," one that upholds sovereign states as Westphalian "insiders" and other actors, particularly politically violent substate actors, as "outsiders."[1]

Often argued as one of the most important criteria of *jus ad bellum*, legitimate authority is also one of the longest standing. Plato and Aristotle articulated that entities, whether individuals or institutions "entrusted with the 'care for the common good,'" were the only authorities that could properly decide on the use of force.[2] Accompanying this idea was the distinction between "good" and "bad" authority. Within a particular community, "good" authority was considerate of the health of the entirety, while "bad" considered the ruler's own good or a smaller party's interests.[3] My concern is that legitimacy is still derived from "morality" and such "morality" is defined and limited to a specific way of acknowledging and constructing politics and international affairs.[4]

Miranda Fricker argues that epistemic injustice is a particular way of denying people epistemic authority based off of their identity.[5] Said theory of epistemic injustice is applicable to the Just War tradition's reliance on Western ideas of statehood, war craft, and moral legitimacy. This chapter owes a debt to Virginia Held and Tarik Kochi for helping construct a criticism of the present binary between sovereignty/legitimacy and substate actors/illegitimacy necessary to applying the philosophical concept of "epistemic injustice" to international affairs.[6]

DUAL NATURE: AUTHORITY AND LEGITIMACY

In such a brief section it would be impossible to create a comprehensive understanding of the development of legitimate authority. Instead this section seeks to introduce the reader to the definition, historical development of procedural authority, and the conflation of sovereignty with moral credibility. Broadly conceived, legitimate authority is the highest political authority that can make the decision to go to war: "competent" or "legitimate" authority is described "as whatever authority happens to be in place within a state."[7] The dual element criterion is often viewed as one of the most important to *jus ad bellum*.[8] The first element resides in the political authority of the sovereign to call the military to war and then to call it back.[9] Such an understanding is often referenced as "procedural" authority and is distinguished from the moral/ethical values embedded within legitimacy.[10] Legitimacy is explicitly normative and often conceptualized as doing what is right or good for a particular community; in the contemporary writings of Michael Walzer and Alex J. Bellamy legitimacy is tied to democratic states.[11]

A brief timeline of legitimate authority highlights its evolution from sovereign monarch or government to sovereign state. Articulations of legitimate authority, as previously stated, began in the Western tradition in Ancient

Greece with Plato and Aristotle conceiving of authority as the entity with highest or supreme authority to act for a political community. When St. Augustine communicated his own basic formulations of the Just War tradition, procedural authority to go to war resided in the monarch as the highest authority in the Holy Roman Empire.[12]

In the Middle Ages, some scholars saw authority to declare war as diffused across secular authorities. The Catholic Church also claimed some degree of legitimate authority with respect to the right to declare a Holy War. St. Aquinas continued the thinking of St. Augustine, who believed the most important criterion was the sovereign's legitimate authority, placing it above two other early (*jus ad bellum*) criteria, just cause and right intention.[13] (In contrast, James Turner Johnson argues that currently legitimate authority is secondary to just cause.[14]) As natural law replaced Christian theology and as the Westphalian system took shape, authority became more explicitly linked to the sovereign state.[15] The marriage of (legitimate) authority to the sovereign state remained stable between the mid-1600s to the mid-1900s. The absolute authority that states possessed in this period is in stark contrast to the current understanding of legitimate authority. The Westphalian norms of non-intervention and non-aggression, that to some degree bound absolute authority, became codified in international law by the mid-nineteenth century; this was most evident in the creation of the UN.[16] At this time, the United Nations Security Council (UNSC) was recognized as holding legitimate (procedural) authority to declare war, and a state's (procedural) authority was limited to instances of self-defense.[17]

Two issues in the post–World War II era have complicated and thus somewhat expanded modern legitimate authority. The first expansion of legitimate authority after the establishment of the UN was reflective of the postcolonial period and the rise of nationalist movements. The 1977 Protocol Additional Geneva Conventions expanded legitimate authority to include anticolonial and territorial-based movements that hold state aspirations, even if these expansions came seemingly late in the postcolonial era.[18] The second expansion reflects the growing awareness of humanitarian crises in the post–Cold War period. The UN's adoption of the "Responsibility to Protect" (R2P) doctrine in 2005 allows for the UNSC to authorize war for humanitarian purposes. The intervening forces could be UN Blue Helmets or states granted permission to intervene for non-self-defensive purposes.[19] Therefore, R2P weakens states going to war only in self-defense while also strengthening the UNSC's authority.

Nonetheless, in contemporary work, procedural authority is often tied to sovereign states, and democratic ones at that. Throughout *Just and Unjust Wars*, Michael Walzer conceives of Just Wars as fought between sovereign, autonomous states (making some exception for nationalist self-determination).[20] While these states may be represented by politicians and lawyers in the international arena, the states themselves are the highest representation of the will of the people.[21] For instance, Walzer argues that the "moral standing" of a state "depends upon the reality of the common life it protects"—a common life that is best if it respects liberties.[22] Thus authority and legitimacy are granted by the people and are a tacit conveyance of a belief in liberalism and the (moral) supremacy of democracy. Walzer's construction of democratic legitimate authority is echoed by Alex J. Bellamy's 2008 book on just war and terror. He creates a near essentializing argument that pits Western democracies, which if they are to be moral agents of legitimate authority should stay true to their democratic values, against radical Islam.[23] This is not to pick a fight with liberalism per se, but to point out that liberal values (democracy, rights, liberties, and prosperity) are a particular way of approaching how to order the world. Liberal values are claimed to be desired universally, yet the violence of colonialism, the proxy wars of the Cold War, and the method for fighting the "War on Terror" negate this (something Bellamy agrees with in his criticism of the Bush administration).[24] The creation of a liberal hermeneutic presents a Manichean vision that delegitimizes other voices, here substate actors. This could broadly be conceived of as an epistemic injustice, as is argued later.

A normative conceptualization of authority leads to the second piece of legitimate authority's dual nature. Even if the conflation of legitimate authority with sovereign, democratic states is a newer development in the Just War tradition, granting authorities moral credentials is certainly not. As stated in the introduction, Ancient Greek thought believed authority was legitimate if it represented the good of a particular *polis*. St. Augustine was the first to imbue it with heavy theological weight—the sovereign was the highest authority precisely because God placed him there. The decision to go to war is discerned through the sovereign's relationship with God: "a right will is in union with the divine law."[25] Since Augustinian legitimate authority rests on the righteousness and piety of the authority, right intention and just cause will follow as a matter of course.

St. Aquinas places a heavy emphasis on sovereign authority because it is the "sovereign's responsibility to seek the good for the society he governs," and limiting authority to the sovereign yields "good" results: "order, justice, and peace."[26] In his challenge to the Catholic Church, Luther argued "rightful authority belonged to secular powers."[27] Still, this secularizing challenge led directly to the Thirty Years War and its outcome: the Peace of Westphalia. It was under Westphalia that the state became the primary actor in international affairs. While states under Westphalia are tacitly bound by norms, there is a certain amount of tension between *raison d'état* and ethical ideals. Overriding the tension, states almost had a free reign in going to war.[28] Thus, the strengthening of the state and its previously held moral credentials led to a binary: states' actions are inevitably viewed as legitimate and substate actors' actions as illegitimate (or less important, valued, credible).

Just War is an inherently ethical framework, meaning that to critique the moral basis is to critique something fundamental within the tradition. It is argued quite well and extensively that the "legitimacy" of an "authority" must be "concretely evaluated" in order to uncover the ethics of a particular potential war.[29] Yet, this represents a certain epistemic perspective that determines what constitutes not only "moral" legitimacy but authority as well. However, as a tradition it is meant to grow and develop. Legitimate authority has become so wedded to Westphalia that perhaps it has a difficult time engaging and understanding substate agents.

EPISTEMOLOGICAL INJUSTICE, WESTPHALIAN STATEHOOD, AND LEGITIMATE AUTHORITY

Epistemic injustice is based within an understanding of power as socially situated (social power), which creates either active or passive (in)justice that further contributes to the marginalization of particular populations. Fricker specifically illustrates two types of interpersonal or intergroup situations: testimonial and hermeneutical injustices, respectively. Yet, even if her examples are micro- and meso-based, this does not mean her argument does not have application to International Relations (IR) and then to the Just War tradition. International Relations and its adherence to the Westphalian system constructs social power as the purview of state actors—a construction leading to the hermeneutical injustice of denying power, credibility, and ultimately legitimacy to nonstate actors. To demonstrate a link between epistemic injustice and global politics, this section explains Fricker's argument before applying it to International Relations.

Fricker's overarching goal is to bring ethics to "our most basic everyday epistemic practices: conveying knowledge to others by telling them, and making sense of our own social experiences."[30] Epistemic injustice occurs when someone is wronged "in their capacity as a subject of knowledge."[31] This can happen in two different ways: 1) as a testimonial injustice, "when a hearer wrongs a speaker in his capacity as a giver of knowledge, as an informant"; and 2) a hermeneutic injustice, which happens when "someone is wronged in their capacity as a subject of social understanding."[32]

Fricker rightly argues that since humans are socially situated and social interactions are imbued with power, there are issues of power and justice that exist between people and in how we try to make sense of one another (epistemic practice).[33] Therefore, social power, or the "idea that power is a socially situated capacity to control others' action," is at the core of epistemic injustice. Within social power is a "subspecies" of power—identity power, "which is directly dependent upon shared social-imaginative conceptions of the social identities of those implicated in the particular operation of power."[34] Identity power is beholden to the self-explanatory "identity prejudice," which ultimately leads to "identity-prejudicial credibility deficit" (italic emphasis removed)— meaning that because a person belongs to a certain group his or her epistemic credibility is doubted or denied.[35] Such an injustice strikes at something "essential to human value."[36]

States have access to "identity power" as the recognized primary actor in IR.[37] Through the development of the state system, focusing especially on the significance of the Treaties of Westphalia, the sovereign, autonomous state has come to represent and be acknowledged as the primary actor in International Relations.[38] As such, this lessens the prominence and perceived importance of other actors.[39] Situating states in this way is dependent upon an acceptance of social power—states acquire and maintain power as a means of influencing other states and asserting their place in the world.

The moral legitimacy that has been invested in states simply by their existence is the problem.[40] States are legal entities that solve problems through the use of power however one wishes to define it: social, structural, or physical power. That the state is the location of various activities, from identity to economics to protection, is not a problem. Yet, to conflate states' legal authority with moral authority "complicates the discussion" and may "contribut[e] to the problem of violence."[41] Legal status (procedural authority) and moral credibility (legitimacy) should be understood differently. Walzer does make this differentiation: if a political community shows promise of self-governance, it may constitute a legitimate authority.[42] Arguably, however, few such substate actors are actually recognized as being credible enough for self-governance. Even though the Chechens won their first war for national self-determination against Russia, with both sides using terroristic violence, Russia is seen as (slightly) more competent and far more legitimate (at least) as a state. This is an identity prejudice, speaking to a hermeneutical injustice.

State behavior may be constrained by norms, but as privileged actors, those who control state behavior are free to ignore norms at will depending on how much power, whether military or economic, that state possesses. Therefore, the leaders and elites of states decide whether or not that state will follow a certain standard. This can be seen in both the flaunting of norms or acquiescence to them: ranging from the United States invading Iraq in 2003 against the UNSC decision to the United States adhering to World Trade Organization (WTO) rulings, even if it went against U.S. financial interests.

Granted, the physical entity that is a state does not possess knowledge nor does it judge another actor's capacity for knowledge. But the politicians, advisers, and academics who determine how the global system is going to run determine this based on an epistemic construction of how it should be run. Thus, those in privilege are going to maintain a system that protects said privilege. Such privilege and power are based within a particular epistemology that exists because those who create and maintain policy in the international system grant "truth" to the primacy of the state and thus to the "logic" and "reality" of Westphalia. Further, such actors who guide state behavior are going to maintain, limit, and therefore privilege those with legitimate access to power. States are in. Nonstate actors are out—or are in only to the degree that states decide they are important, like the United States accepting WTO rulings. Substate actors are granted legitimacy when it serves the purposes of those with power.[43]

Finally, as the Just War tradition has developed, it is particularly beholden to how norms and values shift, and such norms and values shift according to epistemic beliefs of those contributing to the tradition. The construction of the tradition has consistently conflated the political operation of the state with a moral one.[44] Thus, the Just War tradition's acceptance of state primacy carries with it a problematic ethical weight that creates exclusionary boundaries related to the identity politics of state versus substate actors. This would not necessarily be a problem, except that most of the wars in the world today are not fought between states; they are fought within states or by nonstate actors. Despite both the aforementioned 1977 Additional Protocols Geneva Conventions and its roots in Lockean thought (i.e., if the state has become tyrannical, a group of citizens has the right, nay the obligation, to rebel), groups that utilize political violence are still not satisfactorily theorized in the Just War tradition.[45] There is an epistemic bias that exists toward "terrorist organizations" that deny legitimacy to their violence and to their entire raison d'être.[46]

By no means does this chapter seek to argue that all dissatisfied peoples everywhere take up arms—there are better and more productive solutions.[47] Yet, once a substate group begins to arm, "terrorism" is most often the label given to it. A politically violent substate actor may receive international support if opposition to the regime already exists. Take, for instance, the support given to the Libyans against Muammar Gaddafi as opposed to fundamental lack of support granted to the Tamilese against the Sri Lankan state—both involve state-conducted genocidal acts and ethnic cleansing against substate actors. Furthermore, Nelson Mandela was considered a terrorist until the international community finally recognized and sought to end the injustice of South African apartheid. Hence, the perception of legitimacy, which shifts and is fluid in time, is derived from identity power.

HERMENEUTICAL INJUSTICE: POLITICALLY VIOLENT SUBSTATE ACTORS IN INTERNATIONAL RELATIONS

Actors who choose to use political violence as a means of bringing attention to their cause or as a way of furthering it do invite judgment upon themselves. There is an ethical dilemma in using violence—it is harmful and destructive and typically only adds to or begins a cycle of violence. This goes for states as well.[48] Yet, state violence or war is seen as more acceptable, legitimate, and credible than substate violence. This hypocrisy drives international affairs, and it both feeds and is fed by hermeneutical injustice.

Explained in another way, hermeneutical injustice happens when "members of hermeneutically marginalized groups are left inadequately conceptualized and so ill-understood [that] . . . the content of what they aim to convey" is "not heard as rational" and therefore is discounted or dismissed.[49] While many terrorism studies scholars argue that terrorism is a rational activity, the discourse that surrounds agents and actors who challenge Westphalia belies this.[50] Terrorism lacks a universally acceptable definition because it is a subjective term used to discredit groups that challenge the state system. It is not difficult to find work that deconstructs the label of "terrorist"/"terrorism" as delegitimizing and discrediting.[51] Substate groups that choose to use political violence against the state are inadequately conceptualized and ill understood because they create fear and anxiety by challenging the status quo. The denial of credibility to substate actors is arguably a hermeneutical injustice because they lie outside of Westphalian norms in two ways: they are substates, and they challenge the monopoly on violence.[52]

Fundamentally, recognizing substate agents as credible, legitimate actors is difficult. While Heinze and Steele's recent volume on Just War and nonstate actors does a tremendous job in creating an unbiased definition of nonstate actors, it is still hard to overcome the fundamental problems in defining what exactly constitutes terrorism. Heinze and Steele grant legitimacy to nonstate actors by identifying them as "entities that are potentially emerging as challengers to the prevailing authority, or who are filling a voice where such authority is weak or contested."[53] They include "substate rival communities" (U.S. Civil War), "organized armed groups" (Hizbollah), and "terrorist organizations" (Al Qaida).[54] Nevertheless, whereas identifying the authority may be easy, explicating any legitimacy is not.

Most terrorism studies scholars are willing to admit that the term "terrorist" is pejorative, loaded, and ultimately problematic.[55] This is often blown off with the cliché one person's freedom fighter is another's terrorist. While such explanations are watery, it is a dilemma that is not going to be easily resolved—although many are trying to reduce the watery dilemma to one centered on the targeting of civilian populations. For instance, Bellamy recognizes that the label of terrorism is often prone to subjectivity and cliché, but he maintains that terrorism is a "moral definition." While moral definitions are tricky because "they have to be universizable,"[56] nonetheless Bellamy sets out to establish that terrorism is distinguishable from other forms of political violence. Terrorism is illegitimate and immoral "in every circumstance" because it intentionally targets noncombatants for political purposes.[57] Yet, Virginia Held argues that using the noncombatants-as-targets as a basis for defining terrorism is deeply problematic (see also Harry Gould's chapter in this volume).[58]

Kochi argues that Just War still holds a particular moral vision that marginalizes other kinds of violence, most specifically non-Western and terrorist violence. Therefore, he argues that a person subscribing to or critical of Just War might be better served by asking a series of questions that speak back to the hegemony of the Westphalian tradition:

> What might be some of the forms of right that a theorist would need to consider? A non-exhaustive list might include: the question of "legitimacy" of the state and international law; competing notions of sovereignty; moral and legal justifications of violence and coercion; differing accounts of individual and group rights; secular and religious conceptions of political community; differing forms of ethical life; and, competing notions of the "good," "democracy" and "freedom" enunciated both historically and in the present.[59]

Both Kochi and Fricker argue for changing our epistemic practices; he calls for "epistemic labor" and she "epistemic virtue." In essence, both are extending a desire to understand the identities and ideas of others and how these construct notions of legitimacy. In this argument, it is necessary to see how different communities think differently about sovereignty and the right of the community that may lay outside of Western/Westphalian constructions of the state, morality, and credibility.

Notes

I owe an enormous debt to my undergraduate research assistant, Colin Barnard, who investigated the historical development of legitimate authority in the Just War tradition during his senior year at Abilene Christian University.

1. Chris Brown, *Sovereignty, Rights, and Justice: International Political Theory Today* (Cambridge: Polity Press, 2002), 21.

2. See Henrick Syse and Helene Ingierd, "What Constitutes a Legitimate Authority?," *Social Alternatives* 24, no. 3 (2005): 11–16, 12.

3. Ibid., 12.

4. See Virginia Held, *How Terrorism Is Wrong: Morality and Political Violence* (Oxford: Oxford University Press, 2008); Tarik Kochi, *The Other's War: Recognition and the Violence of Ethics* (Abingdon: Birkbeck Law Press, 2009).

5. Miranda Fricker, *Epistemic Injustice: Power and the Ethics of Knowing* (Oxford: Oxford University Press, 2007).

6. Held, *How Terrorism Is Wrong*; Kochi, *The Other's War*.

7. James Turner Johnson, "Aquinas and Luther on War and Peace," *Journal of Religious Ethics* 31, no. 1 (Spring 2003): 5.

8. Ibid., 7.

9. Ibid., 10; Syse and Ingierd, "What Constitutes a Legitimate Authority?," 12; Robin Lovin, "Reasons of State," *Christian Century*, October 10, 2001: 6–7, 6.

10. See Johnson, "Aquinas and Luther on War and Peace," 5; Syse and Ingierd, "What Constitutes a Legitimate Authority?," 12; Eric A. Heinze and Brent J. Steele, "Introduction: Non-state Actors and the Just War Tradition," in Eric A. Heinze and Brent J. Steele, eds., *Ethics, Authority, and War: Non-state Actors and the Just War Tradition* (New York: Palgrave Macmillan, 2009), 1–20, 5.

11. Michael Walzer, *Just and Unjust Wars: A Moral Argument with Historical Illustrations* (New York: Basic Books, 1977); Alex J. Bellamy, *Just Wars: From Cicero to Iraq* (Cambridge: Polity Press, 2006).

12. Johnson, "Aquinas and Luther on War and Peace," 6.

13. Ibid., 9.

14. Ibid., 7.

15. Ibid.; Bellamy, *Just Wars*, 124. See also Brown, *Sovereignty, Rights, and Justice*, 27.

16. Johnson, "Aquinas and Luther on War and Peace," 7; Brown, *Sovereignty, Rights, and Justice*, 35.

17. Bellamy, *Just Wars*, 124.

18. Heinze and Steele, "Introduction," 10.

19. International Commission on Intervention and State Sovereignty, *The Responsibility to Protect* (Ottawa: International Development Research Centre, 2001).

20. Walzer, *Just and Unjust Wars*, 31, 45, 51–54, 58, 61–63.

21. Ibid., 53–54; see also Syse and Ingierd, "What Constitutes a Legitimate Authority?," 12.

22. Walzer, *Just and Unjust Wars*, 54.

23. Alex J. Bellamy, *Fighting Terror: Ethical Dilemmas* (London: Zed Books, 2008), 2, 20, 27.

24. Oliver P. Richmond, *Peace in International Relations* (London: Routledge, 2008); Oliver P. Richmond, *Maintaining Order, Making Peace* (Houndsmill, Baskingstoke: Palgrave Macmillan, 2002). See also Kochi, *Other's War*, 41. For commentary on the Bush administration see Bellamy, *Fighting Terror*, 127.

25. St. Augustine, *The Political Writings*, ed. Henry Paolucci (Washington, D.C.: Regnery, 1996), 170; Herbert A. Deane, *The Political and Social Ideas of Saint Augustine* (New York: Columbia University Press: New York, 1963) 158; see also James F. Childress, "Just-War Criteria," in *War in the Twentieth Century: Sources in Theological Ethics*, ed. Richard B. Miller (Louisville: Westminster/John Knox Press, 1992), 351–72, 358.

26. Johnson, "Aquinas and Luther on War and Peace," 10.

27. Ibid., 14.

28. Bellamy, *Just Wars*, 124.

29. Syse and Ingierd, "What Constitutes a Legitimate Authority?," 12.

30. Fricker, *Epistemic Injustice*, 1.

31. Ibid., 5.

32. Ibid., 5, 7.

33. Ibid., 3.

34. Ibid., 4.

35. Ibid.

36. Ibid., 5.

37. See, for instance, Laura Sjoberg, "Gender, Just War, and Non-state Actors," in Heinze and Steele, *Ethics, Authority, and War*, 151–76.

38. Brown, *Sovereignty, Rights, and Justice*, 35.

39. See J. Ann Tickner, *Gender in International Relations* (New York: Columbia University Press, 1992); Christine Sylvester, *Feminist International Relations: An Unfinished Journey* (Cambridge: Cambridge University Press, 2002).

40. See Bellamy, *Just Wars*.

41. Brown, *Sovereignty, Rights and Justice*, 7–9; Brent J. Steele and Jacque L. Amoureux, "'Justice Is Conscience': Hizbollah, Israel, and the Perversity of Just War," in Heinze and Steele, *Ethics, Authority, and War*, 177–204, 179.

42. Walzer, *Just and Unjust Wars*, 87–91; see also Heinze and Steele, "Introduction," 11; Christopher J. Finlay, "Legitimacy and Non-state Political Violence," *Journal of Political Philosophy* 18, no. 3 (2010), 287–312.

43. Kochi, *Other's War*, 255.

44. Ibid., 253.

45. John Locke, *The Second Treatise on Civil Government* (1690); Held, *How Terrorism Is Wrong*, 11.

46. Kochi, *Other's War*, 250.

47. Maria Stephen and Erica Chenoweth, "Why Civil Resistance Works: The Strategic Logic of Nonviolent Conflict," *International Security* 33, no. 1 (2008): 7–44.

48. Held, *How Terrorism Is Wrong*, 15.

49. Fricker, *Epistemic Injustice*, 6–7.

50. Martha Crenshaw, "The Causes of Terrorism," *Comparative Politics* 13, no. 4 (1981): 379–99; Bruce Hoffman, *Inside Terrorism* (New York: Columbia University Press, 2006); Robert Pape, "The Strategic Logic of Suicide Terrorism," *American Political Science Review* 97, no. 3 (2005): 343–61. Caron E. Gentry, "Governing Emotion: (Ir)rationality and Counter-terrorism," paper presented at A Decade of Terrorism and Counterterrorism Conference, University of Strathcylde, September 9–11, 2011.

51. See Caron E. Gentry, "The Neo-Orientalist Narrations of Women's Involvement in Al Qaeda," in *Women, Gender, and Terrorism*, ed. Laura Sjoberg and Caron E. Gentry (Athens: University of Georgia Press, 2011), 176–93; Richard Jackson, *Writing the War on Terrorism* (London: Routledge, 2005); Lee Jarvis, *Times of Terror: Discourse, Temporality and the War on Terror* (London: Palgrave Macmillan, 2009).

52. Gentry, "Gender and Terrorism."

53. Heinze and Steele, "Introduction," 12.

54. Ibid.

55. Hoffman, *Inside Terrorism*; Jackson, *Writing the War.*

56. Bellamy, *Fighting Terror*, 29.

57. Ibid., 30.

58. Virginia Held, "Legitimate Authority in Non-state Groups Using Violence," *Journal of Social Philosophy* 36, no. 2 (2005): 175–93.

59. Kochi, *Other's War*, 28.

CHAPTER TWO

Strategizing in an Era of Conceptual Change

Security, Sanctioned Violence,

and New Military Roles

Kimberly A. Hudson and Dan Henk

MILITARY PROFESSIONALS EXERCISE the state's monopoly on the "management of violence,"[1] a role that remains important in the early twenty-first century. Yet violence is manifestly not the only expectation of contemporary military establishments and, in light of significant expansions in thinking about security and sovereignty violence, may no longer be the military's primary role. There is a striking modern irony in the escalating transformation of institutions created to win armed conflict into those now equally responsible for attenuating, intervening in, or preventing it.

This chapter explores some of the conceptual shifts behind the changes in roles and missions of security sector actors. As notions of security have changed significantly over the past several decades, so have notions of just cause, and as missions have changed, what is required for success has also changed. The international community's expectations of state militaries may now exceed their present capacity, and the Just War criteria of proportionality and likelihood of success require that security strategists align capabilities to expectations and discern realistic security ends against which they can apply feasible ways and available means. Those feasible ways and means will involve significant change in the security sector itself—including changes in structure, force development, focus, and ethos.

The international community has embraced new *jus ad bellum* norms regarding the use of force, including intervention in support of fundamental human rights. The "human security" paradigm means that security is no longer narrowly focused on the inviolability of the state but is instead also concerned with human welfare. These new *jus ad bellum* norms create *jus in bello* problems in that they frequently require combatants to carry out functions that are significantly different from those they performed in the past. To avoid causing harm both to themselves and to others, the manner in which military personnel carry out these new functions will also need to evolve.

WHAT IS DRIVING THE CONCEPTUAL CHANGE?

Security sector roles and missions are undergoing a dramatic transformation.[2] The recent expansion in military roles is relatable to the issue of ends, and this calls attention to a worldwide evolution in contemporary thinking about security and public sector accountability. Since the early 1980s, scholars and practitioners have engaged in a fascinating series of debates about the meaning of security.[3] The trajectory of this change has been away from earlier conceptions of national, regional, or international military security and toward the broad new conception of "human security."[4] These debates soon overlapped and eddied with scholarly conversations about related concepts such as development, democratic peace, and (later) Responsibility to Protect (R2P).[5]

At first, the new security conceptualizations were offered as analytical frameworks to identify the root causes of human suffering, but they were rapidly embraced by humanitarian activists who saw an opportunity to reframe security to support various advocacies. The enthusiastic embrace of the new ideas by the United Nations in the early 1990s and by policymakers in a number of states resulted in at least two rather different communities.[6] While a number of G-77 and many non-aligned members worried that emphasis on human security would pose a threat to the norms of sovereignty and non-intervention, a number of nations, most notably Japan and Canada, and at least one grand alliance—the European Union—sought to make human security a guiding principle.[7] Some scholars remained uncomfortable with the state's embrace of human security, preferring to see the paradigm remain a conceptual tool for scholarly analysis.[8]

It is difficult to overstate the importance of the ongoing shift in thinking.[9] Policymakers have agonized over conflicting mandates of protecting state interests and sovereignty on the one hand and fulfilling the growing global demand for a broad new vision of security—including issues of human security—on the other. Two noteworthy trends are evident. The first is a change in the international community's thinking about the "referent object" of security. This is no longer exclusively taken to be the state. Rather, local communities—or even individuals—assume center stage as rights-bearing entities. Safeguards for individuals are now widely acknowledged as an inherent obligation of individual states and of the international community. The principle of Responsibility to Protect was unanimously affirmed by all UN member states in the *Outcome Document of the United Nations High-Level Plenary Meeting (the 2005 World Summit)*. A few years earlier, the world community had unambiguously withdrawn almost any grounds for individual claims to impunity for atrocity crimes in war, with the Rome Statute (adopted in 1998) and the resulting creation of the International Criminal Court.[10]

The second noteworthy trend is a growing acceptance of a much broader definition of international peace and security than was prevalent before the mid-twentieth century so that the concepts no longer apply exclusively to the inviolability of national sovereignty and borders, maintenance of governing elites, or even protection of communities from external aggression.[11] As defined by the influential International Commission on Intervention and State Sovereignty (ICISS), true security is human security, including "physical safety, . . . economic and social well-being, respect for [the] dignity and worth [of] human beings, and the protection of . . . human rights and fundamental freedoms [of individuals]."[12] The human security debate has been advanced by the adoption of Responsibility to Protect, along with the Rome Statute and the International Criminal Court (ICC), which form a basis upon which the international community is obligated to respond to egregious affronts to human security. The bedrock value underlying Responsibility to Protect and the Rome Statute is a prioritization of the human being as the referent object of security. The obligation of the international community to protect human security within the borders of a state that is unwilling or incapable of doing so itself arguably leads a revised threshold of just cause for transgressing sovereign borders with coercive force.

In this new paradigm, "international peace and security" are not simply the absence of war and refugee flows or the security of state borders. The broadest definitions of security now encompass the ultimate objectives of universal freedom from want and fear, with a variety of necessary contributing ends.[13] These include the following:

- Access to a decent standard of living for all members of a community (income security);
- Availability of sufficient food and clean water to adequately nourish all members of a community (food security);
- Access to adequate health care and freedom from the scourge of epidemic disease (health security);
- An environment that is not toxic and from which all members of the community receive equitable benefits (environmental security);
- Freedom from violence to persons, property, and dignity (personal security);
- Individual human rights of all members of the community respected and protected;
- Community norms and values that are safeguarded against rapid, destabilizing change;
- Governance that is accountable to all members of the community, including universal access to justice and fair dispute mediation.

A broad new definition of security leads naturally enough to a new categorization of threats; if the perception of "security" is increasingly broad, so is the list of factors or circumstances that threaten it.[14] Not all of these threats can be successfully countered with military intervention. On the contrary, statements on R2P, including the ICISS report and the 2005 World Summit outcome document have purposely sought to encourage a broader range of responses to humanitarian crises, marking a distinct break with the earlier concept of humanitarian intervention. Nevertheless, even these statements acknowledge that some disasters will require the use of force. The broader notions of security in the new thinking are interrelated with expanding notions of accountability and responsibility (and human rights).

Significantly, under the new models, states themselves can threaten international peace and security without aggressive intent, simply by their inability to deliver competent governance. Some of this is little more than the elaboration of earlier themes in human history; for instance, an amplification of the concept of a social contract between rulers and the governed that gained currency in Europe's Enlightenment or models of ethical conduct in war rooted in Augustine, Aquinas, and Grotius, now generally categorized under the rubric of Just War (*jus ad bellum* and *jus in bello*).[15]

Yet despite these continuities with the past, the most progressive contemporary views are unprecedented in scope—going well beyond the state-centric notions of earlier eras. The most progressive new thinking now posits a responsibility within the world community as a whole for safeguarding people everywhere from the depredations of nature, human strife, or even the ambitions of local leaders. These new responsibilities will not always involve the use of force, and some of the tenets of human security require restraint, but the expanded scope of security does potentially broaden the scope of just causes for which force may be used. Such expectations may still be more pious hope than reality, but they nonetheless represent a growing, novel vision of mutual global accountability.

While the worldwide understanding of security has shifted remarkably since the mid-twentieth century, the institutions responsible for delivering "security" under the old models have not. The state remains the key security actor on the international scene, and not all states are interested in accepting the responsibilities implied by the new security thinking. Even within sympathetic states, the security establishments are not necessarily amenable to the new ideas.[16] Here, the largest, most expensive actors are still the military establishments, and some of these bear a remarkable resemblance to the eighteenth-century armies of King Frederick II of Prussia or King George III of Great Britain. This is true not only of their form and ethos but also of their articulated purpose. In many parts of the world their basic role is still to provide ruling elites with the ultimate capacity to apply irresistible lethal coercion against their enemies, including fellow citizens. To be sure, military roles and missions (along with military capabilities) have expanded significantly since the eighteenth century, but in the minds of many governing elites the newer roles are either irrelevant or little more than add-ons to the "sovereign control of the means of violence." Where states are unable or unwilling to comply with the broad new visions of security within their borders, the international community may now recognize a responsibility to protect, but the "international community" has no army to enforce it.

A HISTORICAL PERSPECTIVE

"War makes states and states make war" is American sociologist Charles Tilly's memorable aphorism, and state borders in modern Europe bear mute testimony to its applicability. Since the formation of the modern state, nation-states typically maintain war-making establishments. Until the middle of the twentieth century, only a few were reluctant to describe government oversight as the Ministry of War or War Department. The presumed key role of national military forces themselves was to engage in "war"—to project violence on behalf of the state when so ordered by duly constituted authorities. The main responsibility of the technocrats carrying out military orders was to do so efficiently and successfully.

It is worth noting that the move in the mid-twentieth century to retitle the government managerial and oversight agencies as the Department of Defense or Ministry of Defense fell in line with the ascendance of an aggressor-defender paradigm in Just War conceptualizations. This paradigm posited that all offensive wars were unjust, while all defensive wars were just. Just War thinking in recent years has challenged that view, suggesting that offensive use of military force is sometimes permissible (or even obligatory) in defense of grave threats to human security—for example, in the case of humanitarian disaster. Yet this thinking also rejects the notion that narrow state interests provide justification for offensive war.

The new thinking emphasizes legitimate authority, proportionality, and likelihood of success to justify lethal coercion for justifiable objectives.[17] In the aggressor-defender paradigm, where all and only defensive wars were considered just, emphasis on proportionality, likelihood of success, and last resort was negligible. Likelihood of success and proportionality in wars of humanitarian intervention require protection of the noncombatants whose security is the war's aim, as well as postbellum operations to maintain that security.

Some such roles and missions for military organizations are not entirely new. America's small nineteenth-century regular army served, among many other roles, as a frontier constabulary, developer of national transportation infrastructure, facilitator of settlement, and accumulator of scientific data. European colonial military officials performed similar functions in nineteenth-century empires. In more recent times, military organizations around the world have served as labor pools for various needs of the state. Equipment acquired for military usage has been regularly redirected to other national priorities. The expertise of military planners has been diverted to humanitarian emergencies and other roles not directly related to the management of violence. But this does not mean that military professionals necessarily accede with equanimity to roles and missions outside the core of what they consider their legitimate expertise.[18]

By the 1950s, military planners were anticipating the possibility of massive conventional and nuclear war and preparing their militaries accordingly. Yet though general war was a contingency requiring readiness, it was also an almost unthinkable last resort. In fact, the most fundamental role for most of the military establishments engaged in the Cold War was to prevent war, not to conduct it. The lead "instrument" of state in this effort was diplomacy, with military activity simply an adjunct in a coordinated portfolio of options and elements of power. Here, the military's principal role was to project credible deterrence through presence rather than resort to force. Its core competency was not so much "management of violence" as "preservation of stalemate" and to ensure that general war would be a bona fide last resort.

During the Cold War, peace support operations were at best tangential to the military roles and missions of the key contestants. By the early 1970s, peacekeeping had evolved largely into a niche role for countries whose political alignments were relatively inoffensive to the major Cold War powers. Non-aligned countries such as Finland, Sweden, and India were able to develop considerable expertise in this field. Other less developed countries found that commitment of troops to UN peacekeeping missions provided military training opportunities, served to keep military forces gainfully employed, and provided a lucrative source of revenue. Missions for peacekeeping forces were deliberately limited. The UN preferred the permissive environments of "Chapter VI" mandates with the typical role of separating cooperative former combatants. The Security Council was notably more reluctant to invoke "Chapter VII" for peace enforcement—authorizing coercion against recalcitrant armed actors. Peacekeeping could envision securing the activities of humanitarian organizations but did not typically imply any military responsibility for the needs of local civil society or any deep commitment to national reconstruction.

The aftermath of the Cold War brought new roles and missions into the mainstream of the larger military actors. The "new" kinds of conflicts were not really unique to the human experience but were now unconstrained by the pressures of Cold War competition. Therefore, they engaged the attention of the developed world in a new way. Somalia in the early 1990s offered both the United Nations and the United States a rude awakening to the disjunction between humanitarian impulses and likelihood of success.

By that time, military establishments still were "managing" (and applying) violence stalemates (as in Korea). But military interventions—for example, in Kosovo—were now legitimated by agreement between coalitions of partner states. Military personnel were expected to work harmoniously with coalition partners toward human security ends with an array of nonmilitary public and private sector actors, including international and nongovernmental organizations and civil societies.[19] Success in these roles depended on productive relationships with coalition partners and local populations. The key role of military forces was now to project values rather than force. In addition to the management of violence, likelihood of success required the management of trust.[20]

DEFINING AND PRIORITIZING THE ENDS

Contemporary security sector agencies—particularly military establishments—are now being employed in a range of novel roles, whether or not the military members are developed with those roles in mind. Therefore this chapter is interested in the ends for which security sector agencies are suited—or could be suited if developed and managed in a visionary way. Or framed as a question: How may a society best use its most sophisticated and expensive public assets? That leads inexorably to further questions: What roles and missions are appropriate to security establishments, and how should these be trained, equipped, led, and dispatched to properly fulfill those roles and missions when required? If the rationales for just cause have expanded, and the types of roles and missions for military members have also changed, does it follow that military organizations must possess expanded competencies to satisfy the Just War criteria of likelihood of success and proportionality?

Leaving aside for a moment the concern of who within a governing elite exercises the prerogative to order the deployment of security sector agencies, a key issue is the coherence of the process for defining and prioritizing "security" ends—in other words, the ends against which "security" agencies conceivably could be used. Some of those ends would almost certainly include protection of those things that the governing elite and the larger society hold most dear, which returns to the definition of "security" itself. A clear definition of security is a critical first step in any rational effort to defend against the things that undermine or threaten it and should precede any conversation of the appropriate roles of security sector actors.[21]

Whether a society defines its "security" ends narrowly or broadly, its security sector will almost inevitably play some role in pursuing them. However, it is when the military or police engage outside the national borders that the broad new security thinking comes particularly into play. In a negative sense, security sector personnel conducting international operations are now subject to previously unknown levels of scrutiny, with growing pressure to uphold high standards of ethical conduct.[22]

SOME IMPLICATIONS FOR DEVELOPING THE FORCE

Senior security sector officials, with their unique education and experience, offer management capacities rarely duplicated elsewhere in the public sector. This is particularly true of their ability to coordinate complex systems and their ability to perform threat and mission analysis. In other words, they should be able to take conflicting and ambiguous orders (or demands and expectations) and discern clear end states along with the subsidiary objectives required to arrive at those end states, factoring societal expectations and accommodating them in things like rules of engagement. They also should be uniquely qualified to coordinate the development and implementation of plans to attenuate, avoid, and overcome threats and obstacles. Senior security sector personnel—particularly senior military officers—are routinely expected to organize complex, divergent processes into a unified effort. It is rational to give such officials key leadership roles in humanitarian interventions of almost any variety. But there is still a question of whether even these officials are adequately prepared for the growing expectations.[23]

Military education emphasizes critical times and places at which concentrated effort can be directed to achieve decisive results—the tactician's *schwerpunkt*, or main emphasis. The challenge here is to broaden their perspective to apply this expertise to decisive results involving diverse communities of actors in a culturally complex environment—to seek social *schwerpunkts* whose outcome is human well-being, harmonious human relations in general and productive civil-military relations in particular. Of particular value would be senior security sector officials able to visualize and pursue ends as broad as self-sufficient societies able to peacefully resolve internal differences with mutually advantageous linkages to the wider international community.[24]

Transformation of a security sector to succeed in the evolving new roles, even at the low end of existing expectations, may not be possible. At best, it is no simple prospect. Military establishments play roles sanctioned by long peculiar histories—often with substantial emotional investment by the host society. Security sectors themselves tend toward the traditional and conservative, reluctant to embrace social change and even more reluctant to lead it. Nor is there any real consensus among the global attentive public on the specifics of security sector renovation. Then, too, the changes to accommodate the new security thinking, both in expectations and in actual performance, have hardly been uniform and consistent. Military organizations themselves have yet to prove beyond a shadow of a doubt that they are capable of meeting the evolving expectations. All that said, if security sector agencies—particularly military and civilian police—rise to the challenge, they will be obliged to consider changes both in organizational structure and in the development of individual members of the profession.

Structural change is arguably the most difficult challenge to articulate and achieve, largely because of the previously mentioned conservatism and the difficulty in anticipating the full range of challenges a security sector may be expected to address. It is unlikely that the capacity for warfighting—application and management of violence—will cease to be a core expectation. Modern security institutions are suited to this role, and security sectors in the developed countries are adept at producing military professionals capable of managing those institutions. It is the new roles and missions that seem to demand rethinking, whether structural or otherwise. The real issue is how to employ institutions originally designed to kill people and break things into organizations that attenuate violence by projecting values and managing trust.[25]

Some of the most innovative thinking on this topic has come from the European Union (EU), which commissioned a study in 2003 to explore the prospects for a human security approach to its European Security Strategy. The resulting study was overseen by London School of Economics scholar Mary Kaldor.[26] Its recommendations were at once visionary and radical. The authors started with a fundamental assumption that the international community has an unavoidable obligation to intervene in situations of severe insecurity and that the primary goal of such intervention would be "cessation of violence in order to provide space for political solutions." The immediate objectives would be to "protect people, calm violence, and establish a rule of law." Kaldor's study proposed a fifteen-thousand-person EU Human Security Response Force, fully a third of which would be comprised of "police officers, human rights monitors, humanitarian aid workers, civilian administrators and others." It envisioned a core group of five thousand, maintained at high readiness with constant training for immediate intervention; the remaining ten thousand members would train together periodically for follow-on augmentation of the initial core group. The structural diversity was intended to produce a "new ethos combining the traditional military values like heroism, sacrifice and excellence with the civilian qualities of listening and enabling others."[27] In 2011, seven years after the publication of the study, there was little evidence that the EU intended to implement its recommendations or that any individual country was experimenting with such radical restructuring, but a significant restructuring vision had been introduced into the mainstream of ideas about new military roles and missions.[28]

The United States has endeavored to adapt its military to the new roles and missions since the turn of the century, although its military profession still exhibits substantial ambivalence about those roles. Some American analysts suspect that the global security environment of the early twenty-first century is little more than a "strategic pause" preceding the resumption of more traditional military competition between superpowers. All indications are that the United States intends to maintain substantial warfighting capability for the foreseeable future. It has tried to accommodate the "building trust" missions largely within its traditional structures. Still, there are at least four very public indications of some new thinking: first, the appearance of calls for new capabilities since about 2004 in policy documents such as the Quadrennial Defense Review; second, the publication of the U.S. Army and Marines' new counterinsurgency (COIN) field manual;[29] third, the U.S. Army creation of the Human Terrain System, providing army combat commanders with small teams of nonmilitary experts charged with connecting combat forces to local communities or societies; and fourth, a growing emphasis by about 2006 on developing much more foreign language capability and understanding of culture in the general purpose forces.[30] In other words, the American approach currently places more emphasis on developing the people (human capacity) than changing the structure (structural capacity) to accommodate the new roles and missions.

Regardless of any structural change, it is unlikely that military organizations will be adequate for the new roles and missions without inculcating new understandings, values, and skills in military members. For the most part these are additions to—not substitutes for—existing capabilities, and the missing components almost all have to do with human relations. Military education in developed countries already pays attention to the human relations both of military leadership and of expected behavior of service members. What is novel is the additional attention to the relations between members of the military and the full range of human actors in the contemporary operational universe outside of the military organization itself. To adequately fulfill these new expectations, somewhat different sets of capabilities are required by military members of different rank and responsibility, of course—one developmental size cannot possibly fit the needs of all members. But it is possible to generalize at least four categories of required new knowledge and skills required for likelihood of success in mass atrocity response operations: ethical conduct, personality and social pathology, cross-cultural competence, and community living processes.

One of the most fundamental—and minimum—requirements in new capabilities is a basic awareness of emerging new global expectations of accountability to local communities and noncombatants. This is irrespective of the intensity of combat operations or the brevity of military intervention. The new expectations go well beyond traditional criteria of *jus in bello*. They include restraint not only in use of force and limitation of collateral damage but also expectations of succor for victims of trauma, sustainment of basic human needs (including physical safety), avoidance of activity that undermines the future health and safety of local populations, and safeguarding of cultural heritage. And there is more. The global attentive public expects military members not only to uphold standards of personal and organizational behavior but also to recognize and call attention to war crimes and crimes against humanity, wherever they occur and whoever the perpetrators may be.[31]

The gist of the new roles and missions is building trust and projecting values. This carries an assumption that actors of widely different backgrounds and perspectives will work effectively together toward common goals, generally with a military organization serving as the planning, logistic, and security glue that binds the whole. Given the potential diversities of agendas and cultures, the human relations aspects of these expectations can be daunting. Nor is it possible in advance to accurately anticipate all the possible permutations of personality and culture that will be encountered. If security sector personnel are deliberately and adequately prepared for the new roles, they require generalizable knowledge, skills, and attitudes that can be applied in almost any circumstance of complex human relations. This places a considerable challenge on military education and training programs. However, the expectations are not unreasonable and the task is not impossible.[32]

The requirement for military cross-cultural competence (often described in somewhat different words but meaning the same thing) has stimulated quite a bit of discussion among military practitioners and educators over the past decade. The heart of this issue is the expectation that security sector personnel successfully perform their duties in circumstances of significant cultural complexity that include differing organizational cultures and members of different nationalities and people groups. The challenge is rendered more complex by worldview differences often encountered within larger societies, reflecting differences of religious belief, class, generation, gender, and similar factors. A minimum set of capabilities required for this kind of competence would be:

- Perspective taking: an ability to suspend judgment and see reality through the "cultural filter" of another, along with a nuanced understanding of how one's own values, assumptions, beliefs, and expectations may impede the ability to see the "other's" reality.

- Cross-cultural communication: an ability to transmit and receive accurate messages across cultural boundaries, including a basic understanding of the role, use, and interpretation of nonverbal forms of communication.

- Relationship building: an ability to build productive working relationships in which all participants—regardless of culture or organizational affiliation—are motivated to work together effectively and harmoniously toward common objectives.

- Conflict management: an ability to analyze causes of interpersonal and interorganizational conflict and empowerment with an inventory of conceptual tools to resolve or attenuate the conflict, including skill in interest-based negotiations.

Beyond the particular skills of cross-cultural competence is a requirement for military personnel in the new missions to deal effectively with key cultural issues. Two examples are illustrative. One issue is social organization. At a minimum, this entails an ability to analyze how a local society conceives of its internal social connections, organizes collective activity, and allocates rights and responsibilities, while recognizing that these norms may have been changed or destroyed by conflict. At issue here is how collective decisions are made and disputes resolved. Within this framework, a military observer would want to know the local differences between coercive power, authority, prestige, and legitimacy and how to intersect, restore, or protect local governance and mediation. A second issue would be issues of livelihood, economic exchange, and the connection between the cultural environment and the natural environment, focusing on livelihood capacities that a community still has—so as not to engage in programming that dilutes or substitutes for it.

Here, the military observer would want to know how to encourage the continuation of a community's agricultural and commercial rhythms and restore or protect traditional relations of production. Again, this is not to infer that all infantrymen should be social anthropologists and agricultural economists. Rather, it is to infer that an intervention force should contain some members with sufficient expertise that it can work with, not against, local social organization and local economic processes. Even better would be a "reach-back" capability in which military members can quickly access deep expertise, as required, to deal with operational problems.[33]

The foregoing discussion of competencies for the emerging new roles and missions will undoubtedly strike some members of professional military askance, as it represents a substantial deviation from tradition. American military leaders often talk about "legacy" weapons systems—expensive armaments still in the U.S. inventory but better suited to the requirements of earlier conflicts. However, much worse than legacy weapons are legacy ideas—prevalent models of human organization and human behavior no longer appropriate to the needs of the human family. These are particularly problematic when it comes to security. Given the priority and resources that societies devote to this requirement, legacy ideas are not merely unfortunate; they rob the future of its possibilities. Legacy ideas about "security" may be one of the most difficult issues faced by strategists.

At the same time, this discussion may also seem at odds with most thinking within the Just War tradition. *Jus in bello* norms, as they have been formulated, focus on making distinctions between military personnel and civilians and on minimizing harm to the latter. The focus has been on minimizing physical harm, based on the assumption that the military's key role is in the projection of force. As this chapter argues, the military's role has shifted so substantially that the projection of force is no longer the only—or perhaps even the central—function of the military. As its functions evolve, the military potentially causes other types of harm to the civilians it encounters. As such, the competencies that we discuss above are significant not only for the ultimate success of an operation but also in terms of minimizing harm resulting from these new functions.

Notes

1. Harold Lasswell, "The Garrison State," *American Journal of Sociology* 46, no. 4 (1941): 455–68; Samuel Huntington, *The Soldier and the State: The Theory and Politics of Civil-Military Relations* (Cambridge, Mass.: Belknap, 1957).

2. G. John Ikenberry and Anne-Marie Slaughter, *Forging a World of Liberty under Law: U.S. National Security in the 21st Century: Final Report of the Princeton Project on*

National Security (Princeton: Woodrow Wilson School of Public and International Affairs, Princeton University, 2006).

3. Jessica Tuchman Mathews, "Redefining Security," *Foreign Affairs* 68, no. 2 (1989): 162–77; Stephen Walt, "The Renaissance of Security Studies," *International Studies Quarterly* 35, no. 2 (1991): 211–39; David Baldwin, "The Concept of Security," *Review of International Studies* 23, no. 1 (1997): 5–26; Barry Buzan, Ole Weaver, and Jaap de Wilde, *Security: A New Framework for Analysis* (London: Lynne Rienner, 1998); J. Peter Burgess and Taylor Owen, eds., "What Is 'Human Security'?," special section of *Security Dialogue* 35, no. 3 (2004): 345–71. For a succinct but excellent overview of the evolution of this new thinking, see Annette Seegers, "The New Security in Democratic South Africa: A Cautionary Tale," *Conflict, Security & Development* 10, no. 2 (2010): 263–85 (esp. 265–68).

4. S. Neil MacFarlane and Yuen Foong Khong, *Human Security and the UN: A Critical History* (Bloomington: Indiana University Press, 2006).

5. Oliver Richmond, "The Problem of Peace: Understanding the 'Liberal Peace,'" *Conflict, Security & Development* 6, no. 3 (2006): 291–314.

6. High-Level Panel on Threats, Challenges, and Change, *A More Secure World: Our Shared Responsibility*, Report of the Secretary-General's High-Level Panel on Threats, Challenges, and Change (New York: United Nations, 2004); United Nations Development Programme (UNDP), *New Dimensions of Human Security*, Human Development Report 1994 (New York: United Nations, 1994), http://hdr.undp.org/en/reports/global/hdr1994/ (accessed March 1, 2013).

7. See, for instance, P. H. Liotta and Taylor Owen, "Sense and Symbolism: Europe Takes on Human Security," *Parameters* 36, no. 3 (2006): 85–102.

8. See, for instance, "Human Security: Safety for People in a Changing World" (Ottawa: Department of Foreign Affairs and International Trade, 1999), http://www.summit-americas.org/canada/humansecurity-english.htm (accessed March 1, 2013); Bert Edström, "Japan's Foreign Policy and Human Security," *Japan Forum: The International Journal of Japanese Studies* 15, no. 2 (2003): 209–25; Rialize Ferreira and Dan Henk, "'Operationalizing' Human Security in South Africa," *Armed Forces & Society OnlineFirst* 35, no. 3 (2008): 501–25.

9. Tara McCormack, "Power and Agency in the Human Security Framework," *Cambridge Review of International Affairs* 20, no. 1 (2008): 113–28.

10. Human Security Report Project, *Human Security Report 2009/2010: The Causes of Peace and the Shrinking Costs of War* (New York: Oxford University Press, 2011).

11. Carsten Stahn, "Responsibility to Protect: Political Rhetoric or Emerging Legal Norm," *American Journal of International Law* 101, no. 1 (2007): 99–120; Stephen Marks and Nicholas Cooper, "The Responsibility to Protect: Watershed, or Old Wine in a New Bottle?" *Jindal Global Law Review* 2, no. 1 (2010): 86–130.

12. Gareth Evans and Mohamed Sahnoun, *The Responsibility to Protect: Report of the International Commission on Intervention and State Sovereignty* (Ottawa: International

Development Research Centre, 2001). Of course, R2P as it relates to military intervention applies only in egregious cases of "freedom from fear," not the "freedom from want" issues associated with human security.

13. Simon Chesterman has recorded the practical expansion in the use of the term "threat to international peace and security" by the United Nations Security Council in Simon Chesterman, *Just War or Just Peace? Humanitarian Intervention and International Law* (Oxford: Oxford University Press, 2002). See also Elizabeth Reid, "A Future, If One Is Still Alive: The Challenge of the HIV Epidemic," in *Hard Choices: Moral Dilemmas in Humanitarian Intervention*, ed. Jonathan Moore (Lanham, Md.: Rowman & Littlefield, 1998), 269–86.

14. High-Level Panel on Threats, Challenges, and Change, *More Secure World*.

15. See, for instance, Hugo Grotius, *The Rights of War and Peace; Including the Law of Nature and of Nations* (B. Boothroyd, 1901). The contemporary notion of "sovereignty as responsibility" cites an old concept. The oft-quoted eighteenth-century scholar Emerich de Vattel, while plainly affirming the autonomy of the sovereign state (particularly the moral equality of small and weak states to large and powerful ones), attached responsibilities to sovereignty: "If tyranny, becoming insupportable, obliges the nation to rise in their own defense,—every foreign power has a right to succour an oppressed people who implore their assistance."

16. Ibid.; Ferreira and Henk, "'Operationalizing' Human Security in South Africa."

17. Kimberly A. Hudson, *Justice, Intervention and Force: Re-assessing Just War Theory in the 21st Century* (Oxford: Routledge, 2009): 19–21.

18. Janine Davidson, "Giving Peacekeeping a Chance: The Modern Military's Struggle over Peace Operations," *Small Wars & Insurgencies* 15, no. 2 (2004): 168–84.

19. This coincided with "second generation" peacekeeping in the late 1980s and 1990s (and later, third-generation peacekeeping, which combined not only robust force but also wider mandates involving civilian protection and, in some settings, state-building beginning in the mid-1990s). The notion of integrated missions emerged from these experiments. Interview with Melissa T. Labonte, October 24, 2011. See also Margaret Karns and Karen Mingst, *The United Nations in the Post–Cold War Era* (Boulder: Westview Press, 2000); Michael Doyle, "War Making and Peace Making: The United Nations' Post–Cold War Record," in *Turbulent Peace: The Challenges of Managing International Conflict*, ed. Chester Crocker, Fen Osler Hampson, and Pamela Aall (Washington, D.C.: United States Institute of Peace, 2001); Ramesh Thakur and Albrecht Schnabel, "Cascading Generations of Peacekeeping: Across the Mogadishu Line to Kosovo and Timor," in *United Nations Peacekeeping Operations: Ad Hoc Missions, Permanent Engagement*, ed. Ramesh Thakur and Albrecht Schnabel (Tokyo: United Nations University Press, 2001); Oliver Richmond, *Maintaining Order, Making Peace* (New York: Palgrave, 2002).

20. The author is indebted to Canadian military scholar Al Okros (Captain, Canadian Navy, retired) for this elaboration of expectations of security sectors. It is particu-

larly his thinking that identified the "projection of values" and "management of trust" as contemporary responsibilities of military organizations.

21. Baldwin, "Concept of Security"; Buzan, Weaver, de Wilde, *Security*.

22. See, for example, Carol Allais, "Sexual Exploitation and Abuse by UN Peacekeepers: The Psychosocial Context of Behaviour Change," *Scientia Militaria* 39, no. 1 (2011): 1–15; Prince Zeid Ra'ad Al-Hussein, "A Comprehensive Strategy to Eliminate Future Sexual Exploitation and Abuse in United Nations Peacekeeping Operations," United Nations A/59/710, http://cdu.unlb.org/Portals/0/Documents/KeyDocs.pdf (accessed September 28, 2011).

23. Barak A. Salmoni, Jessica Hart, Renny McPherson, and Aidan Kirby Winn, "Growing Strategic Leaders for Future Conflict," *Parameters* 40, no. 1 Spring 2010): 72.

24. Remi Hajjar, "A New Angle on the U.S. Military's Emphasis on Developing Cross-Cultural Competence: Connecting In-Ranks' Cultural Diversity to Cross-Cultural Competence," *Armed Forces & Society* 36 (2010): 247.

25. Taylor Seybolt, *Humanitarian Intervention: The Conditions for Success and Failure* (Oxford: Oxford University Press, 2007).

26. Ulrich Albrecht, Christine Chinkin, Kemal Dervis, Renata Dwan, Anthony Giddens, Nicole Gnesotto, Mary Kaldor, et al., *A Human Security Doctrine for Europe: The Barcelona Report of the Study Group on Europe's Security Capabilities*, presented to EU Secretary-General Javier Solana, September 25, 2004.

27. Mary Kaldor, "A Force for Intervention: A Human Security Doctrine for Europe, and Beyond," *New York Times*, 30 September 2004, http://www.nytimes.com/2004/09/30/opinion/30iht-edkaldor_ed3_.html (accessed September 28, 2011). The EU's motivation in commissioning the study, and the tenor of the recommendations, seemed to have had the earlier EU-sponsored intervention in the Democratic Republic of Congo in mind. However, the timing of the study also suggested EU discomfort with the U.S. intervention in Iraq and a desire to distance European countries from the U.S.-led coalition and its more conventional military approach.

28. This view reflects the cosmopolitan security model envisioned by many EU elites and now under fire from some quarters. See reference to Ulrich Beck in Mary Hampton, "Living in a World of Dangers and Strangers: Changing EU and German Perception," *German Politics & Society* 29, no. 3 (2011): 73–96.

29. U.S. Army/Marine Corps Counterinsurgency Field Manual (Chicago: University of Chicago Press, 2007), 3–24.

30. All of these efforts have provoked controversy. Negative reactions in American academe include David Price, *Weaponizing Anthropology: Social Science in Service of the Militarized State* (Oakland, Calif.: AK Press, 2011); Roberto Gonzalez, *American Counterinsurgency: Human Science and the Human Terrain* (Chicago: University of Chicago Press, 2009).

31. Jared Tracy, "Ethical Challenges in Stability Operations," *Military Review* 89, no. 1 (2009).

32. Ben Connable, "All Our Eggs in a Broken Basket: How the Human Terrain System Is Undermining Sustainable Military Cultural Competence," *Military Review* 89, no. 2 (2009).

33. Allison Abbe and Stanley Halpin, "The Cultural Imperative for Professional Military Education and Leader Development," *Parameters* 39, no. 4 (Winter 2009–10): 20–31; see also *Counterinsurgency*, Field Manual 3-24 (Washington, D.C.: Department of the Army and Headquarters, United States Marine Corps, 2006).

CHAPTER THREE

Is Just Intervention Morally Obligatory?

Luke Glanville

THE IDEA THAT HUMANITARIAN INTERVENTION is not only permissible but obligatory is a central tenet of the "responsibility to protect" that has rapidly emerged in international discourse over the last decade. This concept was first developed by the International Commission on Intervention and State Sovereignty (ICISS) in 2001.[1] As numerous scholars had done in the 1990s,[2] the ICISS laid out principles for humanitarian intervention according to widely accepted Just War criteria. These included just cause, right intention, last resort, proportionality, reasonable prospects for success, and right authority.[3] However, whereas earlier scholars had suggested that the satisfaction of Just War criteria could generate a right of intervention, the ICISS claimed that it actually generated a responsibility to intervene. The commission asserted that in those instances where intervention was permissible, it was also obligatory. Nevertheless, the ICISS provided little justification for this claim, simply implying that such intervention was demanded by our "common humanity" and by the need to deliver "practical protection for ordinary people, at risk of their lives, because their states are unwilling or unable to protect them."[4]

In this chapter, I outline a defense of the claim that humanitarian intervention, where just, is morally obligatory. I consider some arguments in favor of this proposition and suggest that to the extent that intervention can ever be justified, it is obligatory by virtue of the duties-generating character of human rights. Although some have argued that such a duty is "imperfect" since it does not fall on any potential intervener in particular, I claim not only that the duty can in theory be "perfected" by appropriate and equitable distribution of obligations but that states, regional organizations, and international institutions already behave as if they recognize the duty to protect to be largely distributed in this way. The chapter, therefore, goes some way toward responding to claims long heard that we have only a minimal duty to assist and protect strangers and foreigners and that the duty ought to instead be understood as a discretionary right lest it impose an excessive burden upon particular actors.

MORAL OBLIGATION IN JUST WAR THINKING

Cicero, one of the earliest Just War theorists, wrote of duties of assistance and protection owed to foreigners. In a work that profoundly influenced the subsequent development of Western political thought, *On Duties*, the Roman philosopher developed an account of the obligations that we owe to each other by virtue of our common humanity. Cicero argued that a man is not to harm another, and he is also not to stand by when harm is being perpetrated against another: "the man who does not defend someone, or obstruct the injustice when he can, is at fault just as if he had abandoned his parents or his friends or his country."[5] He insisted that duties are owed universally, declaring it absurd to say that justice and fellowship obtain between family members but not between fellow citizens, and equally absurd that account should be taken of fellow citizens but not of foreigners. Those who suggest otherwise "tear apart the common fellowship of the human race."[6]

However, Cicero believed that duties owed to family and fellow citizens take priority over those owed to strangers and foreigners. "It seems clear to me," he observed, "that we were so created that between us all there exists a certain tie which strengthens with our proximity to each other. Therefore, fellow countrymen are preferred to foreigners and relatives to strangers."[7] He accepted that the performance of a duty to defend others would at times require some degree of self-sacrifice, and he reprimanded those who neglect their duties out of a desire to avoid "enmities, or toil, or expense."[8] Yet he indicated that duties that were owed to strangers were limited to those instances where "assistance can be provided without detriment to oneself." After all, "the resources of individuals are small, but the mass of those who are in need is infinitely great." We need to be measured in our generosity, therefore, so that "we shall still be capable of being liberal to those close to us."[9]

Cicero's account of duties contributed in no small measure to the subsequent development of Just War theorizing. His universal duties of assistance and protection were commonly combined with arguments about the legitimacy of pun-

ishing tyrants for breaches of natural law in order to justify extensive intervention by states in each other's affairs, and particularly by European states in the
New World. Sometimes intervention was framed merely as a right, but often it
was articulated in terms of a duty. Gentili asserted a universal duty "to protect
men's interests and safety" and, defending war on behalf of others, maintained
that "the subjects of others do not seem to me to be outside of that kinship of
nature and the society formed by the whole world."[10] Some appealed to the limits that Cicero placed on the duties owed to foreigners in order to emphasize
the discretion that states could rightfully exercise. Grotius, for example, emphasized the natural right of self-preservation and, citing Cicero for support, suggested that rescue of peoples from injury and oppression was obligatory for a
state only insofar as it could be carried out with "convenience" to itself.[11] Vattel similarly allowed intervention in support of peoples resisting tyranny while
cautioning, "The duties of a nation towards itself, and chiefly the care of its own
safety, require much more circumspection and reserve, than need be observed
by an individual in giving assistance to others."[12]

During the nineteenth and twentieth centuries, as the sovereign right of
non-intervention became firmly entrenched in international law, the focus of
debate about "humanitarian intervention" was whether it was permissible at
all, not whether it was mandatory. Since the end of the Cold War, however, as
notions of conditional sovereignty and the permissibility of humanitarian intervention have come to be widely accepted within the society of states, attention
has again turned to whether and in what circumstances such intervention is
morally obligatory.

THE MORAL OBLIGATION TO INTERVENE

Clearly, intervention can be morally obligatory only insofar as it is morally permissible, and there are several powerful arguments against intervention that
ought to make us pause. Some theorists, such as Las Casas in the sixteenth
century, observed that wars in defense of people risk creating more harm than
good and costing more lives than are saved.[13] Others, such as Pufendorf in the
seventeenth century, have warned that a right of intervention could be subject
to self-interested abuse and lead to increased instances of unjust war.[14] Others
still, such as J. S. Mill in the nineteenth century, have criticized the notion of
intervention as a violation of the right of communities to self-government.[15]
Nevertheless, I wish to cautiously proceed on the assumption that there are

occasionally extraordinary situations, such as the 1994 Rwandan genocide, in which military intervention in defense of humanity satisfies Just War criteria and should be permitted. It does not automatically follow, however, that permissible interventions are obligatory.

Some have argued, particularly since the terrorist attacks of September 11, 2001, that realist logic produces a moral obligation to intervene to protect populations from mass atrocities since the occurrence of atrocities so frequently spawns flows of refugees and conditions that facilitate arms and drug smuggling, the proliferation of weapons of mass destruction, and the spread of international terrorism, each of which threatens international order and stability and therefore national security.[16] This realist argument, however, suffers from a serious limitation in that while it may be persuasive in certain cases like Kosovo, it will be less persuasive in cases like Rwanda in which the material self-interests of powerful states are not clearly affected. We need, therefore, an argument for the morally obligatory nature of intervention that does not rely on a coincidence of national interests with the interests of strangers.

One such argument suggests that standing by while some members of human society are harmed in fact harms us all in some moral sense. In the sixteenth century, Gentili justified war in response to violations of the "common law of humanity" and the "law of nations" on the grounds that "in the violation of that law we are all injured."[17] More recently, in the 2008 U.S. presidential campaign, Barack Obama asserted that "when genocide is happening, when ethnic cleansing is happening somewhere around the world and we stand idly by, that diminishes us."[18] This kind of argument is certainly appealing, but, to be honest, I do not know what it means.

A less abstract and more persuasive argument rests on the simple observation that human rights generate duties. To the extent that there are universal human rights, there are duties that fall upon us all to protect them, and insofar as it is permissible to intervene beyond borders to protect human rights in exceptional and tragic circumstances, we are morally obliged to do so. We may not agree on where human rights come from.[19] Nevertheless it is agreed that all individuals have rights by virtue of their humanity. The first article of the Universal Declaration of Human Rights, to cite one example, declares, "All human beings are born free and equal in dignity and rights." Moreover, we hold human rights to be so important, so fundamental, that we are sometimes permitted to set aside the sovereign right of non-intervention to defend them when they are threatened on a massive scale. This is the argument upon which theorists justify the permissibility of humanitarian intervention and upon which actual instances of such intervention have been justified by states. It would seem to me that if in a particular situation human rights are threatened to the extent that a state can be said to no longer rightfully enjoy freedom from outside intervention, then the duty-generating character of human rights imposes a duty upon other states to act to protect the population.[20]

Human rights such as the right to life and freedom from violence and injury are properly understood as claim rights, and claim rights generate duties. Cicero suggested that justice requires both that we refrain from harming others and also that we act to defend others who are being harmed. Human rights generate duties in both of these senses: negative duties to refrain from harm and positive duties to assist and to protect from harm. If we are to take the idea of universal human rights seriously—and it would seem that we believe we should given how many conventions and declarations are adopted in their name—then we are required not only to refrain from violating them but also to act to protect them. Henry Shue has persuasively defended such a claim in his classic work, *Basic Rights*, in which he develops a typology of duties: to avoid depriving, to protect from deprivation, and to assist the deprived.[21] Moreover, Shue makes clear that such duties do not fall on only the sovereign state. Using precisely the language that the iciss would later adopt, he acknowledges that the "primary duty" to protect human rights lies with the state, but he insists that external actors possess "default duties" to act to protect populations when states prove unwilling or unable to do so.[22] James Nickel concurs, suggesting that "a morally justified right does not just disappear, or cease to direct behaviour, when it is systematically violated. In such a case, the right's capacity to generate obligations may shift so as to increase the responsibilities of the secondary addressees."[23] There are a range of actions that external actors may undertake to discharge their default duty. They might condemn the violations of human rights, apply diplomatic pressure, or impose economic or military sanctions. However, in those extraordinary situations in which the seriousness of the human rights violations and the context of the crisis are such that military intervention is understood to be permitted as a just response of last resort, it would seem reasonable to suggest that such intervention is morally obligatory since it is the only means of effectively discharging the duty to protect.

Cicero suggested that duties owed to those close to us take priority over duties owed to distant strangers. Such arguments are often heard today in discussions of global justice. A response to the claim that intervention is morally obligatory might be that while there are universal human rights, the duty of the state to provide for and to protect the rights of the national population takes priority over the duty to protect those outside of the state. I would tend to endorse the "strong cosmopolitan argument" advanced by Martha Nussbaum among others that insists that nationality is a "morally irrelevant characteristic" and that national boundaries are "morally arbitrary."[24] While there may be good reasons for individuals to prioritize the duties owed to family and friends, it is not at all clear to me why we should prefer the rights of co-nationals to the rights of those beyond our borders.[25] Nevertheless, we do not need to accept this strong version of cosmopolitanism to accept that we possess duties beyond borders. David Miller defends the moral relevance of nationality and the idea that a nation-state has a particular duty to promote the well-being of its own population, yet he also recognizes that all humans have basic rights that generate duties not only to refrain from harm but, in extraordinary situations, to assist and protect. Miller concludes that nations are bound to limit their pursuit of domestic objectives, at least to some degree, in order to carry out their global obligations.[26] It would seem clear that extraordinary human rights violations are precisely the kinds of situations in which we are obliged to restrain our pursuit of national well-being and act to rescue strangers.

ASSIGNING THE OBLIGATION TO INTERVENE

Numerous scholars have charged that while there may indeed be a moral duty to intervene to protect populations from mass atrocities, it is an "imperfect duty," meaning that it is not one that can be morally demanded of any particular actor. Michael Walzer puts it well: "The general problem is that intervention, even when it is justified, even when it is necessary to prevent terrible crimes, even when it poses no threat to regional or global stability, is an imperfect duty—a duty that doesn't belong to any particular agent. Somebody ought to intervene, but no specific state in the society of states is morally bound to do so."[27] This would seem to render the notion of a universal right to protection meaningless. As Onora O'Neill observes, "When obligations are unallocated it is indeed right that they be met, but nobody can have an effective right—an enforceable, claimable or waiveable right—to their being met. Such abstract rights are not effective entitlements. . . . [They] are empty 'manifesto' rights."[28]

What is required is that the duty to intervene be allocated to particular actors in particular circumstances. The duty to protect human rights is not a universal duty in the sense that the duty to refrain from injuring others is. We are all expected to refrain from doing harm, but we cannot all be expected to individually contribute to everyone else's protection. Nor do we need to be. To paraphrase O'Neill, the universal right to be protected from injury can be fully met so long as *somebody* provides such protection.[29] As Shue suggests, "Universal rights, then, entail not universal duties but full coverage. Full coverage can be provided by a division of labor among duty-bearers."[30] What is required to make the notion of universal rights meaningful is that the duty to protect must be distributed and assigned to particular actors and thereby "perfected." Moreover, it would seem that such distribution is itself a perfect duty. While international actors may not all have a perfect duty to intervene in every instance to ensure every individual's protection, they arguably do have a perfect and universal duty to work together to ensure that the duty of intervention is distributed efficiently and equitably.[31]

How might the duty to intervene be appropriately and fruitfully assigned? Moral theorists suggest two key ways to assign such a positive duty. The first, and least satisfactory, way involves identifying an actor that stands in a *special relationship* with those in need of protection or that has a *special capability* for protecting them. This idea is based on the concept of "backward-looking" and "forward-looking" responsibility allocation developed by Robert Goodin,[32] and it has been applied to the subject of military intervention by a number of philosophers including Kok-Chor Tan.[33] An actor who has one of these special qualities may be understood to bear a particular duty to intervene. Looking backward, a state might be understood to stand in a special relationship with people in need of protection in another state by virtue of shared historical ties, including perhaps past injustices. Tan observes that former colonial powers are often understood to bear a particular responsibility to ensure the ongoing peace and stability of a former colony. Alternatively, looking forward, responsibility might arise due to the state's military strength or its geographical proximity to the people in need. The argument, then, is simply that we may be able to identify actors that "stand out" and bear a particular duty to intervene on behalf of the society of states.[34]

I suggest that this means of responsibility distribution is already accepted in practice in certain instances. States often recognize that they bear a particular burden of responsibility to intervene in response to mass atrocities either by virtue of their special relationship with the victims or their special capacity to rescue. In 2003, for example, President George W. Bush acknowledged that the United States' "unique history with Liberia" had "created a certain sense of expectations" that the United States would act to end the violence in the country.[35] And in 1994, the Clinton administration tacitly acknowledged that it bore a particular obligation to act to end the violence in Rwanda, presumably because of the military capability of the United States and its role as a leading power, when it actively sought to frame the violence as an intractable civil war rather than as a genocide in order to avoid the sociopolitical costs of failing to act. However, this means of distributing responsibility has important limitations. The existence of special relationships can be patchy and contested, and the burdens imposed upon those with special capacity can at times be unreasonable.[36]

The second and more satisfactory means of allocating responsibility is institutionalization. This idea was outlined by Shue in a well-known article, "Mediating Duties."[37] Shue suggests that we need institutions to mediate the duties that all actors have to protect the rights of others, both for reasons of efficiency and also in order to provide respite for actors who might otherwise be unfairly burdened. Institutions assign duties to particular actors and specify their content. Thus, they transform "imperfect" duties into "perfect" duties that can strictly bind actors. He claims that the development of institutions to mediate duties for the protection of the rights of others is itself a duty that we all bear: "If institutions are players of as much importance as I have maintained throughout and can implement positive duties effectively, among the most important duties of individual persons will be indirect duties for the design and creation of positive-duty performing institutions that do not yet exist and for the modification or transformation of existing institutions that now ignore rights and the positive duties that rights involve."[38] As noted earlier, Shue acknowledges that the institution that bears the "primary duty" for the protection of populations is the sovereign state. However, since it is clear that states are often unwilling or unable to discharge their responsibilities, Shue argues, it is necessary to develop institutions beyond the state that can carry out "default duties" to protect populations when required. A number of scholars have applied this concept of institutionalization to the subject of intervention in recent years.[39] They argue that if we accept that intervention is at times a moral duty, then all actors within the society of states have an obligation to "perfect" the duty by developing institutions that can effectively undertake or facilitate such interventions. After all, as O'Neill suggests, universal rights are "easy to proclaim, but until there are effective institutions their proclamation may seem a bitter mockery to those who most need them."[40]

I again suggest that this argument for the allocation of duties is not merely plausible in the abstract, but international actors already behave as if duties of intervention are allocated in this way. Particular states, regional organizations, and international institutions bear particular duties to either undertake or facilitate intervention in particular instances due to the institutionalization of the duty. Such distribution of duties may not yet be optimal in terms of efficiency or equitability, but it does mean that particular actors can at times be identified who bear a particular obligation to act and who can be appropriately subject to blame when they fail to do so. In Article 4(h) of its Constitutive Act, for example, the African Union (AU) has declared for itself "the right . . . to intervene in a Member State pursuant to a decision of the Assembly in respect of grave circumstances, namely: war crimes, genocide and crimes against humanity." In claiming the *right* to develop "African solutions to African problems," the AU has arguably taken upon itself the *obligation* to do so on behalf of the society of states. The role of the AU with respect to the crisis in Darfur was repeatedly framed in this way by both African and non-African states until it became clear in 2006–7 that the organization was not able to effectively discharge its obligations and that the UN Security Council would need to authorize the deployment of a hybrid UN-AU force.[41]

The Security Council, in turn, is an international institution that is understood to bear the particular obligation to authorize coercive measures in response to mass atrocities, where appropriate, by virtue of its right to decide on such matters under the UN Charter.[42] Certainly, the Security Council should exercise discretion in determining the most appropriate way of responding to individual crises. However, in claiming the exclusive right to authorize the use of military force, it also takes on the obligation to do so when necessary.[43] Moreover, it would seem to follow that council members have a moral obligation to table and facilitate the passage of appropriate resolutions, and the five veto-wielding permanent members of the council have a duty to refrain from impeding the council by vetoing or threatening to veto draft resolutions that would authorize the effective protection of populations.

While the obligation to intervene and facilitate intervention is already assigned to particular actors in particular circumstances, such distribution is not yet optimal. Cicero and several theorists who followed him suggested that intervention for the protection of others from injury could be morally obligatory only so long as it could be performed without excessive cost to oneself. Consideration of what is excessively costly to a state is beyond the scope of this chapter. Nevertheless, it seems reasonable to suggest that there are limits to the costs that we can expect states to bear in protecting those beyond their borders. After all, a state cannot be expected to intervene to rescue strangers if such intervention seriously undermines its capacity to protect the rights of its own populations. However, all international actors do have a duty to cooperate and coordinate to institutionalize the duty of intervention so that it may be most efficiently and fairly distributed such that it *can* be effectively discharged without any particular actor bearing excessive cost. As Shue suggests, "one wants institutions that function effectively to honor rights while imposing only duties that make fair demands of those who bear them. . . . We simply must find out whether both [of these principles] can be satisfied together in practice, being as imaginative as we can."[44] The demand that intervention not be excessively costly does not allow us to ignore the duty to intervene. Rather, it obliges us to distribute the duty more fairly and effectively. Of course, it is conceivable that there could be instances in which, even with equitable distribution of responsibility among capable actors, justifiable intervention will be excessively costly.[45] Our duty is to distribute the obligation to intervene effectively and fairly so that such instances arise as infrequently as possible; so that the moral obligation to intervene may be discharged and so that universal rights may be vindicated.[46]

~

In this chapter I argue that to the extent that intervention to protect populations is ever permissible, it is morally obligatory. I justify this by appealing to the duties-generating character of human rights. If we are to take the idea of universal human rights seriously, then we need to accept that their protection is not merely a discretionary right but a moral duty. I suggest that regardless of whether we think that duties owed to those close to us should take priority over those owed to strangers, the obligation to protect those beyond our borders is surely generated in those instances where violations of human rights are so severe that external intervention is permitted. I observe that the obligation to intervene does not fall on every actor, but rather that it falls on particular actors in particular ways, and that every actor has a duty to cooperate and to institutionalize the duty so that the burden is distributed appropriately and fairly and so that it can be discharged effectively. And I suggest that states, regional organizations, and international institutions already appear to recognize the obligation to intervene to be distributed in fairly clear ways, if not always in the most efficient or equitable ways. This is not to say that relevant actors always faithfully discharge their obligation, but merely that it is at least widely recognized upon whom the obligation falls. We have a universal duty to continue to work together to further ensure that the obligation to intervene is best distributed so it can be performed as far as possible without excessive costs to particular actors.

Of course, it is to be lamented that there ever arise instances in which military intervention is required. Even when it saves the lives of many, intervention typically costs the lives of some. Moreover, the obligation to intervene always follows a tragic failure to prevent a crisis in the first place. There is an overwhelming case, therefore, for imploring international actors to carry out their prior moral obligation of assisting states to protect their populations from grave violations of human rights so that mass atrocities are prevented and intervention does not need to occur. In recent years, advocates of the "responsibility to protect" have endeavored to reorient discussion about the protection of populations away from the controversial issue of intervention and toward a focus on the prevention of mass atrocities through assistance, capacity building, and institutional reform. Such a move holds the promise not only of avoiding contentious debates about the rights and duties of intervention but also of saving more lives.

Notes

1. International Commission on Intervention and State Sovereignty (ICISS), *The Responsibility to Protect: Report of the International Commission on Intervention and State Sovereignty* (Ottawa: International Development Research Centre [IDRC], 2001).

2. See, for example, Mona Fixdal and Dan Smith, "Humanitarian Intervention and Just War," *Mershon International Studies Review* 42, no. 2 (1998); Nicholas J. Wheeler, *Saving Strangers: Humanitarian Intervention in International Society* (Oxford: Oxford University Press, 2000).

3. ICISS, *Responsibility to Protect*, xii.

4. Ibid., 2, 11.

5. Cicero, *On Duties*, ed. M. T. Griffin and E. M. Atkins (Cambridge: Cambridge University Press, 1991), I.23.

6. Ibid., III.28.

7. Cicero, *De Amicitia*, qtd. in Richard Tuck, *The Rights of War and Peace: Political Thought and the International Order from Grotius to Kant* (Oxford: Oxford University Press, 1999), 36.

8. Cicero, *On Duties*, I.28.

9. Ibid., I.51–52.

10. Alberico Gentili, *De Iure Belli Libri Tres*, trans. John C. Rolfe, vol. 2 (Oxford: Clarendon Press, 1933), I.XV, I.XVI.

11. Hugo Grotius, *The Rights of War and Peace*, ed. Richard Tuck (Indianapolis: Liberty Fund, 2005), II.XXV.7(1).

12. Emer de Vattel, *The Law of Nations*, ed. Bela Kapossy and Richard Whatmore (Indianapolis: Liberty Fund, 2008), II.I.3.

13. Bartolome de Las Casas, *In Defense of the Indians*, trans. Stafford Poole (DeKalb, Ill.: Northern Illinois University Press, 1992), ch. 31.

14. Samuel Pufendorf, *The Law of Nature and Nations*, trans. Basil Kennett (London, 1729), VIII.VI.14.

15. See J. S. Mill, "A Few Words on Non-intervention," in *The Collected Works of John Stuart Mill*, vol. 21, *Essays on Equality, Law and Education* (London: Routledge and Kegan Paul, 1984).

16. See, for example, Michael Wesley, "Toward a Realist Ethics of Intervention," *Ethics and International Affairs* 19, no. 2 (2005).

17. Gentili, *De Iure Belli Libri Tres*, I.XXV.

18. Qtd. in James Pattison, *Humanitarian Intervention and the Responsibility to Protect: Who Should Intervene?* (Oxford: Oxford University Press, 2010), 177.

19. Referring to agreement reached on human rights by "proponents of violently opposed ideologies" within UNESCO soon after the Second World War, Jacques Maritain famously observed that "we agree on these rights, *providing we are not asked why.*" Jacques Maritain, *Man and the State* (Chicago: University of Chicago Press, 1951), 77. I would contend that the only plausible grounds for holding that we all possess rights is that we are all conferred with moral worth by a loving God. See Nicholas Wolterstorff, *Justice: Rights and Wrongs* (Princeton: Princeton University Press, 2008). I recognize, however, that many believe that universal rights can be justified on alternative grounds.

20. This argument is derived from Kok-Chor Tan, who suggests: "If rights violations are severe enough to override the sovereignty of the offending state, which is a cornerstone ideal in international affairs, the severity of the situation should also impose an obligation on other states to end the violation." Kok-Chor Tan, "The Duty to Protect," in *Humanitarian Intervention*, ed. Terry Nardin and Melissa S. Williams (New York: New York University Press, 2006), 90.

21. Henry Shue, *Basic Rights: Subsistence, Affluence, and U.S. Foreign Policy*, 2nd ed. (Princeton: Princeton University Press, 1996).

22. Henry Shue, "Afterword: Rights-Grounded Duties and the Institutional Turn," in *Basic Rights*.

23. James Nickel, "How Human Rights Generate Duties to Protect and Provide," *Human Rights Quarterly* 15, no. 1 (1993): 85.

24. Martha C. Nussbaum, "Patriotism and Cosmopolitanism," in *For Love of Country: Debating the Limits of Patriotism*, ed. Joshua Cohen (Boston: Beacon Press, 2002), 5, 14.

25. For an argument endorsing this view, see Simon Caney, *Justice beyond Borders: A Global Political Theory* (Oxford: Oxford University Press, 2005).

26. David Miller, *National Responsibility and Global Justice* (Oxford: Oxford University Press, 2007). Miller, however, emphasizes that this is a "humanitarian duty" whose performance is unenforceable rather than a "duty of justice" (248, 73). For Kantian arguments that intervention is in fact a duty of justice, see Carla Bagnoli, "Humanitarian Intervention as a Perfect Duty," in *Humanitarian Intervention*, ed. Terry Nardin and Melissa S. Williams (New York: New York University Press, 2006); Heather M. Roff, "A Provisional Duty of Humanitarian Intervention," *Global Responsibility to Protect* 3, no. 2 (2011).

27. Michael Walzer, *Just and Unjust Wars*, 3rd ed. (New York: Basic Books, 2000), xiii.

28. Onora O'Neill, *Bounds of Justice* (Cambridge: Cambridge University Press, 2000), 126.

29. Ibid., 103.

30. Henry Shue, "Mediating Duties," *Ethics* 98, no. 4 (1988): 690.

31. O'Neill, *Bounds of Justice*, 103.

32. Robert E. Goodin, *Protecting the Vulnerable: A Reanalysis of Our Social Responsibilities* (Chicago: University of Chicago Press, 1985), 117–35.

33. See Pattison, *Humanitarian Intervention*; Roff, "Provisional Duty"; Tan, " Duty to Protect."

34. Tan, " Duty to Protect," 98, 101.

35. Elizabeth Bumiller and Eric Schmitt, "Bush Insists Liberian President Go before Troops Come," *New York Times*, July 4, 2003. Tan also offers this example in Tan, "Duty to Protect," 114n23.

36. Tan, " Duty to Protect," 101–2.

37. Shue, "Mediating Duties."

38. Ibid., 703.

39. See Bagnoli, "Humanitarian Intervention"; Pattison, *Humanitarian Intervention*; Roff, "Provisional Duty"; Tan, "Duty to Protect."

40. O'Neill, *Bounds of Justice*, 105.

41. See UNSC Resolution 1769 (July 31, 2007).

42. How this exclusive right of the Security Council can be reconciled with the right of intervention claimed by the AU is not altogether clear under international law.

43. Indeed this function of the Security Council is framed as a "responsibility" in Article 24(1) of the Charter.

44. Shue, "Afterword," 166.

45. I would suggest, however, that it would usually be the case that excessively costly interventions are actually unjustifiable on grounds of proportionality and likelihood of success in the first place.

46. It is sometimes suggested that while states may in certain circumstances bear a moral obligation to intervene, the same cannot be said of individual soldiers who are asked to risk their lives to protect the lives of strangers. For a compelling discussion, see Daniel Baer, "The Ultimate Sacrifice and the Ethics of Humanitarian Intervention," *Review of International Studies* 37, no. 1 (2011): 301–26. I would suggest that this is no truer of humanitarian intervention than it is of any other kind of war. If we accept that soldiers can ever be asked to risk their lives in war on behalf of their state, there is no reason, it seems to me, to suggest that asking them to do so as part of a humanitarian intervention is any more problematic than any other justly waged war.

CHAPTER FOUR

Private Military Companies and the Reasonable Chance of Success

Amy E. Eckert

ASSESSING THE REASONABLE CHANCE of success, one of the ancillary criteria of *jus ad bellum*, has become more complicated with the increasing reliance of states on private force. With the emergence of the private military industry, states and other actors can now hire additional capabilities to augment their own forces. Private military companies (PMCs) provide a range of services from logistical support to combat, all of which enhance their clients' ability to wage war. The capabilities that actors can secure on the open market can transform their ability to wage war, and these potentially transformative services are available to both wealthy and poor actors. The availability of wealth from mineral resources and other state assets can pay for private force so that even states without access to the cash to pay for services can hire PMCs. This means that the complications for assessing the reasonable chance of success apply across the board, virtually without limitation. The complications of enhanced capabilities apply to all states and rebel movements, without regard to their wealth or poverty.

The function of the Just War tradition generally, and *jus ad bellum* norms in particular, is to limit the unjust use of force. Certainly the use of force is unjust if it is deployed in service of an unjust cause. But even where a state has just cause to wage war, its use of force may still be unjust where the state has no reasonable prospect of achieving its cause. Where a state lacks this reasonable chance of success, the pursuit of even a just cause takes on the nature of a quixotic endeavor that inflicts harm without achieving any morally redeeming result. This principle is sometimes characterized as a prudential principle rather than a moral one. Alex J. Bellamy characterizes the reasonable chance of success as a prudential *jus ad bellum* criterion that provides a check on the waging of an otherwise justifiable war.[1] While this particular principle does require a strategic assessment of a potential opponent's capabilities, it is at its core a moral principle. The use of force without a realistic chance of obtaining the (presumably just) cause is not merely imprudent but also unethical.

The application of this principle does require the state or, in the context of a civil war, the rebel movement to make an assessment of both its own capabilities and its potential adversary's strengths. Success, defined as the military triumph over the enemy, is essential to obtaining the just cause that initially motivated the war. While events may take the war in an unpredictable direction, initiating a war that cannot possibly succeed is at odds with the central concern of *jus ad bellum* principles, the limitation of unjust force. If the principle of reasonable chance of success is to be satisfied, a state must have at least some realistic possibility of prevailing.

Making this assessment requires that states be able to judge the capabilities of their potential adversaries with some degree of accuracy. Such an assessment is difficult under any circumstances because of the nebulousness inherent in the concept of power itself. Power is difficult to calculate under any conditions, but the availability of private force means that even an accurate assessment of power could quickly become obsolete. The use of private force in Sierra Leone's civil war bears out the transformative role that PMCs can play in war. On its own, the government of Sierra Leone could not defend itself against a challenge from the Revolutionary United Front (RUF). After hiring the PMC Executive Outcomes (EO), the government's fortunes improved substantially, to the point that the government was able to compel the RUF to negotiate a settlement. These gains resulted solely from the involvement of EO, as the aftermath of EO's withdrawal establishes. While the case of Sierra Leone and the role of EO is an instance in which the contributions of private force were particularly dramatic, PMCs always enhance the capabilities of their clients. Even the performance of logistical functions frees the military personnel who would otherwise perform those tasks, allowing them to assume more combat-related functions. The potential of PMCs to enhance their clients' military capabilities makes the estimation of power and the chances of success more difficult than ever.

This chapter considers the emergence of the private market for force and how the ability of states to hire PMCs complicates the application of this principle of reasonable chance of success. The discussion begins with an overview of the principle of reasonable chance of success. It then discusses the rise of the private market for force. Participating in the private market for force can radically transform a state's capabilities, at least over the short term. The involvement of EO in Sierra Leone illustrates the potential for such transformation. Finally, this chapter looks at the potential for the principle to apply even within these increasingly complex circumstances. The emergence of the market for private force has complicated the strategic assessment that this moral principle requires. For reasonable chance of success to be meaningful and useful, it must account for this growing complexity. Specifically, I argue that the potential for states to enhance their capabilities by acting in concert with PMCs must be recognized by the formulation of this principle.

REASONABLE CHANCE OF SUCCESS

A state must be pursuing a just cause in order to satisfy the *jus ad bellum* test, but just cause alone is insufficient for the overall decision to wage war to be considered just. The decision to wage war must also satisfy the ancillary *jus ad bellum* criteria, one of which is reasonable chance of success.

Since this *jus ad bellum* principle involves an assessment of the military capabilities on both sides, reasonable chance of success is sometimes treated as a prudential consideration rather than a moral one. That going to war without a meaningful chance of prevailing is imprudent certainly seems beyond question. However, this decision would not be merely imprudent but also immoral. The goal of the Just War tradition is the limitation of war.[2] Waging war, even for a just cause like self-defense or defense of others, involves destruction of lives and property. Without a reasonable chance of success, waging war would inflict its destructive effects without achieving any good effects to mitigate these harms. To invite this harm on one's own state is suicidal and imprudent; to impose this harm on the target state is homicidal and unjust. Reasonable chance of success is thus a moral principle albeit one that implicates strategic and prudential considerations.

The reasonable chance of success raises the question of what success really means in this context. Ultimately, success requires achieving the just cause that motivated the war. In a more immediate sense, success requires prevailing militarily. If the just cause could be obtained without resort to force, then the nonmilitary means to that end would be utilized as required by the *jus ad bellum* principle of last resort. In the absence of a nonforcible avenue to achieving the just cause, force is the only remaining possibility for achieving the cause. As such, the question of success often focuses somewhat narrowly on the likelihood of military success, or what Clausewitz would call "the overthrow of the enemy."[3] Michael Walzer criticizes this view, arguing that war (or at least fighting) should terminate when the goals of the Just War are within political reach.[4] At that point, he argues, success has been obtained. Similarly, James Turner Johnson emphasizes the understanding of success as the reestablishment of postwar order.[5]

But even when success is defined more broadly in terms of achieving the cause that motivates the war, that understanding of success entails some degree of success in military terms. Assuming that the other *jus ad bellum* criteria have been satisfied, and war is truly the last resort by which the state can attain its just cause, then the successful use of coercion is necessary to achieve the just cause that motivated the war. If success in political terms could be achieved in the absence of military coercion, then war would not truly be a last resort, and the war's justness would have failed to satisfy other *jus ad bellum* criteria.

The possibility of successfully coercing the enemy requires an assessment of the relative capabilities of both potential parties to the conflict. Prevailing militarily depends largely on the possession of more power, a concept that is both central to the study of international politics and ill defined. Nevertheless, the judgment concerning possibility of success remains difficult. Superior military capabilities do not always translate neatly into success in winning the war, as the defeat of great powers by smaller powers throughout history demonstrates. Moreover, information about state capabilities may be concealed or distorted, making the assessment of the chance of success more difficult.

Calculating the possibility of success becomes infinitely more difficult with the availability of private force. As in other aspects of the Just War tradition, thinking about the reasonable chance of success has become crystallized around the state. Caron Gentry's chapter in this volume considers this problem with respect to the principle of right authority, but statism poses problems with respect to reasonable chance of success as well. The presumption that war is conducted by state actors obscures the reality that states often engage in armed conflict in conjunction with nonstate actors who contribute to their capabilities. States and other actors now have at their disposal additional capabilities that can be acquired with a signature on a contract. The potential to easily acquire additional capabilities from the market means that even an accurate assessment of a state's national forces is only a partial picture. The inability to form a true picture of the force at a state's disposal, in turn, distorts any estimate of the possibility of success. The private force that states can obtain may, in certain circumstances, have a truly transformative effect on a state's military capabilities. A state that would have been easily defeated without its PMC partners can become a formidable opponent with them. The experience of the RUF in Sierra Leone, waging war against both the unassisted government and the government acting in concert with EO bears out this point.

This is true across the range of services offered by PMCs, enumerated below, all of which enhance a state's ability to wage war. PMCs now perform a number of functions that state militaries used to perform for themselves exclusively. States may hire PMCs to supplement their downsized national militaries, or they may seek expertise that is lacking within their own armed forces. In many cases, PMCs are hired to perform functions that seem far removed from the battlefield but nevertheless add to state capabilities in a meaningful way. The ability to turn to the market enhances both the numerical strength at states' disposal and, in some cases, their technical expertise as well. As the case studies suggest, the impact of PMCs and their role in combat can be decisive.

THE MARKET FOR PRIVATE FORCE

Private force has previously been an important component of the international system. Prior to the emergence of the national military, rulers often turned to the market to supplement the forces at their disposal. European armies in the Middle Ages contained large numbers of mercenary troops.[6] With the emergence of the state system and especially the state's consolidation of authority over force around the time of the French Revolution, private force was pushed to the margins of the international system. After the Cold War, a new market for private force emerged. The downsizing of national armed forces created a large supply of newly unemployed individuals with military skills. The declining willingness of the West to intervene in conflicts, either unilaterally or multilaterally, created a demand for some other means for meeting these security needs. Finally, an ideological predisposition for market solutions, which the East also began to embrace after the collapse of the Soviet Union, favored the private market for force as the optimal way to satisfy those demands.[7] Collectively, these forces gave rise to a new private market for force.

This market differed in important ways from the mercenaries of the Cold War. One important difference is that PMCs offer a range of services to their clients as opposed to only engaging in combat on behalf of clients. Peter W.

Singer divides PMCs into three categories based on the type of services that they provide.[8] He describes the services based on their proximity to combat using a spear analogy. The firms closest to the tip of the spear are military provider firms or provide other services that are closely related to combat. These are PMCs that will engage in the use of force on behalf of their clients. One step removed from this stage are military consulting firms, which provide training or advice to clients. Furthest from the tip of the spear are military support firms. These are PMCs that provide services like transportation and other logistical functions. While it may be more useful to classify contracts instead of firms,[9] since the same firm can provide different services in different contexts, Singer's typology is a useful way of thinking about the range of services that PMCs provide.

PMC services at all points on the metaphorical spear augment the capabilities of their clients. Military provider firms do so in the most obvious way, as these firms fight alongside the national forces of state clients. In these cases, the services provided by these firms can be transformative, particularly where they are more professional than the military of the state that hires them. But even consulting or logistical services can enhance state capabilities. When PMCs provide consulting or training services, the expertise that they impart can transform the military potential of client states, possibly for the long term. When PMCs provide consulting or training services, they have the potential to make the local militaries to which they provide the services more professional and more capable over the long term. Even firms that provide services that seem far removed from the battlespace, such as transportation or logistics, can enhance national military capabilities, though the effect will not last beyond the expiration of the contract. If nothing else, PMCs acting in this capacity frees up military personnel to form more essential military functions. Prior to the emergence of the PMC industry, military personnel performed the entire range of functions located at all points along the "spear." Placing PMC personnel in these functions rather than soldiers frees the soldiers to perform functions that are more closely tied to combat.

In some cases, the effect of PMCs on the military capabilities of client states can be dramatic. The impact of the PMC Executive Outcomes in Sierra Leone illustrates the kind of impact that private force can have on state military capabilities. EO, a South African PMC that has since shut its doors, was an early entrant into the market for private force. EO formed in the wake of South Africa's postapartheid military cuts. A military provider firm, EO performed functions that were close to the tip of the spear, often engaging in combat alongside its clients. Sierra Leone hired EO to help suppress rebel movements. Although this is a case of internal rather than international armed conflict, the stark difference between the capabilities of the national armed forces with and without EO underscores EO's significant impact on state capabilities.

PRIVATE FORCE IN SIERRA LEONE

Sierra Leone is perhaps the paradigmatic "weak state."[10] After Captain Valentine Strasser seized power in a coup, his government soon faced opposition from a rebel movement, the Revolutionary United Front. The RUF was led by Foday Sankoh, an ally of Charles Taylor, who would eventually become the president of Liberia and who was then the leader of the National Patriotic Front of Liberia, a rebel group that sought to topple the government of Samuel Doe.[11] Sierra Leone's national military had been deliberately weakened under the government preceding the one that Strasser had overthrown. This move, calculated to avoid a coup, left the government forces ill equipped to fend off the RUF's assault.

The national forces came to be known as "sobels," reflecting the fact that they were an amalgamation of soldiers and rebels.[12] In terms of their conduct, both sides engaged in looting and other attacks on the civilian population. In some cases, individuals literally switched back and forth between the two sides, as soldiers were lured by the prospect of economic gain. One of the consequences is that the national forces alienated the civilian population. As a result of the government forces' weakness and their lack of civilian support, by the end of 1991 the RUF controlled two-thirds of Sierra Leone's territory.

The government's ineffectiveness in combating the RUF was a major factor in the coup that brought the Strasser regime to power. Yet the Strasser regime fared little better. By 1995 the RUF made significant military gains against the government, advancing to within twenty kilometers of Freetown, Sierra Leone's capital. In April 1995, Strasser hired EO to conduct offensive operations against the RUF.[13] The Strasser government reportedly hired EO by granting mineral concessions. EO was part of Strategic Resource Corporation, which engaged in "security services for private and corporate clients, in air charter, and, directly or indirectly, in mining."[14] EO also had ties to Branch Energy, which engaged in oil exploration and mining in politically unstable regions.[15] EO's corporate ties, and Sierra Leone's limited ability to pay, fueled considerable speculation about the financial arrangements connected to the contract. This speculation includes the possibility that payment to EO took the form of mineral concessions to Branch Energy.[16] While David Shearer maintains that Sierra Leone paid EO in cash, he acknowledges that EO performed its services in areas rich in minerals because these minerals provided the government with important sources of revenue.[17] Whether Sierra Leone paid EO with mineral concessions to its corporate cousin or used the revenue flowing from those mineral-rich areas to pay EO, the Strasser government was drawing on resources that belonged to the state in order to procure EO's services for the purpose of prolonging its own existence.

In strategic terms, EO had a number of military objectives, including securing Freetown, regaining control of key resources, destroying RUF headquarters, and clearing out remaining RUF occupation.[18] Sierra Leone's military played only a supporting role in these operations.[19] The involvement of EO altered the strategic picture in Sierra Leone and brought a period of relative peace to the country. This allowed for the holding of parliamentary and presidential elections in 1996. A further consequence of the gains made by EO, was that the RUF was forced to the bargaining table. In November 1996, the government and the RUF signed the Abidjan Peace Accord. This agreement created a mechanism for consolidating peace. It also provided for the disarmament of the RUF and the integration of rebels back into society under conditions of amnesty. Importantly, the Abidjan Peace Accord included terms requiring that EO leave Sierra Leone.[20]

These gains were short lived. With the departure of EO, the strategic picture allowed the RUF to recommence their attacks. By May of the next year, the new civilian government was overthrown, and the new government promptly aligned itself with the RUF. The ousted government fled to Guinea, where it hired Sandline, another PMC, to help it lead a countercoup. There was considerable continuity in terms of personnel and control between EO and Sandline, making Sandline a successor company to EO.[21] Sandline's involvement in the crisis was both controversial and inconsequential. The controversy stemmed from Sandline's shipment of weapons and ammunition to the exiled government and peacekeepers from the Economic Community of West African States Monitoring Group (ECOMOG).[22] This shipment violated an arms embargo and came to be known as the Arms to Africa scandal. Before either the arms or personnel from Sandline could arrive, the ECOMOG peacekeepers had already overthrown the governing junta.[23]

THE FUTURE OF REASONABLE CHANCE OF SUCCESS

The transformative effect that EO had on Sierra Leone's capabilities against the RUF underscores the complications that private force can pose for applying the principle of reasonable chance of success to privatized conflicts. The difference between a state's capabilities with and without the assistance of PMCs can be significant. The government's capabilities with EO differed starkly from its capabilities without EO, a fact of which both the government and the rebels were keenly aware. An adversary that might prevail easily against unassisted national forces may find itself unable to defeat those same forces augmented by even a small number of PMC personnel. The capabilities of Sierra Leone's national forces at three key points in the conflict with the RUF illustrates the striking impact that EO's participation had on the government's potential to prevail over the RUF.

At the point immediately before the Strasser government hired EO, the government was on the verge of defeat by the RUF, which controlled most of the country's territory, including key mineral resources, and nearly had Freetown within its grasp. An assessment of Sierra Leone's capabilities at that point would have found that the government's forces were undisciplined and ineffective. The national forces of Sierra Leone, in the absence of outside assistance from a PMC, were a relatively easy target, and the chance of prevailing against them was high.

Augmented by a small number of EO personnel, the government forces' capabilities transformed radically. With EO fighting alongside the national troops, the government was able to secure Freetown and retake control of the mineral-rich areas from the RUF. These strategic reversals brought the RUF to the bargaining table, and the resulting peace agreement established a new government. Fighting alongside EO, the forces of Sierra Leone were a much more formidable adversary than they were previously. The chances of success against Sierra Leone's forces in cooperation with EO would almost certainly be much lower than they would have been against the national forces alone.

The peace agreement between the RUF and the government also required that EO leave Sierra Leone. While the civilian government would eventually hire Sandline and secure assistance from peacekeeping troops, for a period of time the national forces were unassisted by any PMC. During this time frame, the new government of Sierra Leone was overthrown and forced into exile. An assessment of the capability of Sierra Leone's national forces would again be quite different. If the chance of success against the national forces with EO would be lower, the chance of success against those same forces after the departure of EO would be considerably higher. This was evidenced by the RUF's success in toppling the newly elected government shortly after the departure of EO.

It may be tempting to treat EO's impact in Sierra Leone as a marginal case, particularly since EO was engaging in offensive operations on behalf of its client. Most PMCs do not provide this type of assistance but focus instead on providing consulting and training to national militaries or performing logistical support for them. While military provider firms like EO do not make up the bulk of the private military industry, all PMCs contribute to the ability of their clients to engage in the use of force. Under the national military model of the Westphalian state system, the military was a self-contained entity that performed all functions related to war. To the extent that any of these functions are now performed by the private sector, this shift frees up military personnel to engage in combat functions. The outsourcing of even transportation functions of the operation of lodgings enhances the capability of a force beyond its size. Furthermore, a PMC does not need to engage in combat to have a transformative effect on the ability of the state to do so. Providing training or consulting services can also radically enhance the ability of a state to wage war. With respect to considerations of justice and war, this is not inherently just or unjust. If a state or rebel movement is waging war for a just cause, such as intervention to prevent an act of genocide, then facilitating the attainment of that cause, even through the use of private force, would certainly be a positive.[24] By contrast, if the private force is used on behalf of an unjust cause, such as propping up an illegitimate or even genocidal regime, then the just war implications would clearly be quite different. In either instance, the probabilities for prevailing could differ considerably if private force becomes a factor in the conflict.

An implication of this changing picture is that we need to take a broader view of assessing state capabilities and the chance of prevailing against them. With the growth of the private military industry, state capabilities transform dramatically over a short period of time. Even assuming that an estimate of a state's power at a particular point is accurate, it may become wildly inaccurate quickly. An accurate assessment of Sierra Leone's capabilities prior to the contract with EO would belie the capabilities that the government would have at its disposal once EO personnel were leading the offensive strikes against the RUF. With respect to the chance of success, a military campaign against the national forces alone may be an easy proposition, while a war against the national military and its private partners would be significantly more difficult. The former scenario may offer a reasonable chance of success while the latter does not. The availability of private force, even to a poor state like Sierra Leone, means that state capabilities are more fluid and difficult to assess than they were in the absence of the private military industry. With the rise of private force, a state's capabilities can change drastically and immediately with a signature on a document.

The growing fluidity and opacity of state capabilities in light of the availability of private force alters the way in which this particular *jus ad bellum* criterion should be applied. If the purpose of the reasonable chance of success principle is to limit the destructive pursuit of hopeless causes, assessing state capabilities at a single point is a useless exercise. Rather than making the assessment of a state's capabilities once, prior to engaging in war, the assessment must be continuous and ongoing. At some point, the chances of success may change so dramatically that the likelihood of prevailing all but disappears. What was once a just war, in which a belligerent has a reasonable chance of prevailing, becomes a quixotic and destructive pursuit. In that event, the war would become unjust because it would no longer be winnable. Applying the reasonable chance of success criterion in a continuous manner may well prohibit wars that would otherwise be moral, but refusal to license destruction in pursuit of a futile cause is consistent with the overall *jus ad bellum* goal of limiting needless harm.

Although the focus of this chapter is on the *jus ad bellum* reasonable chance of success, it is important to recognize that the privatization of force has implications for the Just War tradition that extend beyond this principle, and even beyond the body of *jus ad bellum* principles more generally. The introduction into armed conflict of elements that are external to state militaries threatens to undermine the reciprocity and mutuality that underlies the *jus in bello* limitations on armed conflict. Many individuals who work for PMCs have a military background, but this does not necessarily translate into their being socialized according to the rules and norms of armed conflict. On the contrary, some individual participants in the market may come from backgrounds that are problematic with respect to *jus in bello* norms. Early in the emergence of the contemporary market for private force, a major source of labor came from apartheid-era South African forces that had been put out of work with the downsizing of the South African military in the wake of multiracial elections in that state. Nothing inherent in the market prevents PMCs from employing individuals without a military background or with a background of serious human rights violations or war crimes. Furthermore, PMCs lie outside the structure of the militaries that employ them. The U.S. Army Field Manual, for example, specifies that military personnel cannot give orders to civilian contractors. The contract is the mechanism for control over PMCs; once signed, PMCs may operate alongside but apart from national militaries. To the extent that practices of reciprocity are tied in with military identities, this divide threatens the application of Just War norms, at least in their present state, more broadly.

~

The private military industry has already become an important factor in armed conflict, with the involvement of EO in Sierra Leone being just one example. The Just War tradition, which predates the emergence of the Westphalian state system by many centuries, is certainly capable of accounting for this diffusion of the use of force. Recognizing that states increasingly wage war in cooperation with private partners is an important step in the evolution of the tradition. Because the precise level of PMC involvement, as well as the impact of that involvement, is so fluid and unpredictable, the only meaningful way to assess the reasonable chance of success is to do so on an ongoing basis.

A rigorous application of *jus ad bellum* criteria will not have the effect of licensing every war. In light of the availability of private force and the potentially transformative effect of that force, a continuous application of *jus ad bellum* criteria, including the requirement that a war have a reasonable chance of success in order to be just, will have the effect of licensing even fewer wars. It may even be the case that an initially Just War becomes unjust at some point and should be terminated. The limited justification for war is consistent with a resistance to excessive permissiveness. Any other application of this criterion would be inconsistent with the goal of restricting the harm of war to the level necessary to achieve the war's just cause.

The Just War tradition is an evolving body of principles rather than a static body of rules. One way in which the tradition becomes extended is through the application of its core principles—including the limitation of unjust war—to new circumstances like the emergence of the PMC industry. Despite the beginnings of the reversal of state monopoly over the legitimate use of force, the body of *jus ad bellum* rules can nevertheless provide a response that achieves this vital moral purpose.

Notes

1. Alex J. Bellamy, *Just Wars: From Cicero to Iraq* (Cambridge: Polity Press, 2006), 123.

2. Ibid., 3.

3. Quoted in Michael Walzer, *Just and Unjust Wars: A Moral Argument with Historical Illustrations*, 3rd ed. (New York: Basic Books, 2000), 110.

4. Walzer, *Just and Unjust Wars*, 110.

5. James Turner Johnson, *Can Modern War Be Just?* (New Haven: Yale University Press, 1984), 28–29.

6. Janice E. Thomson, *Mercenaries, Pirates, and Sovereigns: State-Building and Extraterritorial Violence in Early Modern Europe* (Princeton, N.J.: Princeton University Press, 1994).

7. P. W. Singer, *Corporate Warriors: The Rise of the Privatized Military Industry* (Ithaca, N.Y.: Cornell University Press, 2003).

8. Ibid.

9. Deborah D. Avant, *The Market for Force: The Consequences of Privatizing Security* (Cambridge: Cambridge University Press, 2005).

10. Ibid., 82.

11. Because of his support for the RUF, Charles Taylor is currently facing charges before the Special Court for Sierra Leone. He is charged with crimes against humanity committed by the RUF in Sierra Leone.

12. Jeremy Harding, "The Mercenary Business: 'Executive Outcomes,'" *Review of African Political Economy* 24, no. 71 (1997): 92.

13. Ulric Shannon, "Private Armies and the Decline of the State," in *Violence and Politics: Globalization's Paradox*, ed. Kenton Worcester, Sally Avery Bermanzohn, and Mark Ungar (New York: Routledge, 2002), 35.

14. Harding, "Mercenary Business," 88.

15. David Shearer, *Private Armies and Military Intervention* (Oxford: Oxford University Press, 1998), 44.

16. Harding, "Mercenary Business," 93.

17. Shearer, *Private Armies and Military Intervention*, 40.

18. Ibid., 49.

19. Shannon, "Private Armies," 35.

20. David J. Francis, "Mercenary Intervention in Sierra Leone: Providing National Security or International Exploitation?," *Third World Quarterly* 20, no. 2 (1999): 327.

21. Charles Dokubo, "'An Army for Rent', Private Military Corporations and Civil Conflicts in Africa: The Case of Sierra Leone," *Civil Wars* 3, no. 2 (2000): 60.

22. Francis, "Mercenary Intervention in Sierra Leone," 328.

23. Christopher Kinsey, *Corporate Soldiers and International Security: The Rise of Private Military Companies* (New York: Routledge, 2006), 78.

24. Eric A. Heinze, "Private Military Companies, Just War, and Humanitarian Intervention," in *Ethics, Authority, and War: Non-state Actors and the Just War Tradition*, ed. Eric A. Heinze and Brent J. Steele (New York: Palgrave Macmillan, 2009).

Jus in Bello

CHAPTER FIVE

Postheroic U.S. Warfare and the Moral Justification for Killing in War

Sebastian Kaempf

> We had five hundred casualties a week when [the Nixon administration] came to office. America now is not willing to take casualties. Vietnam produced a whole new attitude.
>
> HENRY KISSINGER, 1999

> During the Gulf War, it was more dangerous to be a young man back in the United States, with all its car accidents and urban murders, than to serve in combat. Thus, almost three hundred soldiers had their lives saved by serving in Desert Shield and Desert Storm. The United States effectively saved American lives by going to war.
>
> CHRIS H. GRAY

THIS CHAPTER INVESTIGATES the theoretical challenges that the advent of "risk-free" (casualty-averse and posthuman) American warfare poses to both the laws of war and the ethics of the use of force. It thereby focuses on the *jus in bello* question of when it is permissible for a soldier to kill another combatant in war rather than the more specific question of when it is permissible for the same soldier to kill a civilian. If the fundamental principle of the morality of warfare that legitimizes the killing of another soldier arises exclusively on the basis that such killing constitutes the right to exercise self-defense within the conditions of a mutual imposition of risk, then the emergence of asymmetrical risk-free warfare represents a deep challenge. This unprecedented challenge is posed by contemporary U.S. warfare: the United States is the first actor in recent history who can kill without suffering the risk of dying in return. Such a scenario (as it has unfolded since the 1990s, from the First Gulf War, through conflicts in Kosovo, Afghanistan, and Iraq, to the recent intervention in Libya) propels us well beyond the principles underlying the laws and the ethics of warfare. The recent risk-free deployment of American military force might be justified politically, but it raises the more fundamental problem that we might no longer be able to appeal to the morality of warfare to justify this mode of combat.

The chapter makes this argument by first establishing how reciprocity (the condition of a mutual imposition of risk) is the key conceptual condition upon which the moral and legal permission for killing in war rests. It then demonstrates how reciprocity implicitly assumes a certain degree of symmetry between warring factions. Third, the chapter argues that in the case of contemporary U.S. warfare, conditions of asymmetry have emerged on such a historically unprecedented scale that they have started to push beyond the conditions of reciprocity. Paradoxically, this American drive toward risk-free warfare has coincided with a systematic attempt—on the part of contemporary U.S. warfare—to comply with the moral and legal provisions set by and codified in Just War thinking and the Laws of War. Exploring this paradox, the chapter argues that while the United States has come to comply with Just War theory and the Laws of War, the removal of risk from its own mode of warfare (by undermining the principle of reciprocity) no longer allows the U.S. military to justify the killing of enemy combatant along existing moral and legal lines. The chapter concludes by outlining a constructive way for the Just War tradition to address this unprecedented challenge.

THE MORAL PERMISSION TO KILL IN WAR AND THE PRE-REQUIREMENT OF RECIPROCITY

In civil life, killing another human being is generally not sanctioned by law but instead is considered to be murder or manslaughter. By contrast, in times of war, killing another human being (who happens to be an enemy combatant) is indeed sanctioned by both the Just War tradition and International Humanitarian Law (IHL) as a legitimate act.[1] So the question arises as to why exactly soldiers are permitted to kill one another without such an act to be considered murder.

The moral paradox about war is that the right for combatants to injure and kill one another is not based on the judgment of their personal moral guilt. They do not fight each other because they hate their adversaries or because one has personally wronged the other. Instead, they find themselves confronting each other because they have been given orders by their political leaders to fight. They are in that sense no more than instruments of the state.[2] Yet equally, the right of warriors to injure and kill one another is not founded on judgments of the moral evil of the state or the political authority on whose behalf they are fighting. While soldiers are held personally accountable for how they conduct themselves in war (*jus in bello*), they are not held responsible for the outbreak of the particular war in which they are fighting (*jus ad bellum*).[3] Instead, they are assumed to be morally innocent, an assumption arising out of what Michael Walzer calls the "moral equality of soldiers."[4]

What, then, gives soldiers the moral and legal right to kill other soldiers? The answer found from within the various strands of the Just War tradition (be it the Christian/Western, Islamic, or African traditions) and IHL is very precise: combatants are permitted to kill one another precisely because they stand in a relationship of mutual risk.[5] The acceptance of the reciprocal imposition of risk establishes the internal morality of the relationship between soldiers. Only this reciprocal condition morally and legally licenses the warrior to kill another warrior.[6] Each warrior thereby possesses the license to kill because each acts in self-defense vis-à-vis the other.[7] This requirement of reciprocity lies at the heart of the moral reality of war and constitutes the condition upon which the moral and legal right to kill in war is founded and what binds warriors together in a brotherhood of death.

In other words, the warrior's moral privilege to kill another warrior (without the killing being interpreted as a crime or murder) is subject to a condition of reciprocity. This means, furthermore, that a warrior is not sanctioned to kill noncombatants (civilians and POWs alike) precisely because he or she cannot justify the killing of civilians as an act of self-defense. Because noncombatants, by definition, are unarmed, killing them (directly and deliberately) is considered to be murder and a war crime.[8] It is only under conditions of the reciprocal imposition of risk that the soldier's moral privilege to kill arises. Without the reciprocal imposition of risk, there is neither a moral nor a legal basis upon which to justify the injuring or killing in war.[9]

Reciprocity of such risks implies the existence of some degree of symmetry between opposing adversaries.[10] Symmetry implies that—to some degree—both adversaries enjoy similar military capabilities and face similar levels of vulnerabilities. Only under conditions of symmetry can the condition of reciprocity exist. Two qualifications are important at this stage: first, pure levels of symmetry probably exist only in theory, not in practice. Military historians would argue that there has hardly ever been a war in history where pure levels of symmetry between opposing armed forces was a reality (though we might point to the duels between ancient Greek warriors or between hoplite phalanxes or to the stalemate on the western front during World War I). This might have something to do with the second qualification—namely, that due to the interactive dynamic that lies at the heart of the nature of war, each adversary naturally strives to create an asymmetrically advantageous situation in which the enemy suffers greater risks of injury and death while its own forces remain relatively safe.[11] In essence, the interactive nature of war results in forces that avoid symmetries and aim at creating asymmetric advantages for themselves.[12]

This means that, on the one hand, pure levels of symmetry might never actually exist. On the other hand, certain levels of asymmetry are always created as a result of the interactive nature of war. Yet, the fundamental moral (the Just War tradition) and legal (International Humanitarian Law) principles of war are founded on the assumption of relative symmetry: that on the overall strategic level, both adversaries actually kill in self-defense vis-à-vis their enemy.[13]

If the fundamental principle of the morality of warfare is founded on the right to exercise self-defense within the conditions of a mutual imposition of risk, then the emergence of extreme forms of asymmetrical warfare represents a deep challenge. Extreme forms of asymmetry would arise when one adversary—on a strategic level—was able (through long-distance, highly sophisticated weapons technology, for instance) to kill the enemy's military forces without suffering the risk of dying in return. Under such conditions of extreme asymmetry, an insurmountable imbalance of reciprocity between adversaries would be created. Such a scenario would undermine the principle of reciprocity and thereby push us well beyond the existing moral and legal foundations that justify killing in war. As the next section demonstrates, such a scenario has started to arise in the case contemporary U.S. warfare.

MOVING BEYOND RECIPROCITY: VIETNAM AND THE ELIMINATION OF RISK IN CONTEMPORARY U.S. WARFARE

Contemporary U.S. warfare has gained the technological capacity to apply overwhelming force globally without suffering the risk of reciprocal injury.[14] From the 1991 Gulf War to the current intervention in Libya, the U.S. military has enjoyed such overwhelming and historically unprecedented technological superiority that it has effectively gained the ability to wage wars without suffering (hardly) any risks to its own soldiers.[15] For instance, "Operation Allied Force" over Kosovo in 1999 constituted the first war waged by the U.S. military that saw zero combat casualties (the only fatalities were caused by accidents or friendly fire). And while Kosovo might—thus far—have remained the exception, it constitutes merely the culmination of a much wider trend at work in U.S. warfare over the last twenty years: between the 1991 Gulf War and the 2003 overthrow of Saddam Hussein's regime in Baghdad, not only were U.S. casualty figures extremely low (both in terms of absolute numbers as well as in historical comparison, ranging in the tens and hundreds rather than in the tens of thousands), but also the majority of U.S. fatalities in most of these conflicts were not caused by enemy fire but friendly fire and accidents (see table 5.1). This implies that the biggest threat to the lives of U.S. service personnel has come less from U.S. adversaries than from within U.S. warfare itself. The same period also saw more NGO workers killed than American soldiers. And during "Operation Enduring Freedom," the American military succeeded in toppling the Taliban regime with a mere 214 CIA operatives and Special Forces on the ground by the time the regime collapsed at the end of November 2001.

Those critiquing the factor of casualty aversion and risk-free American warfare tend to point to the wars in Afghanistan and Iraq as evidence of the U.S. military's and public's willingness to actually pay a high blood price.[16] And while the overall casualty figures among U.S. military personnel in these wars (1,961 in Afghanistan and 4,422 in Iraq as of August 16, 2012) seem at first sight to support their argument of a move away from riskless warfare to an acceptance of higher number of casualties, those figures need to be put into perspective. First, the American military succeeded in overthrowing the regimes in both countries at virtually no risk: in Afghanistan, 40 soldiers lost their lives between October 7, 2001, and the end of March 2002 (8 of which were combat related). In Iraq, 139 U.S. soldiers died between March 19, 2003, and the president's "Mission Accomplished Speech" on May 1, 2003 (31 of which were combat related). In both cases, therefore, the U.S. military was able to bring about the overthrow of regimes at virtually no threat from its adversaries. Second, while the casualty figures the U.S. military subsequently incurred in both Iraq and Afghanistan are significantly higher than any of those seen since 1991, they remain significantly low not only by historical comparison but also given the fact that these two major wars have been waged for eight and a half years and eleven years, respectively, at the time of writing.

TABLE 5.1   U.S. Military Casualty Figures from the Civil War to Iraq

War	Overall casualties	Accidents & friendly fire	Combat casualties
U.S. Civil War (1861–1865)	625,000		
World War I (1914–1918)	53,402*		
World War II (1941–1945)	291,557[†]		
Korean War (1950–1953)	53,686		
Vietnam War (1955–1975)	47,424		
Lebanon (1982–1984)	266[‡]	9	257
Desert Storm (1991–1992)	382[§]	235[|]	147
Somalia (1992–1994)	43[#]	14	29
Bosnia (1995)	0**	2[††]	0
Kosovo (1999)	1	1	0
Afghanistan—Phase I (7 October 2001–March 2002)	40[‡‡]	32	8
Afghanistan—Overall (7 October 2001–16 August 2012)	1,961[§§]	328	1,633
Iraq—Phase I (19 March–1 May 2003)	139[||]	108	31
Iraq—Overall (19 March 2003–18 December 2011)	4,422[##]	934	3,488

* "America's Wars: U.S. Casualties and Veterans," Information Please Database, http://www.infoplease .com/ipa/A0004615.html (accessed 14 August 2011).
[†] Ibid.
[‡] "US Military Operations: Casualty Breakdown," GlobalSecurity.org, http://www.globalsecurity.org/ military/ops/casualties.htm (accessed 17 August 2011).
[§] Ibid.; "America's Wars."
[|] Dennis Cauchon, "Why U.S. Casualties Were Low," http://www.usatoday.com/news/world/iraq /2003-04-20-cover-usat_x.htm (accessed 17 August 2011).
[#] "US Military Operations."
** Richard Holbrooke, "Was Bosnia Worth It?," Washington Post, 19 July 2005, http://www .washingtonpost.com/wp-dyn/content/article/2005/07/18/AR2005071801329.html (accessed 17 August 2011).
[††] "Two Die in Apache Crash," BBC News, 5 May 1999, http://news.bbc.co.uk/2/hi/335709.stm (accessed 13 August 2011).
[‡‡] Martin Shaw, "Risk-Transfer Militarism and the Legitimacy of War after Iraq," n.d., http://www .theglobalsite.ac.uk/press/402shaw.htm (accessed 16 August 2012); http://siadapp.dmdc.osd.mil /personnel/CASUALTY/castop.htm (accessed 16 August 2012).
[§§] U.S. Department of Defense, casualty figures, www.defense.gov/news/casualty.pdf (accessed 18 August 2012); http://siadapp.dmdc.osd.mil/personnel/CASUALTY/castop.htm (accessed 18 August 2012).
[||] "Casualties in Iraq," Antiwar.com, http://antiwar.com/casualties/ (accessed 10 August 2011).
[##] U.S. Department of Defense, casualty figures, http://www.defense.gov/news/casualty.pdf (accessed 18 August 2012).

This technology-driven mode of warfare, which is fundamentally structured around the avoidance of casualties among U.S. military personnel, has started to push beyond reciprocity. From the perspective of U.S. decision makers, this is not a coincidence but rather the intended result stemming from the reforms undertaken as a direct consequence of the Vietnam War.[17] It was due to the disastrous experience in Vietnam that the U.S. mode of warfare was deliberately reformed in ways that aimed at overcoming the risk of dying for U.S. soldiers through the use of overwhelming and superior technology. In other words, following the Vietnam War the deliberate decision was taken to move beyond reciprocity by creating unprecedented asymmetries in military capabilities and vulnerabilities that have started to come to the fore since the 1990s. To help readers understand the scale and scope of this trend, the following pages demonstrate how the outcome of the Vietnam War triggered a set of reforms that ultimately aimed at minimizing the combat risks for U.S. soldiers and at thereby removing reciprocity from U.S. warfare.

Vietnam constituted a fundamental watershed. The nation that had entered the war in Indochina was different from the one that left it. The war had changed the mental and spiritual landscape of America. In the Civil War, World Wars I and II, and the Korean War, America had been prepared to expend vast numbers of lives, yet casualty aversion had not been the central issue. In Vietnam, however, it became the central issue.[18]

When the conflict developed in unexpected ways, the true nature of the larger ideational purpose of America itself was increasingly doubted. Widely held national myths such as innocence were challenged and the belief in exceptionalism fundamentally shaken.[19] Vietnam became, according to Arnold R. Isaacs, "the era's most powerful symbol of damaged ideals and the loss of trust, unity, shared myths and common values."[20] On the deepest ideational level, it was waged not only on a distant battlefield but also in the unchartered depth of the American psyche and soul. It disrupted America's story, its own explanation of the past and vision of the future.[21] "Vietnam," as Richard Nixon observed, "tarnished our ideals, weakened our spirit and crippled our will."[22] Ideational foundations like containment, the domino theory, and the spreading of liberty, which had not only mobilized the nation in the past but had also legitimized sacrifice, were demolished.[23]

Historical sociologists explain this disruption with the past more generally through the rise of reflexive or liquid postmodernity.[24] The modern age, according to thinkers such as Ulrich Beck, Anthony Giddens, and Zygmunt

Bauman, forced societies to undergo a dual process of dis-embedding and re-embedding.[25] Modernity dis-embedded religious absolutes in order to re-embed them into the secular religions of nationalism and ideology. By the 1970s, however, this dual process was starting to be disrupted and replaced by the emergence of risk society where processes of dis-embedding were no longer followed by processes of re-embedding.[26] This, according to Bauman, meant that societies started moving from the era of pre-allocated reference groups into the epoch in which the destination of individuals has remained undetermined.[27] Postmodernity no longer furnished any beds for re-embedding the dis-embedded individuals. As a result, the modern ideational foundations that had mobilized the American people were giving way to postmodern individualization.[28]

This means that the transformation of the U.S. heroism in Vietnam coincided with the rise of America as a postmodern society structured around the avoidance and management of risks.[29] Distributional conflicts over "goods" such as jobs, social security, and income (which dictated the traditional agenda of modern politics) have given way to distributional conflicts over "bads"— that is, the risks created by threats to individual life, health, and well-being.[30] By transforming from a modern into a postmodern society, the United States has become increasingly risk averse. American politics and the way politicians have conducted war have been about the control and prevention of such risks.[31] These societal changes in conjunction with the transformation of heroism translated into an unwillingness to sacrifice, thereby increasingly turning the United States from an inherently heroic society into what Edward N. Luttwak called a "post-heroic society."[32] Reflecting the emergence of risk society, casualty aversion has become institutionalized in the way in which the United States has waged wars ever since.[33]

In its attempt to reinvent itself and to retrieve legitimacy for the use of force following the Indochina War, the U.S. military devised a new doctrine, acquired sophisticated new weapons systems, and made large-scale changes to organizations and tactics (as evidenced by the introduction of an all-volunteer force in 1973, the "Total Force" policy, the new AirLand Battle doctrine and the Weinberger Doctrine in the early 1980s, the so-called Revolution in Military Affairs in the 1990s, and what is known today as netcentric warfare). The driving force behind these post-Vietnam reforms that led to the contemporary U.S. approach to warfare was to bring the use of force in line with what was perceived as a casualty-averse public. Advanced technology was used to reduce American exposure to the risks of combat while heralding lesser risks to enemy noncombatants. It aimed at producing a new grammar of killing in which the spilling of American blood became de-emphasized.[34]

This journey of renewal developed over the period of a decade, and its cumulative effects were fully unveiled for the first time during Operation Desert Storm.[35] Operation Desert Storm was the first American war in which, from the beginning, securing the goal of high levels of casualty aversion was a key operational objective.[36] The formulation of war aims and the conduct of military operations were governed by the fear among American leaders that the loss of too many American military lives (and Iraqi civilian lives) would erode public and congressional support for the war.[37] To the extent that American military and political decision makers were haunted by the memories of Vietnam and were preoccupied with avoiding a repetition of the same mistakes, the 1991 war was fought not only to overthrow Saddam Hussein's aggression against Kuwait but also to conquer and overcome America's troubling memories of Vietnam.[38] The Gulf War, according to George Herring, "was more about Vietnam than Kuwait for a political and military leadership that sought vindication, to prove that they had learnt from their failures in Vietnam."[39] Close adherence to and internalization of the Weinberger Doctrine (which conceived public support as being conditional upon a minimum number of U.S. casualties) ensured that the ghost of Vietnam would not cast its shadow over the Gulf War. Starting from the buildup to the war, President George H. W. Bush and his administration set out to mobilize public support with a conscious and explicit campaign to free the country from the legacy of Vietnam. The president had repeatedly stated that Iraq would not be "another Vietnam" and that the paralysis this war had caused would be overcome.

The successful performance by the U.S. military in winning quickly and with a minimum of casualties certainly vindicated the reforms undertaken in response to Vietnam in the 1970s and 1980s. President Bush emphasized this point in his victory speech on March 1, 1991, when he triumphantly declared the Vietnam Syndrome to be kicked once and for all: "The spectre of Vietnam has been buried forever in the sands of the Arabian Peninsula."[40] Senior military officers also situated Desert Storm in this larger story of redemption. "This war didn't take one hundred hours to win," Major General Barry McCaffrey stated, "it took fifteen years."[41] These and other statements from American officials implied that the historical judgment that had lingered ever since the defeat in the jungles of Vietnam had been overturned.[42]

Yet, by complying to the letter with the Weinberger Doctrine, the United States was far from kicking the Vietnam Syndrome. On the contrary, the American military had succeeded in reinventing warfare in a way that has made it acceptable to the U.S. public, politicians, and the military. It thereby helped restore the respect and prestige of the armed forces within American society and provided a longed-for opportunity for redemption. The U.S. conduct of war post-Vietnam therefore embodied rather than defeated the Vietnam Syndrome.[43]

Beginning with the 1991 Gulf War, the potential death of U.S. military personnel has been instrumentalized as a risk to be avoided, which is profoundly at odds with the principle of reciprocity underpinning the Just War tradition and the Laws of War. America's postmodern society, which is structured around the avoidance of risk in every aspect of social life, has started to wage its wars in ways that aimed at minimizing precisely these risks.[44] In this new postmodern warfare, most servicemen and women are no longer soldiers in a conventional sense. Instead, they have become machine- and technology-assisted agents, trained for and fighting a particular mission by virtual reality and computer simulation.[45] Such virtual wars, Andrew J. Bacevich writes, are "not conducted by specially empowered and culturally distinctive 'warriors' but by computer-wielding technicians."[46] Trained in and assisted by such technology, they are no longer required to feel courage, to experience fear, to face combat risks, or to show the type of endurance that was regarded as the defining marker of soldiering.[47]

As a result, American warfare has achieved lethal perfection with a degree of impunity that is unprecedented. Waged increasingly by computer technicians and high-altitude specialists, it is becoming increasingly abstract, distanced, and virtual. New networked computer systems, simulations, and precision-guided weapons systems have created an experience of war that no longer requires heroism and therefore can be experienced virtually without the need to accept the risks of dying.[48]

Victor D. Hanson interpreted this lack of heroism in today's U.S. warfare as the ending of the warrior tradition of ancient Greece. Greek warriors despised the archers and javelin throwers of the Persian armies for their lack of heroism as they could kill effectively from a distance but with little risk to themselves. Avoiding close infantry battle, something that was disdained by the ancient Greeks, had become one of the central tenets of U.S. military campaigns since the early 1990s. During the Gulf War, for instance, relying on weeks of massive aerial bombardment and precision-guided missile technology before a mere four days of ground campaign brought an end to the war, the United States avoided fighting at close quarters and instead waged war from afar with little risk to its own soldiers.[49] Like the Persians, Hanson concluded, the Americans "suffered from that most dangerous tendency in war: a wish to kill but not to die in the process."[50] Due to its technological might, the United States military has come close to realizing this wish, for it now has the capacity to apply force without suffering the risk of reciprocal injury.[51] At the heart of the postmodern U.S. warfare that evolved since the end of Cold War, James Der Derian writes, "is the technical capability and ethical imperative to threaten and, if necessary, actualize violence from a distance—*with no or minimum casualties.*"[52] The internal logic of this brave new risk-free war was illustrated nicely by one particular statistic, according to which it was more dangerous to be a young man back in the United States with all its automobile accidents and urban murders than to actively serve as a soldier in the liberation of Kuwait. According to Charles Law of the University of California, Berkeley, almost three hundred U.S. soldiers had their lives *saved* by their service in the war.[53] So, whereas risk taking in the past was an illustration of bravery, the hallmark of a soldier's true nature, by the end of the Cold War it had become a measure of irresponsibility for American decision makers and the average citizen.

Taking this postheroic trend even further, American leadership has started replacing soldiers in battle with machines and robots.[54] The current use of predator drones in Pakistan, Yemen, Somalia, or Libya might be indicative here, but it only provides us with a temporary impression of the wider specter of posthuman warfare in which the Pentagon has invested for over fifteen years. Again, the key driving force behind the rapidly expanding army of robots on land, air, and sea is the effort to reduce American deaths and injuries. According to Thomas Killion, the army's deputy assistant secretary for research and technology, the U.S. forces "want unmanned systems to go where we don't want to risk our precious soldiers."[55] In 2004 the army had 150 combat robots; in 2005 the number had grown to 2,400 and grown again to 4,000 by the end of 2006. Before 9/11, the U.S. military had around 200 drones in its arsenal. Ten years later, that number had risen to over 7,000, accounting for 31 percent of all American fighter planes.[56] By 2010, the U.S. Air Force for the first time was training more drone pilots than fighter pilots.[57] In 2006, the Defense Department's Quadrennial Defense Review declared that in the near future, 45 percent of the air force's future long-range bombers will be able to operate without humans on board. And it is estimated that by 2015, 33 percent of the army's ground combat vehicles are supposed to be unmanned.[58]

All this does is to indicate that post-Vietnam trends toward minimizing the combat risks of U.S. military personnel seem likely to continue, if not even accelerate in the near future. But even at its current level, such extreme forms of asymmetry have already arisen that allow the American military to kill the enemy's military forces without suffering the risk of dying in return. As a result of such extreme conditions of asymmetry, an insurmountable imbalance of reciprocity between adversaries is created. What makes U.S. warfare such a particular challenge therefore to the Just War tradition and the Laws of War is that its own mode of warfare has started to undermine the principle of reciprocity to such an extent that it pushes U.S. warfare well beyond the moral and legal foundations that justify killing in war.

THE CRUX / THE PUZZLE

The sheer dimension and novelty of this particular challenge posed by contemporary U.S. warfare comes to light through historical comparison. Similarly extreme levels of military asymmetry could last be found during colonial wars in the age of European empire. Equipped with superior weapons technology, colonial powers were able to conquer (and—for a long time—control) indigenous peoples in a risk-free manner.[59]

One of the most powerful examples can be found in the infamous Battle of Omdurman (in today's Sudan) in 1898 when the British Imperial Army under the command of General Horatio Kitchener was attacked by the indigenous Madhist forces. Even though Kitchener's forces were vastly outnumbered, the combined effects of British military discipline and the newly developed Maxim machine gun resulted in what Winston Churchill, a youthful participant, called "the most signal triumph ever gained by the arms of science over barbarians."[60] In the course of the battle, eleven thousand Sudanese forces were killed and another sixteen thousand wounded (and subsequently slaughtered), while Kitchener's forces suffered a mere forty-eight deaths.[61] It was a battle without reciprocity as the imperial forces could kill their indigenous adversaries without (barely) facing the risk of dying in return. Omdurman symbolized the vast asymmetric military predominance that had allowed Europeans to dramatically expand their territorial empires in the nineteenth and early twentieth centuries.

Historically, therefore, the lack of reciprocity found in contemporary U.S. warfare is not dissimilar to the one enjoyed by European imperial armies. Yet, the key difference between these two epochs lies in the moral and legal implications. In the age of colonialism and European empire, Just War criteria and their nascent legal codifications applied only to wars between fellow white and Christian Europeans (so-called civilized nations) but did not extend to wars against non-European "savages" and "barbarians."[62] This particularistic nature of the moral and early legal codes of warfare at the time was based on the distinction between Bellum Civile and Bellum Romanum. The former codified the normative restraints on the use of force in order to maintain a high level of discrimination in war. In contrast, Bellum Romanum was a type of "warfare in which no holds were barred and all those designated as enemies, whether bearing arms or not, would be indiscriminately slaughtered."[63] This type of warfare was inherently indiscriminate.[64]

The reason why Bellum Romanum rather than Bellum Civile was practiced against non-Europeans was located in a limited notion of humanity. Those living inside the respective historical conception of humanity were regarded as human beings and therefore subjected to the principles of Bellum Civile. Those living outside the conception of humanity were seen as subhumans to whom neither moral nor legal standards and judgments applied.[65] Lying outside the confines of Just War thinking and the Laws of War, "savages" and "barbarians" were consequently subjected to the principle of Bellum Romanum. The limits and boundaries of humanity were the fault lines between Bellum Civile and Bellum Romanum.[66] This means that in the wars of European empire against non-Europeans, as at the Battle of Omdurman, no moral or ethical issues arose over the lack of reciprocity. In other words, from within Just War thinking, the question of how one could justify the killing of enemy soldiers in the absence of any reciprocity of risks never arose.

This issue, however, arises today precisely because of two historically significant developments. First, in the course of the twentieth century, the principles of Just War thinking as well as the Laws of War have become universalized and therefore lost their particularistic nature.[67] And second, the United States, which for most of its history had conducted wars along the Bellum Romanum and Bellum Civile divide, has—over the past few decades following the Vietnam War—revamped its mode of warfare to systematically comply with those very same universalized moral and legal standards.[68] This has resulted in a paradoxical situation where contemporary U.S. warfare has come to comply with the Just War tradition and the Laws of War and has justified its own combat behavior along these legal and moral lines,[69] while at the same time developing a mode of warfare that undermines the very same foundation (reciprocity as a condition for legitimate killing) upon which those moral and ethical principles rest. This means that the current U.S. mode of war has started to violate the fundamental principle that establishes the internal morality of warfare (and that also constitutes the basis of IHL): self-defense within conditions of reciprocal impositions of risk. If asymmetric warfare increasingly enables the U.S. military to kill without facing the risk of death in return, then the U.S. military can no longer draw on existing moral and legal frameworks to justify the killing of enemy soldiers. In what ways, then, can this unprecedented challenge posed by the emergence of risk-free U.S. warfare be resolved?

CONSTRUCTIVE WAYS FOR JUST WAR THEORY TO ADDRESS THIS CHALLENGE

This final section offers various ways in which this particular challenge can be addressed by Just War theory. If existing levels of extreme asymmetry push beyond reciprocity to such an extent that they no longer permit the current U.S. mode of warfare to draw on moral principles to justify killing in war, then two possible solutions emerge.

The first solution would require a deliberate reversal of the casualty-averse approach to war by increasing the risks faced by U.S. soldiers. Such a rebalancing of risks would reintroduce the fundamental principle of reciprocity that provides the moral precondition upon which Just War theory (and the Laws of War) permit the killing of enemy combatants. Given the nature of the transformation of U.S. warfare post-Vietnam, the larger American inclination toward employing technological solutions to overcome problems of combat risks, and the general fear among U.S. decision makers that public support for U.S. wars is conditional upon zero or very few U.S. casualties, such a policy change seems unlikely. Yet, with the current mode of warfare hitting an impasse in Iraq and the subsequent introduction of the "surge manual" (which emphasizes the need for higher combat risks—the "human factor"—in order to win "hearts and minds" in counterinsurgency operations),[70] we might be witnessing the beginning of precisely such a trend that gradually would reintroduce higher degrees of reciprocity into U.S. warfare in the future. It needs to be pointed out, however, that the surge manual's attempt to increase the combat risks of U.S. soldiers has neither been driven by deontological moral values nor by a recognition of the lack of available moral justifications of killing, but rather as a way to avoid losing the Iraq War. The conceptually challenging questions arising for the Just War tradition are about the threshold of reciprocity: How much asymmetry is permissible for a particular mode of warfare to remain within the confines of existing moral norms? Exactly how much rebalancing of risks would U.S. warfare need to undergo to fall back into the confines of Just War thinking? And is there a moral obligation for military forces to create symmetries in order to allow them to wage war?

Second, if such a rebalancing of combat risks were not to occur and instead the U.S. military were to continue to pursue along the lines of wider casualty-averse trends, then justifying the killing of enemy combatants could not be justified by existing moral and legal conventions. Instead, the U.S. military would have to wage wars without killing. This could be done by either exclusively employing nonlethal weapons or by engaging in policing activities rather than actual warfighting. The former destroys properties and debilitates weapons systems rather than killing human beings, while the latter prioritizes the arrest of enemies over killing them.[71] Whether either of these two options is feasible militarily and therefore in the interest of U.S. decision makers is at worst questionable and at best open for debate.

This is why, finally, the Just War tradition needs to take seriously the unprecedented challenge posed by contemporary U.S. warfare. As this chapter has tried to show, the emergence of asymmetrical risk-free warfare in the case of the U.S. military for the first time has propelled us beyond the theoretical confines of the fundamental principles upon which our moral *jus in bello* judgments are based. Will U.S. warfare fall back in line with the principles of reciprocity, or will Just War theory need to rethink its own moral foundations from the ground up?

Notes

1. Michael Walzer, *Just and Unjust Wars: A Moral Argument with Historical Illustrations* (New York: Basic Books, 1992); Geoffrey Best, *Humanity in Warfare: The International History of the Law of Armed Conflict* (London: Methuen, 1993).

2. James T. Johnson, *Just War Tradition and the Restraint in War: A Moral and Historical Inquiry* (Princeton: Princeton University Press, 1981); Walzer, *Just and Unjust Wars*, 36–37.

3. Paul W. Kahn, "The Paradox of Riskless Warfare," *Philosophy and Public Policy* 22, no. 3 (2002): 2–9.

4. Walzer, *Just and Unjust Wars*, 34–40.

5. International Committee of the Red Cross (ICRC), *Spared from the Spear: Traditional Somali Behaviour in Warfare* (Nairobi: International Committee of the Red Cross, 1997); James T. Johnson, *Morality and Contemporary Warfare* (New Haven: Yale University Press, 1999); Best, *Humanity in Warfare*.

6. Kahn, "Paradox of Riskless Warfare," 2–9; Walzer, *Just and Unjust Wars*, 34–44.

7. Johnson, *Morality and Contemporary Warfare*, 124; Kahn, "Paradox of Riskless Warfare," 2–9.

8. Andrew Roberts and Robert Guelff, eds., *Documents on the Laws of War* (Oxford: Oxford University Press, 1999).

9. Kahn, "Paradox of Riskless Warfare," 2–9.

10. Herfried Münkler, "The Wars of 21st Century," *International Review of the Red Cross* 85, no. 849 (2003): 19.

11. Carl von Clausewitz, *On War* (Princeton: Princeton University Press, 1984).

12. Sebastian Kaempf, "Lost through Non-translation: Bringing Clausewitz's Writings on 'News Wars' Back In," *Small Wars and Insurgencies* 22, no. 4 (2011): 550–75.

13. Münkler, "The Wars of 21st century," 19.

14. Michael Ignatieff, *Virtual War: Kosovo and Beyond* (London: Chatto and Windus, 2000); Christopher Coker, *Waging War without Warriors: The Changing Culture of Military Conflict* (London: Lynne Rienner, 2002).

15. Martin Shaw, *The New Western Way of War* (Cambridge: Polity Press, 2005), 79–80; Andrew J. Bacevich, *The New American Militarism* (Oxford: Oxford University Press, 2005), 57; Jeffrey Record, "Collapsed Countries, Casualty Dread, and the New American Way of War," *Parameters* 32, no. 2 (2002), 10–14; Ignatieff, *Virtual War*.

16. Colin Kahl, "In the Crossfire or the Crosshairs?" *International Security* 32, no. 1 (2007), 7–46.

17. Bacevich, *New American Militarism*, 57.

18. Jeffrey Record, "Force-Protection Fetishism: Sources, Consequences, and (?) Solutions," *Aerospace Power Journal*, Summer 2000.

19. Bacevich, *New American Militarism*, 34, 124.

20. Arnold R. Isaacs, *Vietnam Shadow: The War, Its Ghost, and Its Legacy* (Baltimore: Johns Hopkins University Press, 1997), 6.

21. Trevor B. McCrisken, *American Exceptionalism and the Legacy of Vietnam: U.S. Foreign Policy since 1974* (London: Palgrave Macmillan, 2003), xiii–xiv.

22. Nixon, qtd. in Geoff Simons, *Vietnam Syndrome: Impact on U.S. Foreign Policy* (London: Macmillan, 1998), 13.

23. Shaw, *New Western Way of War*, 79–80.

24. Ulrich Beck, *Risk Society* (London: Sage, 1992); Ulrich Beck, Anthony Giddens, and Scott Lash, eds., *Reflexive Modernization: Politics, Tradition and Aesthetics in the Modern Social Order* (Cambridge: Polity Press, 1994); Zygmunt Bauman, *Liquid Modernity* (Cambridge: Polity Press, 2000).

25. Beck, Giddens, and Lash, *Reflexive Modernization*, 23–45.

26. Ulrich Beck, *World Risk Society* (Cambridge: Polity Press, 1999).

27. Bauman, *Liquid Modernity*, 10–17.

28. Richard Rorty, *Contingency, Irony, and Solidarity* (Cambridge: Cambridge University Press, 1989); David Harvey, *The Condition of Postmodernity* (Oxford: Blackwell, 1999).

29. Beck, *Risk Society*.

30. Ibid.

31. Christopher Coker, "Globalisation and Insecurity in the Twenty-First Century: NATO and the Management of Risk," Adelphi Paper 345 (2002), 57–59.

32. Edward N. Luttwak, "Toward a Post-heroic Warfare," *Foreign Affairs* 74, no. 3 (May/June 1995), 109–23; Edward N. Luttwak, "A Post-heroic Military Policy," *Foreign Affairs* 75, no. 4 (July/August 1996): 33–45.

33. Shaw, *New Western Way of War*, 79–80; Bacevich, *New American Militarism*, 57; Jeffrey Record, "Collapsed Countries, Casualty Dread, and the New American Way of War," *Parameters* 32, no. 2 (2002), 10–14.

34. Christopher Coker, "The Unhappy Warrior," *Royal United Services Institute Journal* 150, no. 6 (December 2005): 10–16.

35. Chris Hables Gray, *Postmodern War: The New Politics of Conflict* (London: Routledge, 1997), 36–50; Ignatieff, *Virtual War*, 168.

36. Record, "Collapsed Countries," 4.

37. Karl Eikenberry, "Take No Casualties," *Parameters* 26, no. 2 (Summer 1996): 113.

38. Geoff Simons, *Vietnam Syndrome: Impact on U.S. Foreign Policy* (London: Macmillan, 1998), 20–21; Michael Ignatieff, "The New American Way of War," *New York Review of Books* 47, no. 12 (2000); Record, "Collapsed Countries," 10–14.

39. George Herring, "Preparing Not to Refight the Last War: The Impact of Vietnam on the American Military," in *After Vietnam: Legacies of a Lost War*, ed. Charles E Neu (Baltimore: Johns Hopkins University Press, 2000), 77.

40. Bush, qtd. in McCrisken, *American Exceptionalism*, 150.

41. McCaffrey, qtd. in Bacevich, *New American Militarism*, 34. See also Ignatieff, "New American Way of War."

42. For a listing of various public statements, see Gray, *Postmodern War*, 46; Bacevich, *New American Militarism*, 33–35.

43. Simons, *Vietnam Syndrome*, 6; Record, "Collapsed Countries," 10–14.

44. Beck, *Risk Society*; Coker, *Humane Warfare*, 51–61.

45. See also similar issues raised in chapter 6 of this volume by Brent Steele and Eric Heinze.

46. Bacevich, "Morality and High Technology," 47.

47. Mark Bowden, "The Kabul-ki Dance," *Atlantic Monthly*, November 2002; Luttwak, "Toward a Post-heroic Warfare," 116; Ignatieff, "Battle without Blood," interview by Max Garcone, *Salon*, 4 May 2000, http://www.salon.com/books/int/2000/05/04/ignatieff (accessed April 2, 2004).

48. Ignatieff, *Virtual War*; James Der Derian, *Virtuous War: Mapping the Military-Industrial-Media-Entertainment Network* (Oxford: Westview Press, 2001). See also similar issues raised in Chapter 6 of this volume by Brent Steele and Eric Heinze.

49. Victor D. Hanson, *The Western Way of Warfare: Infantry Battles in Classical Greece* (Berkley: University of California Press, 2000), 6–11.

50. Hanson, *Western Way of Warfare*, 10; see also Paul W. Khan, "The Paradox of Riskless Warfare," *Philosophy and Public Policy Quarterly* 22, no. 3 (2002): 2–9.

51. Kahn, "Paradox of Riskless Warfare," 7; Ignatieff, "Battle without blood."

52. Der Derian, *Virtuous War*, xiv–xv (emphasis in original).

53. Law, cited in Gray, *Postmodern War*, 37.

54. Coker, *Waging War without Warriors*; Peter W. Singer, *Wired for War: The Robotics Revolution and Conflict in the 21st Century* (London: Penguin, 2009).

55. Cited in "Pentagon Works to Increase Its Army of Robots," *Miami Herald*, 14 February 2006.

56. Spencer Ackerman and Noah Schachtman, "Almost 1 in 3 U.S. Warplanes Is a Robot," 9 January 2012, available at http://www.wired.com/dangerroom/2012/01/drone-report (accessed August 15, 2012); Peter Finn, "The Do-It-Yourself Origins of the Drone," *Washington Post*, 24 December 2011, available at http://www.highbeam.com/doc/1P2-30377720.html (accessed August 15, 2012).

57. "Drones Are the Lynchpin of Obama's War on Terror," Spiegel Online International, http://www.spiegel.de/international/world/killer-app-drones-are-lynchpin-of-obama-s-war-on-terror-a-682612.html (accessed August 15, 2012).

58. Coker, *Waging War without Warriors*; Singer, *Wired for War*.

59. Sven Lindqvist, *"Exterminate All the Brutes": One Man's Odysseys into the Heart of Darkness and the Origins of European Genocide*, trans. Joan Tate (London: Granta Books, 2002), 44–47.

60. Winston S. Churchill, *The River War* (London: Prion Books, 1997), 218.

61. John Ellis, *The Social History of the Machine Gun* (Baltimore: Johns Hopkins University Press, 1986), 86–87.

62. Sebastian Kaempf, "Double Standards in U.S. Warfare: Exploring the Historical Legacy of Civilian Protection and the Complex Nature of the Moral-Legal Nexus," *Review of International Studies* 35, no. 3 (2009), 651–74.

63. Michael Howard, George J. Andreopoulos, and Mark R. Shulman, eds., *The Laws of War: Constraints on War in the Western World* (New Haven: Yale University Press, 1994), 3.

64. Michael Ignatieff, *The Warrior's Honour: Ethnic War and the Modern Conscience* (London: Vintage, 1999), 117.

65. Ibid.

66. Colin S. Gray, *Modern Strategy* (Oxford: Oxford University Press, 1999), 275–76; Sven Lindqvist, *A History of Bombing*, trans. Linda Haverty Rugg (London: Granta Books, 2002).

67. Ward Thomas, *The Ethics of Destruction: Norms and Force in International Relations* (Ithaca, N.Y.: Cornell University Press, 2001).

68. Kaempf, "Double Standards in U.S. Warfare."

69. Michael Walzer, *Arguing about War* (New Haven: Yale University Press, 2004).

70. David Petraeus, U.S. Army Counterinsurgency Field Manual, FM 3–24, 2006, available at http://www.fas.org/irp/doddir/army/fm3-24.pdf (accessed March 16, 2013).

71. Kahn, "Paradox of Riskless Warfare."

CHAPTER SIX

From Smart to Autonomous Weapons

Confounding Territoriality and Moral Agency

Brent J. Steele and Eric A. Heinze

ADVANCES IN MILITARY TECHNOLOGY today are frequently described in terms of the extent to which they remove the soldier from the battlefield and increase the precision of the application of force, therefore reducing the costs and suffering associated with waging war. This capability has been further enhanced by the well-documented use of armed unmanned aerial vehicles (UAVs) by the United States in the "global war on terror."[1] The use of unmanned and increasingly autonomous weapons systems, according to some observers, will inevitably lead to autonomous robots being deployed in the battlefield and entrusted with decisions about target identification *and* destruction.[2]

This chapter examines how these advances in military technology confound two fundamental concepts that are critical to making sense of the Just War tradition—those of *territoriality* (or spatiality) and *moral agency*—which we argue has implications for important principles within *jus ad bellum*, *jus in bello*, and *jus post bellum*. Regarding territoriality, we observe that the use of remote weapons in general, and specifically the use of armed UAVs, make the notion of Just War highly problematic because they can be deployed quietly and unofficially, anywhere and everywhere, at any time. In terms of moral agency, we argue that the use of increasingly autonomous weapons substantially frustrates the ability to hold an agent responsible for transgressions of *jus in bello* rules, most notably noncombatant immunity (or discrimination) and proportionality. Furthermore, we contend that the intrinsic ambiguity of morality does not lend itself well to the sorts of predetermined rules that would presumably be the basis for programming autonomous weapons systems to behave "ethically."

THE CENTRALITY OF TERRITORIALITY AND MORAL AGENCY TO THE JUST WAR TRADITION

Territoriality

Territory has played an important role in conflict and war. We often think of territory being the end goal of conflict, not as a constraint on it, but it can be both. For instance, sovereign "spaces" can be thought of as constraining the actions and activities of warfare. One only needs to reflect on the controversy engendered when conflict spills over—deliberately at times—into neutral sovereign states.[3] Thus, sovereignty, especially when connected to territory, serves as an organizing principle of international society.[4]

Even so, territory's role within Just War debates has been, as John Williams remarked in a recent study, "inadequately" engaged.[5] John H. Herz's observation, made over a half century ago, about the "demise of the territorial state" provides us a good starting point toward understanding the problematic delinking of territory from authority and conflict.[6] Herz discusses how in the era of the territorial state, the practice of war "itself . . . was of such a nature as to maintain at least the principle of territoriality."[7] Herz identifies two important phenomena derived from territoriality—legitimacy and nationalism—which "permitted the system to become more stable than might otherwise have been the case."[8] Legitimacy "implied that the dynasties ruling the territorial states of old Europe mutually recognized each other as rightful sovereigns. Depriving one sovereign of his rights by force could not but appear to destroy the very principle on which the rights of all of them rested." Nationalism "personalized" these territories and "made it appear as abhorrent to deprive a sovereign nation of its independence."[9]

These phenomena were transformed beginning with, again, the changing *practices* of warfare, sometime in the nineteenth century and beyond. Among these, Herz notes the two most important and interrelated were air warfare and atomic warfare. Air warfare's "effect was due to strategic action in the *hinterland* rather than to tactical use at the front. It came at least close to defeating one side by direct action against the 'soft' interior of the country, by-passing outer defenses and thus foreshadowing the end of the frontier—that is, the demise of the traditional impermeability of even the militarily most powerful states."[10] And with atomic warfare, Herz finds that the transformation is even more radical, whereas even in the interwar period power could be seen as something "radiating from one center and growing less with distance from that center," by the 1950s "power can destroy power from center to center," thus, "everything is different."[11]

One might read Herz's declaration on the "demise" of the territorial state as simply a cataloguing of the changes technology makes possible both in terms of the practice of war and the understanding of sovereignty, and that this is a process that is defined more by its continuity (technological change and practice adaptation) than its jagged discontinuity or "revolutionary" moments. In this reading, UAVs can be seen as just one more technological change in the practice of war that needs to be taken into consideration within the Just War tradition.

However, we prefer to springboard from Herz's thesis to suggest that the notion of territoriality,[12] while not eliminating the nation-state per se, contained a constraining effect on conflict that was itself "destroyed" by the emerging "nonterritorial" practices of warfare. The point we wish to make is that the *further* we get from the territorial notions of sovereignty—or put another way, the more those notions are radically confounded—the *more difficult* it will be for international society to come to some interpretive (not to mention legal) agreement on legitimate practices of warfare.[13] If there is no official "termination" of war, if it becomes perpetual, then it is difficult to connect such conflict to the original "right intention" (*jus ad bellum*) of an initiated war. Further, by invoking the right to both fly UAVs and deploy force from them, the offensive parties are tacitly compromising the "just authority" of the sovereign states whose spaces are being violated. We discuss this below.

Moral Agency

Another concept that provides much of the moral substance of Just War thinking is that of moral agency, which we understand to be the idea that actors (normally human beings) are capable of behaving in accordance with the precepts of morality, have the ability to make moral choices autonomously, and are considered responsible for the moral choices they make.[14] Moral agency thus entails *autonomy*, which means that agents act independently of the will of others and that their actions originate in them and reflect their ends. It also entails *inten-*

tion, which means that the actors meant to achieve the ends that came about from their actions. It follows, then, that agents can be held individually morally *responsible* for the outcomes of their actions, to the extent that the outcome was intended by the agents and was the result of acting autonomously.

Our account of moral agency, then, is associated primarily with individuals, although we recognize that there are cogent and convincing accounts of collective moral agency that assign moral responsibility to, for example, social and political institutions.[15] Just War theory certainly recognizes the existence of collective moral agency in the *ad bellum* and *in bello* distinction, wherein the former holds institutions ("governments") responsible and the latter holds individuals responsible. It is also the case that institutions are at least in part constituted by individuals, without which it is questionable whether they could truly be held morally responsible for their conduct. Yet we contend that collective moral agency obscures individual moral responsibility—a feature highlighted in the Nuremburg proceedings and subsequent war crimes tribunals—which is why *in bello* concerns focus on individuals, so as to not let their individual immoral conduct go unpunished because they were acting as part of a broader collective war effort. Thus, since our concern in this context is one of *jus in bello*, we proceed with the standard account of moral agency centered on individuals.

Moral agency, thus stated, is required to hold individuals responsible for their conduct in times of war. To the extent that a goal of the Just War tradition is to subject the conduct of war (*jus in bello*) to moral rules, an important precondition to this is the ability to single out the actions of individuals in war for either moral praise or blame. Thus, the concept of moral agency provides a basis to identify individuals and hold them responsible for potentially having violated Just War principles. As Walzer succinctly puts it, "the theory of justice should point us to the men and women from whom we can rightly demand an accounting, and it should shape and control the judgments we make of the excuses they offer."[16] Indeed, the entire enterprise of Just War theory is undermined if we do not have some conception of moral agency as a basis for assigning responsibility for moral transgressions.

Furthermore, the ability to intend to achieve certain ends from one's actions is even *constitutive* of certain Just War principles. The principle of "right intention," for instance, stipulates that an actor must have the proper subjective intention, or state of mind, for an act to be moral. Thus, an actor's intentions and state of mind matter in our moral evaluation of his or her action, and this is possible only if the actor in question is a moral agent. In addition, an actor's intentions are literally what separate war crimes from mere accidents in the context of *jus in bello*. The Double Effect doctrine presumes that noncombatant casualties are permissible (1) if they are unintended and (2) if reasonable precautions are taken to minimize harm by the offensive party.[17] We would generally consider it a far more severe moral transgression if a commander knowingly and deliberately ordered an attack on noncombatants, versus if the commander genuinely believed that they were attacking a legitimate military target. Only the actions of someone with moral agency can be appraised on such a basis.

CONFOUNDING TERRITORY:
PERPETUAL "WAR" IN TIME AND SPACE

The difficulties involved in coming to a consensus about what are or are not the legitimate practices of warfare become especially visible when we catalogue the particular "confoundings" of territory that UAVs make possible. Consider that UAVs have been used most frequently, and recently, in the mountainous "AfPak" region of Afghanistan and Pakistan and thus routinely compromise Pakistan's sovereignty. These seem, on their face, both pragmatic and legitimate—pragmatic because of the global, transnational and "de-territorialized" nature of al Qaeda, and legitimate because of a "hot pursuit" agreement made in January of 2003 between Pakistan and the United States.[18]

And yet two wrinkles emerge more recently with the counterterrorism policies of especially the United States in the region. First, by claiming the right and even necessity of intervening with special forces, missiles, and UAVs, the United States is tacitly asserting that Pakistan is unwilling or unable (because of geography or national politics, or both) to *practice* its own sovereignty by rooting out members of al Qaeda and the Taliban—and, inversely, the United States is therefore invoking such space as within its own authoritative purview—as more than just a "right authority." And yet, secondly, even the United States recognizes that in certain cases, and especially if things go wrong in an operation, it is violating Pakistan's sovereignty by carrying out its attacks, as President Obama recently admitted regarding the "Operation Geronimo" mission that killed Osama bin Laden.[19]

UAVs have been increasingly deployed to the "soft shell" (to borrow Herz's term) areas of sovereign countries that are (at least as of this writing) *not* hostile to the United States. They have, furthermore, reinforced that which covert operations began: the possibility of endless war, temporally and spatially.[20] Any point in space is fair game, and at any moment—the operational space for battle is anywhere and everywhere, and at any time. This limitless war is facilitated even further by the increasingly microtized (smaller with respect to both time and space) nature of UAVs and their targets. The targeting of terrorists depends not on locating just the area of the terrorists, nor even their hideout, but identifying the terrorists. Armed with recognition capacities on the drones, the "space" for UAV targeting transfers from a compound or safe house of terrorists to their *faces*.

Such targeting thus brings us to a second confounding of space made possible by UAVs and their visual acuity—the removal of the "fog of war" in military operations. In a somewhat ironic way, the pilot of such missions has never been simultaneously *further* (in space) and *closer* (visually) to the target.[21] This is similar to but also radically different from what Hans Morgenthau, in delineating the *end* for any chances of an international morality emerging in a context of modern war, called the development of "push-button war." Morgenthau described "push-button war" as being "anonymously fought by people *who have never seen their enemy alive or dead and who will never know whom they have killed.*"[22] In essence, the visual acuity of the UAV provides the pilot a perspective where, in the words of Lauren Wilcox, "such deaths are less like combat deaths, and more like executions viewed at close range. . . . The images show people moving around who seem unsuspecting. . . . The advanced technological killing capabilities that these drones represent can not only bring death in an instant, from an unseen source, but can make this death visible to the operator and an audience of millions. Visibility in instance functions less like a panopticon, and more like a public execution."[23]

Thus, in these situations the pilot faces a situation akin much more to Walzer's examples of "naked soldiers," where the "shooter" faces "deep psychological uneasiness about killing."[24] This confounding of space, then, may explain why some of these pilots, even in their "sterile" environments, "suffer from combat stress that equals, or exceeds, that of pilots in the battlefield."[25]

Yet, this development illustrates something even more profound that dovetails with what Sebastian Kaempf, in his contribution to the current volume, titles a connection of "humanity" in postmodern, asymmetric warfare. This connection was absent in previous asymmetric engagements where a technologically superior power could and would battle an inferior in a "risk-free manner," but also in a way that was free of legal or moral obligations, because such a foe was deemed outside of a group of "civilized nations." And yet, as Kaempf also demonstrates, and as we develop below, while the postmodern context is defined by more universal legal and moral codes, those codes are "undermined" by the "mode of warfare" represented by UAVS. Kaempf notes that since "asymmetric warfare increasingly enables the U.S. military to kill without facing the risk of death in return, then the U.S. military can no longer draw on existing moral and legal frameworks to justify the killing of enemy soldiers."[26] Put another way, there are costs to the U.S. warrior's gains in autonomy and safety in UAVS.

CONFOUNDING MORAL AGENCY: DISCRIMINATION, PROPORTIONALITY, AND THE INDETERMINACY OF MORALITY

The arsenal of remote and unmanned weapons systems—both deployed and in development—can be understood on a sliding scale of autonomy from their human operators. On one end of the scale are those systems such as remote-piloted UAVS, wherein a human pilot makes the decision on when and where to deploy deadly violence (even though other aspects of UAV missions, such as taking off, locating enemy targets, landing, etc., are undertaken autonomously). Such systems are relatively unproblematic for assigning responsibility for transgressions of the laws of war, and we would normally locate such responsibility with the pilot in the same way we would with manned aircraft. Further down the scale are those systems wherein targets are identified by a machine, and then the decision on whether to fire is left to the human operator. Such systems include targeting systems, such as the Aegis Combat System, which are capable of identifying enemy targets by their radar or acoustic signatures and presenting this information to a human operator who then decides whether to "trust" the system and fire on the target.[27] At the far end of the scale, then, are those systems that would be entrusted to identify, as well as destroy, enemy targets without input from a human operator.

These latter two kinds of systems are far more problematic, as the following examples illustrate. First consider Iran Air Flight 655, discussed by P. W. Singer in his book *Wired for War*, which was an Iranian commercial passenger jet shot down in 1988 by a U.S. naval vessel that used the Aegis targeting computer, which mistakenly identified the passenger jet as an Iranian F-14 fighter.[28] In this case, despite other data indicating the aircraft was not a fighter jet, the crew trusted the "judgment" of the computer more than their own and authorized it to fire, thus killing almost three hundred civilians and committing a transgression of the discrimination principle. But who exactly is responsible for this mistake? Normally, we might say the human operators, though surely with the mitigating circumstance of this being a case of mistaken identity, and thus at least partially excusable. But what is interesting about this situation is that it was the *targeting computer* that misidentified the target, and the mistake the human operators made was to trust the computer's judgment over their own. Whereas without this system the human operators might have been culpable for not taking reasonable precautions to ensure that their target was an enemy aircraft, by using these systems and increasingly relying upon them to the detriment of their own decisions, the use of this technology becomes itself the "reasonable precaution" and thus provides a moral buffer between the human operators and their actions. This, in turn, allows those who use such systems "to tell themselves that the machine made the decision,"[29] thus relieving themselves of feeling morally responsible even though it is they, and not the targeting computer, who are the moral agents in this example.

Yet in considering what reasonable precautions combatants must take to minimize risks to civilians, Walzer reminds us that "[w]hat we look for in such cases is some sign of a positive commitment to save civilian lives."[30] If indeed part of this doctrine assumes, as Walzer suggests, that the attacking party must actually put itself in *more danger* to reduce the vulnerability of noncombatants, then UAVs are even more problematic. In order to make such a judgment, one must *locate* and decide whose intentions matters here, for as Jane Mayer notes when it comes to UAVs and their use by the CIA, "there is no visible system of accountability in place," and "the White House has delegated trigger authority to CIA officials."[31] In essence, the intent (turning an expectation into an action) surrounding a UAV's use is diffused through a variety of supporting actors ranging from the CIA, the U.S. president, and the head of the Counter-Terrorist Center to, in an even more radical sense, computer programs.[32] As Mayer describes, "if a school, hospital, or mosque is within the likely blast radius of a missile," then the calculation for estimating civilian casualties with a UAV are all "weighed by a *computer algorithm* before a lethal strike is authorized."[33]

The situation with fully autonomous systems becomes even more problematic. Consider if the Iran Air tragedy had occurred with the targeting computer being entrusted to identify *and* destroy enemy targets *without* human authorization. To the extent that we consider it important to hold some moral agent(s) responsible for this tragedy, even if it was an "honest" accident, it would seem exceedingly difficult, perhaps impossible, to identify one in this case. If a weapon is truly autonomous, which means that it chooses and destroys its own targets without human input, this implies that its orders do not necessarily determine its actions, even if they obviously influence them.[34] This means that the more autonomous a system is, the more it has the capacity to "choose" a course of action that differs from how it was intended to act by both its programmers and those who ordered its use.[35] At some point, the designers and manufacturers of such systems, as well as the officers who ordered their deployment, can no longer control or predict the actions of the system, thus making it difficult to hold them morally responsible. Unless we are willing to imbue a machine with moral agency and hold it morally responsible, which would seem to us to be even more problematic (i.e., how would one "punish" a machine), then there may be no moral agent to hold responsible for potential war crimes, and *all* civilian casualties become ipso facto "excused" as unintended collateral damage.[36]

Let us be clear: the point here is not that UAVs, when "malfunctioning," represent a new problem for the ethics and practices within war, although such malfunctions have indeed occurred with UAV use.[37] Malfunctioning technologies have been a problem for centuries of warfare. The point is, rather, that the location of "intent" for targeting with increasingly autonomous weapons becomes both diffused and confused. Indeed, the very possibility of intent becomes an almost absurd notion when referring to machines, particularly autonomous ones. Even if it were possible (and desirable) to locate moral responsibility with a machine, ascertaining its "intentions" to determine whether it committed a crime may be not be possible. Computers may be said to have "intentions" in terms of their functionality, which is to say that they can act purposefully in that their only "intention" is to carry out what it has been programmed to do, subject to a set of rules.[38] But to say that someone (or something) *intended* to do something is to say that its actions originated with them and reflected their ends, which the agent itself has "chosen" (in some sense) because of its ability to reason and on the basis of past experience.[39] However, granting that a machine can be autonomous in the sense that it may interpret the parameters of its programming in unpredictable ways, the source of its intentions (analogously, its "reason" and "past experience") is human programming. Thus, paradoxically, a weapons system that "chooses" its own targets and then "decides" to destroy them is at the same time an autonomous agent yet lacks true intention. It could, say, mistake a group of civilians for combatants or make a dubious proportionality calculation, but we can never understand its "reasons" for doing so—the essence of intentions—apart from its programming parameters. As Harry Gould suggests in his chapter in this volume, much of the debate over the moral significance of intentions is about competing conceptions of agency.[40]

These examples suggest issues that may be symptomatic of a larger problem with using autonomous weapons systems in accordance with the precepts of just war doctrine, which is that moral behavior in warfare may not be achievable through the delineation of rules in a computer program because of the intrinsic ambiguity in morality itself. It has been claimed that autonomous weapons systems are capable of performing more ethically on the battlefield than human soldiers.[41] Autonomous robots can integrate more information faster and more accurately than humans, they have high-tech sensors to make observations that humans cannot, and they do not suffer from fatigue or emotions that might impede a human soldier on the battlefield. Thus, the solution is simply to program these systems, using extremely precise and clear commands, to behave ethically and in accordance with the laws of war and simply allow the robot's mechanical determinism to follow these rules, resulting in ethical behavior. Whatever behavioral problems ensue, therefore, would be because of the ambiguity of the prior rules, which could be resolved by a continual refining and more precise specification of, for example, who is a combatant.

However, as John Kaag and Whitley Kaufman argue, moral judgment is inherently ambiguous, controversial, and not reducible to a set of rules, and if it were, "it is likely that we would have discovered many or most of these rules long ago."[42] One could even argue that morality is *more* ambiguous in times of war than in ordinary life. Consider a robot programmed with precise instructions to distinguish between civilians and combatants and only engage the latter. Right away one runs into the problem of specifying "civilianness," as the laws of war are extremely ambiguous on the concept of combatancy, and there is almost always room for moral choice within these rules. The first problem is perceptual ambiguity. Computer scientist Noel Sharkey has argued that even the most sophisticated robots would not be able to tell, for example, "whether a woman is pregnant or whether she is carrying explosives," whereas a human soldier would simply use the skill of common sense.[43] Another problem, relating to the indeterminacy of morality, is that sometimes moral behavior requires that one make certain exceptions to the rules. For example, forward observers who provide intelligence required to target enemy forces are clearly taking direct part in hostilities and may be legitimately killed. Yet a robot, programmed as such, making this calculation would presumably not make an exception for the possibility that some armed groups force civilians to engage in this practice against their will. Such was the situation during the Iraq War when the Mahdi Militia used a child for such purposes and U.S. forces declined to shoot the child on moral grounds, despite this being perfectly permissible under the laws of war.[44] A robot is only capable of distinguishing combatants and civilians in the empirical sense, not the normative sense.

WHITHER JUST WAR?

This chapter points out, via the concepts of territory and moral agency, that UAVs and autonomous weapons systems provide distinctive problems for the Just War tradition. Like the rest of the contributors to this volume, we have been assigned to figure out a constructive path for the Just War tradition, in light of the concerns of the chapter, going forward. While we concede that the practice of UAVs within war (per se) may ultimately be handled within the framework of Just War, we ultimately maintain that their use is part of a growing trend of postmodern conflict that makes notions of a Just War increasingly obsolete.

We may consider that UAVs are not the cause but the symptom of a "global war on terror," and thus their use, while bringing somewhat unique dynamics to war, is not per se a unique problem in the practice of war. Yet regarding the notion of space being challenged by UAVs suggests a further consideration for scholars and practitioners alike. UAV usage in a "global war on terror" forces all of us to come to grips with the de-territorialized and postmodern spatial context of the *nature* of this conflict—a conflict that is focused on the identity of individuals, the recognition of their faces rather than territorial spaces. If this is the case, then it is not just the notion of a Just War that's problematic; it is the notion that this is "war" whatsoever. Targeted killing, perhaps; assassination, maybe;[45] but not a war that can be easily categorized, or spoken to, by the tradition of Just War. John Williams gets to the crux of the problematic discourses regarding especially terrorism over the past decade:

> The U.S. government in particular has recast transnational terrorist threats within a statist discourse. Labeling states members of an "axis of evil," ascribing responsibility for combating terrorism to governments—it was governments who were to decide whether they were either "with us . . . or with the terrorists" . . . is telling of a stubbornly "Westphalian" world view. But more

to the point here is that *academic debate about Just War, humanitarian intervention and terrorism*, especially when the latter two are connected, quickly does the same thing.[46]

Our point here is not that we need to return (as if that were possible) to the bygone days of Herz's territorial state, but rather that it seems mere folly to continue to speak of actions like the use of UAVs purely within the language of a Just War tradition that continues to be shackled to principles that have not been properly debated, especially in the context of a "war on terror."

A further point regarding the operational "space" of UAVs takes one of their primary benefits—the safety it provides human operators and thus the minimization of casualties by an attacking party—and turns it into a liability. In the words of Singer, "what seems so logical and reasonable to the side using them may strike other societies as weak and contemptible," leading to assumptions that the UAV-using combatants are "cowardly."[47] In fact, in line with the notions of space discussed above, there is an inverse security relationship that develops with UAVs. While on the one hand those "pilots" flying the UAVs are perfectly safe from their bunkers in Nevada, those parties in the "kill zone" are vulnerable at any time, day or night. And *both* sets of "combatants" know this.

Regarding the notion of moral agency, we would concede that programming autonomous weapons systems to abide by the principle of discrimination seems relatively straightforward compared to programming them to make proportionality calculations. There is really no precise, quantitative way to compare the "good" accrued from neutralizing a certain military object with the "evil" done as a result of incidental collateral damage. Thus, programming a machine to make such a calculation may be an exercise in futility. In some circumstances, the lives of some noncombatants (children) will count more than those of others (munitions factory workers) in making proportionality calculations. For example, some weapons systems in development can be launched like a conventional missile and then "loiter" over enemy territory in order to select and attack their targets by detecting unique radar and mechanical signatures of enemy forces.[48] Will such systems be able to tell if these enemy forces are ensconced in civilian areas and are being protected by human shields (and if so, which humans)? Most importantly, will they be able to calculate whether it is worth killing x number of civilians to take out a single enemy radar? The point is that proportionality calculations epitomize the inherent ambiguity in morality and are extremely context dependent, such that a preprogrammed computer algorithm does not possess the sorts of complex intuitions that humans have about right and wrong behavior that are required to make such calculations.

There are thus two main challenges that Just War theorists must confront regarding the confounding of moral agency if the tradition is to continue to be relevant in an age of increasingly autonomous weapons. First, for those systems where a human decision maker is still involved in deciding to attack but trusts computers to identify targets, it seems fairly clear that moral responsibility still lies with the human operator. The problem is the moral buffer provided by the fact that a computer is identifying targets are to be destroyed, which alleviates the human operator of the important moral burden of deciding whether there is sufficient evidence to conclude that it is legitimate to destroy a particular target. Just War theorists thus need to seriously grapple with the question of whether trusting a supposedly superior computer to make targeting decisions is a suf-ficiently "reasonable precaution" to minimize risks to civilians, and how this implicates the common Just War precept that combatants are expected to put themselves in harm's way to do so.

Second, for those weapons systems that will become *fully* autonomous, the challenge is immense, but we see a couple possible ways to proceed. The most straightforward would be to interpret the Just War tradition as simply forbid-ding the use of fully autonomous weapons. The basic argument would be that the ability to hold agents of war morally responsible for their actions is a nec-essary condition for fighting a Just War. Since autonomous weapons systems make this impossible, and since ethical behavior in war does not lend itself to the sort of mechanistic rule following that these systems are programmed to execute, then deploying autonomous weapons systems is unjust. One could also attempt to reformulate, or excise altogether, the concept of moral agency in order to accommodate actors that are autonomous yet lack intention, although this would fundamentally alter the normative substance of Just War principles and profoundly undermine their ability to provide sound moral guidance, thus possibly relegating them to irrelevance.

Yet given that the deployment of such weapons is likely to occur anyway, and given the centrality of moral agency to the Just War tradition, to argue that the use of such systems is consistent with a Just War requires *at a minimum* that one locate moral responsibility for the actions of these systems. If a machine cannot be held morally responsible, which *people* are responsible for the actions of these machines if they commit moral transgressions and why? Recent lit-erature has explored some ways we might begin to address this issue through the appropriate designing of such systems, whereby clear responsibility would be allocated for each distinct function of the system, as well as the function of the system as a whole.[49] Yet such a responsibility regime would need to be extremely precise and entered into voluntarily by weapons manufacturers and designers so that they know they might be held accountable for a war crime if their system fails.

It is one thing to speak of "more moral" outcomes within war because of advances in technology. It is quite another to think that we (as scholars or practitioners) can effectively locate agency in such a diffuse environment. Territory and agency, we assert here, have both been central in discussions on the "morality" of war. Yet in this case, the centralization of moral blame or praise is no longer possible, as judgment scans past the combatants—the "armchair warrior" piloting a UAV from Nevada, the officer who orders the deployment of an autonomous weapon—and is seemingly back-filtered to the manufacturers of these weapons systems themselves. How are we to speak of "responsibility" within war in such a radically diffused environment? UAVs and autonomous weapons may be more accurate weapons of war and may very well *lead* to the *eventual* reduction of civilian casualties, but the concerns raised in this chapter no longer sit easy within a "tradition" that is at least a millennium old and that prides itself on providing us the means through which we can discuss *a* "morality" of war.

Notes

1. See, generally, Peter W. Singer, *Wired for War: The Robotics Revolution and Conflict in the Twenty-First Century* (New York: Penguin, 2009).

2. Robert Sparrow, "Killer Robots," *Journal of Applied Philosophy* 24, no. 1 (2007): 64; Ronald C. Arkin, "The Case for Ethical Autonomy in Unmanned Systems," *Journal of Military Ethics* 9, no. 4 (2010): 332.

3. See, for example, the international reaction to Germany's invasion of Belgium, an at-the-time neutral country, at the beginning of the First World War. Brent J. Steele, *Ontological Security in International Relations*, (London: Routledge, 2008), chapter 5.

4. See Barak Mendelsohn, "Sovereignty under Attack: The International Society Meets the al Qaeda Network," *Review of International Studies* 31, no. 1 (2005): 45–68.

5. John Williams, "Space, Scale and Just War: Meeting the Challenge of Humanitarian Intervention and Trans-national Terrorism," *Review of International Studies* 34, no. 4 (2008): 581–600.

6. John H. Herz, "Rise and Demise of the Territorial State," *World Politics* 9, no. 4 (1957): 473–93.

7. Ibid., 481.

8. Ibid., 483.

9. Ibid.

10. Ibid., 487.

11. Ibid.

12. Carl Schmitt, in his famous *Nomos* work, asserted in one important passage that "the core of the *nomos* lay in the division of European soil into state territories with firm borders" leading to the notion that this "land had a special territorial status in international law." Carl Schmitt, *The* Nomos *of the Earth in the International Law of the* Jus Publicum Europaeum, trans. G. L. Ulmen (New York: Telos Press, [1950] 2003), 148. It should come as no surprise that Herz cites Schmitt in his article.

13. We recognize, as John Agnew and Stuart Crobridge observed some years ago, that the practice of territoriality has not led to purely uncontested, mutually exclusive claims over space. Agnew and Crobridge, *Mastering Space: Hegemony, Territory, and International Political Economy* (New York: Routledge, 1995), especially chapter 4.

14. See Andrew Eshleman, "Moral Responsibility," *The Stanford Encyclopedia of Philosophy* (Winter 2009 ed.), ed. Edward N. Zalta, http://plato.stanford.edu/archives/win2009/entries/moral-responsibility/ (accessed April 25, 2013).

15. See, for instance, Toni Erskine, ed., *Can Institutions Have Responsibilities? Collective Moral Agency and International Relations* (New York: Palgrave Macmillan, 2004).

16. Michael Walzer, *Just and Unjust Wars: A Moral Argument with Historical Illustrations*, 4th ed. (New York: Basic Books, 2006), 287.

17. Eric A. Heinze and Brent J. Steele, "Introduction: Non-state Actors and the Just War Tradition," in *Ethics, Authority and War: Non-state Actors and the Just War Tradition*, ed. Eric A. Heinze and Brent J. Steele (New York: Palgrave, 2009), 6. See also Harry D. Gould, this volume.

18. Cian O'Driscoll, "From Versailles to 9/11: Non-state Actors and Just War in the Twentieth Century," in Heinze and Steele, eds., *Ethics, Authority and War*, 21–46, 37; "U.S., Pak Agree to 'Quiet' Hot Pursuit," *Indian Express*, January 7, 2003, http://www.indianexpress.com/oldStory/16206/ (accessed April 25, 2013).

19. "Obama on Bin Laden: The Full *60 Minutes* Interview," CBS News, May 8, 2011, http://www.cbsnews.com/8301-504803_162-20060530-10391709.html (accessed April 25, 2013).

20. Jane Mayer quotes Mary Duziak's statement, "Drones are a technological step that further isolates the American people from military action, undermining political checks on . . . endless war." Jane Mayer, "The Predator War," *New Yorker*, October 28, 2009, http://www.newyorker.com/reporting/2009/10/26/091026fa_fact_mayer (accessed April 25, 2013).

21. This perspective can lead to a mystified contextualization of "targets" as well. Singer relates one vignette from 2002, when a tall thirty-year-old Afghan man, Daraz

Khan, was killed in a drone strike because his height—relative to others with him—resembled that of bin Laden: "The men were wearing robes, were at a suspected terrorist hideout, and, most important, one of them was much taller than the others, as bin Laden was thought to be. As best as could be determined from seven thousand miles away, these were the men whom the Predator was looking for. As Pentagon spokeswoman Victoria Clarke explained, 'We're convinced that it was an appropriate target . . . [although] *we do not yet know exactly who it was.*" Singer, *Wired*, 397 (emphasis added).

22. Hans J. Morgenthau, *Politics among Nations*, 7th ed. (1948; New York: McGraw-Hill, 2006), 250 (emphasis added).

23. Lauren Wilcox, "Compulsory Visibility: Violence, Bodies, and the Visual," paper presented at the 2010 annual meeting of the International Studies Association, Northeast, Baltimore, November 2010.

24. Walzer describes these situations generally as "a soldier on patrol . . . catches an enemy soldier unaware, holds him in his gunsights, easy to kill, and then must decide whether to shoot him or let the opportunity pass." Walzer, *Just and Unjust War*, 138–39.

25. Mayer, "Predator War."

26. Sebastian Kaempf, this volume.

27. Singer, *Wired for War*, 124–25.

28. Ibid., 125.

29. Robert Sparrow, "Building a Better WarBot: Issues in the Design of Unmanned Systems for Military Applications," *Science and Engineering Ethics* 15, no. 1 (2009): 183. See also Mary L. Cummings, "Automation and Accountability in Decision Support System Interface Design," *Journal of Technical Studies* 32, no. 1: 23–31.

30. Walzer, *Just and Unjust Wars*, 156.

31. Mayer, "Predator War."

32. Again, Kaempf (this volume) notes in a similar vein that "most servicemen and women are no longer soldiers in a conventional sense. Instead, they have become machine- and technology-assisted agents."

33. Ibid. Peter Singer quotes one robotics expert, "how do we transition authority for lethal action to the machine"? Singer, *Wired for War*, 400.

34. Sparrow, "Killer Robots," 69.

35. Ibid., 70.

36. See Noel Sharkey, "The Ethical Frontiers of Robotics," *Science* 322, no. 5909 (December 19, 2008): 1800–1801. See also John P. Sullins, "When Is a Robot a Moral Agent?" *International Review of Information Ethics* 6 (2006): 23–30.

37. What one 2006 account titled "what is believed to be the world's first incident in which a civilian has been accidentally killed by a military unmanned air vehicle" is the case of a UAV operated by the Belgian army in the Congo. The UAV crashed and killed one woman and injured three others on the ground. See "Belgians in Congo to Probe Fatal UAV Accident," *Flightglobal*, October 10, 2006, http://www.flightglobal.com

/articles/2006/10/10/209752/belgians-in-congo-to-probe-fatal-uav-incident.html (accessed April 25, 2013).

38. Deborah G. Johnson, "Computer Systems: Moral Entities but Not Moral Agents," *Ethics and Information Technology* 8, no. 4 (2006): 201.

39. Sparrow, "Killer Robots," 65. See also Gould, this volume.

40. Gould, this volume.

41. Arkin, "Case for Ethical Autonomy," 332.

42. John Kaag and Whitley Kaufman, "Military Frameworks: Technological Know-how and the Legitimization of Warfare," *Cambridge Review of International Affairs* 22, no. 4 (2009): 601.

43. Quoted by Nic Fleming, "Robot Wars 'Will Be a Reality within 10 Years,'" *Telegraph*, 27 February 2008, http://www.telegraph.co.uk/earth/earthnews/3334341/Robot-wars-will-be-a-reality-within-10-years.html.

44. Kaag and Kaufman, "Military Frameworks," 600.

45. See Avery Plaw, *Targeting Terrorists* (London: Ashgate, 2008).

46. Williams, "Space, Scale and Just War," 595.

47. Singer, *Wired for War*, 312.

48. Noel Sharkey, "Saying 'No!' to Lethal Autonomous Targeting," *Journal of Military Ethics* 9, no. 4 (2010): 370.

49. Sparrow, "Building a Better WarBot," 179.

CHAPTER SEVEN

An Alternative
to Nuclear Weapons?

Proportionality, Discrimination, and
the Conventional Global Strike Program

Alexa Royden

IN THE SPRING OF 2010, the White House confirmed that President Obama supports the development of Conventional Prompt Global Strike (CPGS), a "super" conventional ballistic missile program that would serve as an alternative to, and possible long-term replacement for, U.S. nuclear weapons. Ostensibly, a conventional ballistic missile system would be free of the disadvantages that make nuclear weapons so problematic: indiscriminate destructive power and radiation. And yet, on closer examination, CPGS poses serious problems of its own. These problems stem largely from the fact that CPGS is designed to be used—and used under conditions in which it may be difficult to adhere to the *jus in bello* principles of discrimination and proportionality.

First emerging in 2001 as part of the U.S. Air Force Global Strike Concept in support of the 2002 Quadrennial Defense Review, CPGS would offer the United States a flexible, hypersonic capability that could respond to rapidly evolving threats in approximately one hour. The White House, having prioritized a reduction in the U.S. nuclear arsenal, clearly finds the idea of a usable, conventional capability an important way to bolster U.S. strategic forces while pursuing deep cuts in the existing nuclear stockpile. Further, having a weapon that can be used to rapidly and preemptively respond to the threats posed by rogue states and global terrorist groups fills an existing gap in our military arsenal.[1]

And as a conventional weapon system, CPGS violates none of the norms that have evolved to constrain a potential nuclear encounter.

The assumption, however, that a conventional ballistic missile attack is a more just means of responding to global threats has received little careful attention. Certainly, conventional ballistic missiles are generally less destructive, in a literal sense, than even the smallest nuclear device. However, any weapons system that has even the slightest potential to replace a nuclear capability is likely to pose problems in terms of its legitimate use, particularly if the threshold for its use is significantly lower than the one observed for the use of nuclear weapons. This chapter explores precisely this issue through an examination of the core *jus in bello* principles that are generally cited when critiquing the use of nuclear weapons: discrimination and proportionality. The first section examines the principles generally, as they are commonly understood to date. The next section explores their application to nuclear weapons, including a discussion of nuclear strategy and deterrence. Following, these same concepts are applied to the CPGS program in order to examine the extent to which it meets *jus in bello* criteria. Finally, a concluding section considers responses to these issues in hopes of furthering the utility of the Just War tradition in light of the evolution of conventional weaponry.

JUS IN BELLO: THE PRINCIPLES OF DISCRIMINATION AND PROPORTIONALITY

In the Just War tradition, *jus in bello* principles are concerned with justice in battle. Two criteria are central to the use of missile technologies, be they nuclear or conventional: the principle of discrimination and the principle of proportionality. Both principles have received extensive treatment in academic and professional literatures; however, the emergence of new technologies continues to complicate their application, as weapons have at once become more deadly and more accurate.

The principle of discrimination identifies parameters regarding the targeting of enemy combatants, noncombatants and civilians, including all civilians and members of the military who are either off duty or a member of a protected class, such as medics and chaplains. Simply put, enemy combatants may be justly targeted, while enemy noncombatants and civilians may not. Unfortunately, as war is an undertaking that doesn't always allow for neat distinctions, it is sometimes inevitable, and under certain circumstances permissible, to know-

ingly target locations where noncombatants and civilians may be at risk, as long
as the intended act is generally perceived to be morally good or neutral.[2] For
instance, it has become generally accepted that the targeting of key infrastructures critical to the success of the enemy's war effort is in fact just, as it is likely
to shorten the length of hostilities. Civilians or noncombatants engaged in activities that directly support these efforts may inadvertently become casualties,
but there are likely to be fewer civilian casualties in the long term if the amount
of time engaged in active combat is reduced. Thus the act, while destructive,
could be considered a moral good. The key to this caveat is the doctrine of
Double Effect, or the distinction made between the unintentional targeting of
noncombatants and civilians versus the deliberate targeting of the innocent.
This "collateral damage," while regrettable, is not innately unjust, although it
is subject to further restriction under the principle of proportionality (below).
However, determining the line between critical targets and noncritical targets
has proven complicated. A munitions factory undoubtedly meets the criteria,
while a factory that produces soldiers' uniforms likely does not. More controversial is the targeting of civilian structures and other public spaces where combatants may gather.[3] Thus, the extent to which the principle of discrimination
can be successfully implemented relies heavily upon the acquisition of accurate
and timely intelligence, without which selecting legitimate targets that minimize collateral damage is challenging. And in all cases, it is incumbent upon the
party launching the attack to demonstrate that careful deliberation preceded a
military strike that results in a significant level of collateral damage, even if the
target itself is ultimately deemed just.[4] This allows, unsurprisingly, for a fair
degree of subjectivity in the selection and prioritizing of targets, further fueling
the debate regarding the acceptable casualty rate of civilians in wartime.

The principle of proportionality further limits the actions of those engaged
in combat. While the use of violence by state actors is considered legitimate
under certain conditions, "the bombing will be morally permissible only if the
importance of the military targets equals or outweighs the resulting deaths of
ordinary civilians."[5] In other words, the amount of force utilized must be commensurate with the injury or likely harm the enemy has committed or intends
to commit. Further, the amount of force used should be the minimum amount
of force necessary to achieve the desired end state. It would be immoral to cause
unnecessary injury, and given a range of alternatives, the moral course of action
is to pursue the military strategy that successfully neutralizes the threat while
causing the least harm to the population and the infrastructures necessary to

support the population.[6] Thus, as a practical matter, proportionality posits a base-level cost-benefit analysis. The extent to which this is successful, of course, depends upon the accuracy of the threat assessment. And it is in the assessment of threat that subjective analysis inevitably takes place.

Taken together, the principles of discrimination and proportionality provide broad guidance regarding the moral constraints leaders should observe in the conduct of war. The specifics, however, are vigorously debated. That said, one arena in which there is comparatively little debate is in the use of nuclear weapons. With the bombings of Hiroshima and Nagasaki, it became clear that nuclear weapons were inherently both indiscriminate and disproportional, and most scholars deplored their potential use, even while they recognized the seemingly inevitable reality that was the nuclear arms race. And yet, within the debates of this period emerged an important discussion regarding the "worst case" scenario: global nuclear war. The hypothetical "rules" that would govern its conduct are illuminating and demonstrate the deficiencies inherent in crafting a just strategy for the use of nuclear weapons.

JUST CONDUCT, NUCLEAR WEAPONS, AND THE EVOLUTION OF CPGS

Nuclear weapons are created in the fervent hope that they will never be used. Upon first blush, this makes little sense, but key to an understanding of nuclear strategy is the concept of deterrence. As noted above, Hiroshima and Nagasaki revealed the intrinsic potential of the atom bomb: the ultimate and unsparing destruction of life and everything related to life within the bomb's core blast zone. In addition, beyond the kill zone, the bomb left behind a terrible and entirely uncontainable secondary effect, nuclear fallout from the radiation released in the process of the explosion. Because the consequences were so horrific, it seemed that any military objective would pale in comparison to the likely result of confrontation. The basis of deterrence, then, is the idea that no rational actor would invite nuclear retaliation by actually using a nuclear weapon, much less provoking a nuclear attack.

This is why nuclear weapons are classified by so many as inherently unjust. While a ruling by the International Court of Justice in 1996 seemed to leave open the possibility for the first use of nuclear weapons in the event a state should face supreme emergency, or a truly existential threat to its existence, that decision was deeply controversial and has never fully resolved the debate regarding the use of nuclear weapons.[7] In targeting, it is impossible to discriminate between combatant and civilian, and in proportion, nuclear weapons are truly commensurate only in response to another nuclear attack. Thus, for many, the only possible scenario in which nuclear weapons can be used legitimately is in a "second strike." This, however, is precisely the scenario that scholars and policymakers contemplated during the Cold War. What if deterrence failed? What if the worst-case scenario did happen? How might we respond? And was any response truly just?

There were three primary strategies that evolved around the idea of second strike, or the strategy a state would execute in the event deterrence failed and it was subject to nuclear attack. These strategies—countercity, counterforce, and countercontrol—were retaliatory in nature, as first-strike nuclear attacks were overwhelmingly considered illegitimate.[8] In the event of an attack, however, and in the absence of a conventional response commensurate to the initial aggression, various policies were proposed that were designed to maximize the overall goal of deterrence. These scenarios inevitably drew criticism from ethicists, who argued that no nuclear second-strike strategy could be either discriminating or proportional enough to meet Just War criteria.

The first of these, the countercity strategy, emerged in the early 1950s, when U.S. nuclear weapons were pointed at Soviet cities and vice versa. The assumption, of course, was that neither adversary would act first if their populations were held hostage. And this is exactly why critics objected to the strategy on the grounds that it was indiscriminate. Beyond the fact that nuclear weapons themselves are indiscriminate in their effect, the deliberate targeting of civilians as the base strategy—a strategy designed to maximize, not minimize, casualties— failed as it violated the core condition of discrimination: civilians shall not be targeted with intent. While it is undeniably true that civilian centers remained on the target list of U.S. strategic nuclear forces, this type of response became increasingly delegitimized.[9]

As a result, nuclear strategy evolved to include a counterforce approach. This plan, coming close to a decade after the beginning of the U.S.-Soviet nuclear arms race, was designed to target Soviet military installations, including the missile silos. The policy appears to have been an attempt on the parts of senior leadership to discriminate between military and noncombatant or civilian targets. Again, it doesn't change the inherent nature of the weapon, and this led to a second round of criticism from ethicists concerned with the justness of nuclear retaliation. These objections recognized that any plan for a second strike that hoped to neutralize the enemy's remaining nuclear infrastructure would necessarily involve thousands of bombs, and the effects of those bombs would not be limited to military installations and the combatants that manned them. Inevitably, through either error or overkill, innocent civilians would lose their lives, potentially in great numbers, again violating the principle of discrimination. This objection likely had little effect on the actual plans prepared by the Pentagon, but it did force yet another rethinking of nuclear strategy that resulted in a final iteration of the second-strike concept.[10]

The countercontrol strategy, enunciated by the Reagan administration in the 1980s, would alternatively focus on the elimination of Soviet political and military leadership, under the assumption that the elites were more likely to be concerned with their own survival in the event of nuclear retaliation. Again, however, it is difficult to imagine a countercontrol strategy that would not result in mass civilian casualties, especially as the nucleus of Soviet government activity was embedded within a densely populated urban area, Moscow. It would seem that, even when responding to a nuclear first strike, responding in kind resulted in the indiscriminate targeting of civilians.[11]

Nor do these strategies fully account for concerns regarding proportionality. Over the years, much debate has taken place regarding the degree of retaliation necessary to achieve the military objective, which ultimately was not the end of a nuclear exchange but the deterrence of a Soviet first strike. Some proposed that a limited counterforce second strike may be adequate to prevent an initial attack. And yet, if deterrence was the fundamental military objective, deliberately limiting the scope of one's response might instead be misread by the Soviets as an opportunity to act. Of course, deterrence itself was a calculated bluff, and it only worked if the other side truly believed that mutually assured destruction was a likely outcome. Clearly, this conception has questionable moral implications. Fortunately, these strategies have never been tested, and with the end of the Cold War in the early 1990s, it seemed that the United States could abandon its focus on strategic forces and turn instead to the business of eliminating missile stockpiles.

Unfortunately, the Global War on Terrorism prompted a reassessment of U.S. strategic capabilities. In fact, it is likely that the CPGS program ultimately emerged in response to the Clinton administration's failed targeting of Osama bin Laden at an al-Qaeda training camp in 1998.[12] Discovering that there were no long-range capabilities that would allow the United States to rapidly respond to an evolving security situation short of launching nuclear missiles, the U.S. Air Force began to work on a broad strategic concept called Global Strike. Global Strike, incorporated into the 2002 Quadrennial Defense Review, sought to highlight potential programs for development that would improve the ability of the United States to rapidly respond to a variety of threats in a dramatically shortened time frame. After 9/11, this capability became increasingly critical, and the Pentagon has spent much of the last decade conceiving of various ways in which to bring the concept to fruition. CPGS is the culmination of these efforts, and both the Bush and the Obama administrations have actively encouraged support for the proposal.[13]

CPGS actually encompasses a variety of possible programs, from existing initiatives to tip Trident missiles with conventional warheads to the proposed ArcLight missile system of the Defense Advanced Research Projects Agency (DARPA), which would use a combination of boosters and gliders to deliver conventional weapons at a speed similar to those reached through ballistic technologies.[14] Most of these programs would field missiles in the range of two to eleven tons, including the payload, and those payloads could vary, depending upon the design of the delivery vehicle.[15]

It is worth noting at this point that the missiles envisioned under CPGS are in no way comparable in terms of devastation to nuclear warheads. The Davy Crockett, the smallest nuclear weapon in the U.S. arsenal, had a yield of fifteen to twenty tons, far outstripping most conventional weapons.[16] In addition, the Pentagon has spent considerable effort addressing the issue of accuracy in the development of a conventionally armed ballistic missile. Unlike nuclear weapons, which detonate above the target, a conventional weapon would have to hit the target precisely. Due to advances in GPS technology, this is technically feasible. Thus, it can be assumed that CPGS has the potential to be both more discriminate and more proportional than nuclear-armed ballistic missiles.

What then, is the problem? The answer to this question lies in the underlying concept that defines CPGS and its likely use. Unlike nuclear weapons, which are designed around the concept of deterrence, CPGS is designed to be used, if selectively, as a regular part of the U.S. antimissile and counterterror strategies. They certainly have the potential to create a deterrent effect, but hardly on the scale associated with mutually assured destruction. In addition, CPGS as it is currently envisioned would most likely be deployed preemptively, not as a retaliatory response to a first strike.[17] This poses possible new problems in relation to their just use, even if they are not inherently unjust in the way that nuclear weapons are generally perceived to be.

Specifically, the assumption that CPGS will be discriminate enough to effectively target combatants, while minimizing the harm to noncombatants and civilians, is open to debate. The war in Afghanistan has provided a wealth of data that seems to indicate that despite remarkable gains made in the military's ability to target with startling accuracy, civilians are still inadvertently killed in disproportionate numbers during the course of an attack. Why is this, and is the CPGS program likely to face similar challenges?

Based upon research carried out by the Project on Defense Alternatives and Human Rights Watch (HRW), it is increasingly clear that the ability to successfully discriminate targets correlates strongly with the amount of time taken when identifying a target and authorizing its destruction. As HRW notes in its recent report on U.S. airstrikes in Afghanistan, "whether civilian casualties result from aerial bombing in Afghanistan seems to depend more than anything else on whether the airstrike was planned or was an unplanned strike in rapid response to an evolving military situation on the ground."[18] From 2006 to 2008, HRW tracked planned bombings versus unplanned bombings. They found that in almost all cases, planned bombings resulted in significantly fewer casualties—for example, in 2008 "no planned airstrikes appear to have resulted in civilian casualties."[19] Why? When planning an airstrike, the military generally relies upon a process designed to select targets that uses "civilian mitigation procedures." This process takes place in the hours, and often days, leading up to an air strike and uses both technical and human intelligence to determine the pattern of civilian activity in the area prior to launch. In addition, a planned strike requires visual confirmation of the target, allowing pilots to suspend an attack in the event that civilians are found to be in the area.[20]

Alternatively, airstrikes called in by forces on the ground in response to rapidly evolving threats resulted in a disproportionate number of civilian casualties. This is largely due to the fact that no one was able to determine in advance the location of civilians, as the process of civilian mitigation procedures is suspended in the event that hostile intent is determined to exist and defensive action is taken to mitigate hostile activity. For example, U.S. guidelines define hostile intent as "the threat of the imminent use of force," while NATO defines the same term as "manifest and overwhelming force." Thus, the United States allows ground forces to preemptively call for airstrikes, while NATO requires that hostilities be evident before an airstrike can be approved.[21]

This is particularly relevant as one considers the CPGS program, as it is deliberately designed to be used in response to rapidly evolving threats. It is unlikely, in many cases, that a thorough process of civilian mitigation could take place if the goal is to authorize and execute a strike in no more than an hour. While this may allow us to eliminate high-value targets more effectively, it is also likely to result in significantly greater collateral damage, as leaders will rarely have a fully accurate picture of civilian activity leading up to the operation's authorization.

This leads to the second concern, proportionality. In the scenarios outlined by the administration, be it a strike against a rogue state with evolving missile capabilities or a terrorist leader at the top of the U.S. hit list, the use of CPGS would likely be preemptive in nature. This is very different from the retaliatory, second-strike scenarios envisaged by nuclear strategists during the Cold War. Again, because this technology is designed to be useable, it seems likely that it will be used, and used in rapid response to real time, evolving threats. Because proportionality is assessed relative to the likely benefit attained as a result of an attack, it is critical that the benefit be obvious and confirmable.

While it may seem self-evident that a rapid response conventional strike on North Korea's missile launch facilities would meet the threshold established by Just War theory should preparations for a nuclear missile launch be detected and confirmed, it is less certain that an attack on Iran's nuclear reactor sites meets these same criteria. Preemption assumes that the intent of the adversary is well understood, and the quality and content of the target is clear and verifiable. Because this type of military action is unlikely to take place in response to a specific attack, but in response to our perception of threat, the accuracy with which threat is assessed is critical to the calculation of proportionality in the event of a preemptive strike. Under such conditions, it may be very difficult to determine with any certainty if the number of civilian casualties generated in an attack would be proportionate to the perceived threat and injury *should the threat have been carried out*. As there is ample evidence that threat is not always accurately measured and assessed, most recently demonstrated in the justifications leading up to the war in Iraq, it is possible that a preemptive strike based on an uncertain understanding of the enemy's intent will lead to a response that is disproportionate to the threat.

Thus, while hypersonic conventional missiles have the technical potential to be used justly, the CPGS program is responding to a need that increases the likelihood of indiscriminate and disproportionate use, thereby presenting a significant problem in terms of just conduct.

MOVING FORWARD: THE JUST USE
OF SUPER CONVENTIONAL WEAPONS

The issues associated with the CPGS program identified above indicate areas in which the Just War tradition needs to respond and evolve. In particular, Just War theory has yet to fully accommodate changes necessitated by the rapidly advancing conventional technologies associated with contemporary warfare, nor has it fully addressed issues related to an increased reliance upon preemptive war, especially in terms of just conduct.

This is important, as it seems likely that hypersonic conventional weapons will be used once they are deployed, as conventional weapons are generally not subject to the restrictions associated with their nuclear cousins. As noted by an anonymous administration official, "A U.S. president might be more likely to approve the launch of a Conventional Strike Missile because it would involve fewer negative consequences and less stigma than nuclear weapons."[22] That said, it is also arguably true that the evolution of conventional weapons and the parameters for their future use have escaped rigorous assessment simply because they are not weapons of mass destruction, at least as popularly conceived. If they are to be used justly, what adjustments need to be made?

In the case of CPGS, it will be necessary for the Just War tradition to address the problem of rapidly diminishing timelines. In many cases, it is considered to be the moral duty of an actor to consider thoroughly the likely outcomes of his actions. As Richard J. Regan observes, "The principle of discrimination requires military combatants to weigh carefully the effects of their actions on ordinary civilians. If military combatants either willfully do not consider the effects of their action on ordinary civilians or *act with reckless disregard of those effects*, the combatants violate the principle of discrimination."[23] This is extremely pertinent when considering advancements in military technologies that allow a state to respond to global threats in, at most, a handful of hours. If the assumption is that the technology will demand an inevitably shortened time frame for decision making, can the principle of discrimination be fully, and conscientiously, applied?

The answer is yes, if the intelligence necessary to adequately assess civilian casualties is readily available. It would be helpful, however, if criteria were devised to broadly guide the actions of decision makers, especially in instances where intelligence is lacking. Logically, there should be an inverse relationship between shorter timelines and certainty; that is, the more quickly an attack is authorized, the more robust the requirement for accurate and complete assessments of conditions on the ground. Unfortunately, in practical terms, the opposite is usually true, as demonstrated by recent air campaigns in Afghanistan. As a result, in situations with marked uncertainty, it seems reasonable to encourage more stringent requirements regarding the scope and degree of force utilized when responding to an emerging situation. As rapid response strikes become increasingly common, it will be important to devise specific parameters, perhaps directly correlated to the robustness of certainty, to help increase fidelity with the spirit of the principle of discrimination. Ultimately, in an environment with high certainty, technically advanced weapons have the potential to be highly discriminate, thus their use could be justly authorized, even when acting within a shortened timeline. In an environment, however, where conditions remain opaque, no matter the quality of the technology, the likelihood of indiscriminate casualties is too high. Regardless of the payload, be it nuclear or conventional, launching a hypersonic weapon in this instance is not always a legitimate option.

Of further concern regarding certainty and decision making is the increased reliance on technologies that have the potential to marginalize human judgment from the decision-making process. Over the past decade, the United States has become heavily dependent on unmanned aerial vehicles (UAVs) for surveillance and intelligence collection.[24] UAVs are now capable of autonomous identification and confirmation of targets, and it will be more and more tempting to rely on computer software to determine certainty. This raises serious questions regarding moral agency, as it is difficult to vest moral responsibility in a drone, regardless of its technical potential to function autonomously. While it seems unlikely that a computer will ever be called upon to make the final decision to use CPGS, much of the data that is utilized to support such a decision may be processed with little thoughtful and measured analysis by an actual human being. Especially in a compressed time frame, this could lead to unfortunate errors, as these are emergent technologies with a comparatively recent track record. While beyond the scope of this chapter, the question of moral agency will likely pose an increasingly difficult problem for Just War theory, as conventional systems further delegate important functions to nonhuman actors.

At the same time, while Just War theory has considered in significant depth the question of preemption as it relates to the *jus ad bellum*, or just resort in going to war, criteria; comparatively little has been written on the implications of preemptive action in terms of the *jus in bello* principle of proportionality. In other words, how does a state determine the level of military force to use in a first strike, when the target has yet to commit an aggressive act? In the absence of a definite incident of aggression, determining the appropriate level of force to be utilized in a preemptive strike is an inexact science. While the principle of proportionality already emphasizes restraint in the use of force (i.e., use no more force than necessary to eliminate the target[25]), it remains largely subjective, and often tied to the importance of the target in question or the anticipated military outcome.[26] Alternatively, the amount of force utilized could be determined by the likely level of casualties involved, with the assumption that more force, in some cases, may result in a speedier result and fewer casualties overall, both to the warfighters and to the civilian population.[27]

That said, in the case of CPGS and many other developing technologies, there is little potential for attrition on the side of the state planning the attack, as these missions are unmanned. This makes the use of CPGS dangerously attractive. CPGS allows a state to intervene quickly, decisively, and with significant force, at little to no human cost to the state instigating the attack. While some might argue that the economic costs associated with a program like CPGS will provide a sufficient barrier to its promiscuous use, the Global War on Terrorism has demonstrated the tolerance a society can have for astronomical costs in the face of even the most ambiguous, and comparatively narrow, threats. If you further consider the fact that few states possess the technical capacity to field a system similar to CPGS, you face an acute imbalance in terms of the human cost to be paid as a result of its preemptive use.

This is a distinctively different problem than the one faced by those tasked with designing a just nuclear strategy. The ethics of nuclear warfare were and are fundamentally about human costs. When utilizing a weapon that is essentially indiscriminate, combatants and noncombatants *on both sides* suffer disproportionately. The preemptive use of CPGS and other emerging unmanned systems divorce warfare, to a startling extent, from that mutual suffering and the potential reciprocity that compels a society to consider the consequences of its actions. This absence of reciprocal human costs undermines the just use of CPGS, a system that few actors beyond the United States have the capacity, or political will, to field.

This is a further reason to create clearer parameters for the preemptive use of hypersonic conventional capabilities. Unless criteria are created that require decision makers to consider both certainty and the human cost associated with its employment, CPGS could suffer from precisely the opposite problem encountered when contemplating the launch of nuclear weapons: it will be too easy to authorize an attack. Because there is little real threat of significant retaliation, and because the harm done is unlikely to be catastrophic enough to militate against a preemptive strike, indiscriminate and disproportional casualties can be expected. This is unacceptable. Even if a conventional capability has the potential to be just, it is dangerous to assume that actors will maximize that potential of their own volition. And while CPGS remains a virtual monopoly, there will be even less incentive to do so.

There is a need for the Just War tradition to be more explicit in its response to emerging technologies. The CPGS system is simply one example where this is the case. As advancements in unmanned weaponry change the face of modern warfare, traditional barriers to military intervention will change. It is critical that the Just War tradition recognizes and responds to these changes in order for it to remain resilient. It is no longer the case, if ever it was, that conventional weapons are somehow innately more legitimate than weapons of mass destruction. In fact, the limits on nuclear warfare and other restricted classes of weapons have, if anything, encouraged the production of conventional capabilities with the potential to be overwhelmingly lethal, if increasingly precise. Recent history would show us that state actors are not always able to use these weapons with the degree of restraint necessary to guarantee discrimination and proportionality. Until there are clearer criteria to guide and potentially limit their use, the spirit of the Just War tradition will remain unfulfilled.

Notes

1. Thomas Scheber, "Conventionally-Armed ICBMs: Time for Another Look," *Comparative Strategy* 27 (2008): 336–44. See also Joshua Pollack, "Evaluating Conventional Prompt Global Strike," *Bulletin of the Atomic Scientists* 65, no. 1 (2008): 13–20.

2. Michael Walzer, *Just and Unjust Wars: A Moral Argument with Historical Illustrations* (New York: Basic Books, 1992), 151–54.

3. Richard J. Regan, *Just War: Principles and Causes* (Washington, D.C.: Catholic University of America Press, 1996), 87–95.

4. Walzer, *Just and Unjust Wars*, 154.

5. Regan, *Just War*, 96.

6. L. C. Green, *The Contemporary Law of Armed Conflict* (Manchester: Manchester University Press, 2000), 148.

7. In fact, of the seven votes taken in support of the overall ruling, vote number six, dealing specifically with the issue of supreme emergency, was the only vote to be split down the middle, with seven justices voting for and seven justices voting against. See "Legality of the Threat or Use of Nuclear Weapons, Advisory Opinion," *I.C.J. Reports*, July 1996, 226–67.

8. This is not to say that the potential for first strike was disregarded by policy-makers and the military, but merely that it was generally acknowledged to be morally indefensible.

9. William V. O'Brien, "Just War Conduct in a Nuclear Context," *Theological Studies* 44 (June 1983): 191–220.

10. Regan, *Just War*, 100–106.

11. Ibid.

12. Michele L. Malvesti, "Bombing bin Laden: Assessing the Effectiveness of Air Strikes as a Counter Terrorism Strategy," *Fletcher Forum of World Affairs* 26 (Winter 2002): 17–28.

13. Amy F. Woolf, "Conventional Prompt Global Strike and Long-Range Ballistic Missiles: Background and Issues" (Washington, D.C.: Congressional Research Service, June 2011), 2–18.

14. This proposal involving Trident missiles has repeatedly been met with objec-tions, as there are concerns that Russia and China may be unable to distinguish between a conventionally armed Trident missile and a nuclear-armed Trident missile. To wit, the Senate recently voted to reduce funding for this particular part of the CPGS program.

15. It is difficult to estimate overall yield, as the specific munitions to be used will vary greatly depending upon the delivery vehicle. For specifics, see Noah Schachtman, "Hypersonic Cruise Missile: America's New Global Strike Weapon," *Popular Mechanics*, December 4, 2006, http://www.popularmechanics.com/technology/military/4203874 (accessed August 15, 2010).

16. For example, the MOAB, or Daisy Cutter, yields approximately eleven tons of ex-plosive power. It is also an extremely heavy weapon, weighing almost twelve tons, and it could not be utilized in a rapid response program similar to the CPGS, where the total package (delivery vehicle and payload), in most cases, weighs approximately two tons.

17. Of course, it could be utilized in this capacity. The concept to date, however, fo-cuses upon preemption, and not retaliation.

18. "Troops in Contact: Airstrikes and Civilian Deaths in Afghanistan," *Human Rights Watch*, September 8, 2008), http://www.hrw.org/en/reports/2008/09/08/troops -contact-0 (accessed August 15, 2010), 29.

19. Ibid., 29.

20. Ibid., 29.

21. Ibid., 30–31.

22. Elaine M. Grossman, "Cost to Test U.S. Global-Strike Missile Could Reach $500 Million," *Global Security Newswire*, March 15, 2010, http://www.globalsecuritynewswire .org/gsn/nw_20100315_8655.php (accessed August 15, 2010).

23. Regan, *Just War*, 100–106, emphasis added.

24. For more on the use of UAVs and noncombatant casualties, see "The Civilian Impact of Drones: Unexamined Costs, Unanswered Questions," Modern Issues in Conflict series, Columbia Law School—Human Rights Clinic and the Center for Civilians in Conflict, 2012, http://web.law.columbia.edu/human-rights-institute/counterterrorism /drone-strikes/civilian-impact-drone-strikes-unexamined-costs-unanswered-questions (accessed November 24, 2012).

25. Judith Gail Gardam, "Proportionality and Force in International Law," *American Journal of International Law* 87, no. 3 (1993): 396.

26. Air Force Pamphlet (AFP) 110–34, *Commander's Handbook on the Law of Armed Conflict*, Department of the Air Force, July 25, 1980), para. 3–8.

27. Gary D. Brown, "Proportionality for Military Leaders," Maxwell Air Force Base, Alabama, AU/ACSC/38-1403/2000-04, April 2000): 15–20.

CHAPTER EIGHT

Rethinking Intention and Double Effect

Harry D. Gould

CONSIDER A SCENARIO almost too commonplace to think of as hypothetical: military planners must decide whether to attack a site that contributes significantly to their enemy's war efforts—a site located amid noncombatants. The planners must decide whether to attack the site despite foreseeing that noncombatants will unavoidably be killed as a direct result of that attack. Destroying the enemy facility will contribute significantly to ending the war, but it will do so only at the cost of these noncombatants' lives.

Perhaps the oldest line of reasoning when confronting such situations relies simply on military-instrumental calculation: if the destruction of the site will contribute to the achievement of victory, then other consequences need not be taken into consideration. In this tradition, success is the only relevant metric; this sort of reasoning is the moral sibling of the legal dictum "*silent enim leges inter arma.*"[1]

Just War theory has turned to Catholic moral theology for a test of such a proposed act's permissibility; the Doctrine of Double Effect (DDE) rests on a presumed distinction between the intended effects of an act and the foreseen but unintended effects of that same act.[2] It is, strictly speaking, a deontological approach.[3] Under DDE, if in seeking a morally allowable result you foresee another result that in itself would not be morally allowable, you may act as long as you do not *intend* to bring about that second (otherwise forbidden) result. "According to DDE, it is morally worse for an agent to bring about some intended bad consequence than to bring about that consequence when it is merely foreseen."[4] By the logic of DDE, so long as the intention of the planners is not those (foreseen) noncombatant deaths, the proposed mission is allowable; if, conversely, the intention is to kill the noncombatants, the mission may not morally proceed.

Canonically, DDE is regarded as having been first articulated by St. Thomas Aquinas in a discussion of self-defense in *Summa Theologiae*.[5] It has been the subject of a tremendous amount of discussion, challenge, refinement, and rearticulation over subsequent centuries. Ethics and International Relations (EIR) as a field, however, shows minimal acquaintance with these subsequent discussions; very few commentators refer to sources or formulations more recent than Aquinas.[6] Yet DDE raises a number of interesting questions for EIR beyond just its usage as a test for the permissibility of proposed military action; implicit in the formulations of the Doctrine are issues about agency and intention that speak directly to parallel debates in International Relations (IR).

It is this idea and its underlying logic that this paper addresses, using this hypothetical bombing scenario as illustration. To do so, we must closely parse the intention / foresight (I/F) distinction upon which DDE is predicated. We have to both ascertain their conceptual relation and analyze the extent to which any distinction between them is *morally* relevant. It is my position that while the underlying I/F distinction is prima facie valid and is morally significant, DDE's emphasis on intention is too permissive and allows too much. Although it recognizes responsibility for unintended harms, this is not sufficient.

ANALYZING THE DOCTRINE

Our hypothetical agent (the mission planner) proposes to engage in action A (the attack on the enemy military site) intending effect E_1 (the destruction of that site) but also foresees E_2 (the noncombatant deaths) without specifically intending that E_2 come to be.

The tradition stipulates four criteria for an act like that proposed in our scenario to be permissible:

1. The initial act (A) is per se licit.[7]
2. The foreseen bad effect (E_2) is caused but not intended (or alternately, only the good effect (E_1) is intended).[8]
3. E_2 is neither the means to nor the cause of E_1.
4. The harm caused by E_2 is proportionate to the good motivating A.[9]

We can see that the DDE would provisionally allow proceeding with the attack so long as the intention behind the attack is not the deaths of the non-

Table 8.1   Diagram of Standard DDE Reasoning

If the foreseen morally bad *secondary* effect (E_2) of an otherwise allowable action (A) taken in pursuit of a morally good end (E_1) is:	Intended and Foreseen	Intended but Unforeseen
The act is:	Forbidden	N/A
Notes:	(E_2 is in no meaningful way a "secondary" result as it was sought via A and was foreseen to result from A.)	(An agent cannot intend to bring about E_2 via A if she or he does not believe that A will produce E_2. Foresight is in this narrow sense a precondition of intention.)
If the foreseen morally bad *secondary* effect (E_2) of an otherwise allowable action (A) taken in pursuit of a morally good end (E_1) is:	Unintended but Foreseen	Unintended and Unforeseen
The act is:	Allowed	Allowed
Notes:	(This is the domain of actions to which DDE is held to apply)	

combatants, so long as the destruction of the site is not causally dependent upon their deaths, and so long as the causing of their deaths is proportionate to the benefit to be had by the destruction of the site. Following general usage, we call the mission planner who chooses a war effort–related target, the destruction of which is calculated to have significant effects on the enemy's material capacity to make war, "Strategic Bomber" (SB). SB foresees the loss of noncombatant lives as a result of the strike. These noncombatant deaths are not the purpose of the strike, and they are not any part of the means of the destruction of the target; they result alongside the intended end and are therefore regarded by advocates of DDE as *praeter intentionem*.[10]

A mission planner who seeks out the same target, but in this instance chooses it as a means to kill noncombatants, we will call "Terror Bomber" (TB). TB's sole aim is to kill civilians in order to instill terror as a means to speed the war's end. These civilian deaths are specifically intended and foreseen; the destruction of the military target is incidental although presumably secondarily beneficial.

SB's proposal to attack a military target or a target that directly contributes to the war effort is prima facie allowable in both the *jus in bello* tradition and under the positive Laws of War. The intended effect of the destruction of the legitimate target is also prima facie licit. The noncombatant deaths are neither intended nor are they a means to achieving the intended end of destroying the target. All that remains is the question of the proportionality of the foreseen noncombatant deaths to the value of the destruction of the target.

TB's proposed act is materially identical; however, his or her underlying intention differs from SB's. Unlike SB, for TB the civilian deaths are intended; this is per se illicit because noncombatants are never legitimate targets in either the *jus in bello* or under the positive laws of war. Because TB *intends* the non-combatant deaths rather than merely foresees them as the concomitant of bringing about E_1 the proposed act is impermissible.[11]

Advocates of DDE hold that in this hypothetical situation, materially identical acts are permissible in the first case and impermissible in the second. The basis of the differentiation is the motivating intention. Intending to destroy a military-related target for the purpose of weakening an enemy's war-making capability is allowable even if civilian noncombatants are killed as a fully foreseen secondary effect. Intending to destroy the same target with the aim of killing those same civilians is, however, impermissible. The civilian deaths are excused in SB because they are incidental to the legitimate aim, but they serve to prohibit the *materially identical* attack in TB because they are intended; because of the illicit end motivating the proposed act, the act is forbidden.

There is a complex issue related to establishing the intent of the agent in doing A—establishing that the agent intends the coming-to-be of E_1, and that the agent does not intend E_2. This has led to an enormous body of literature discussing the proper way to conceptualize intention. Is intention purely a subjective mental state? Is it a fact external to the mind of the agent or any other actor? Are there criteria for identifying the presence or absence of intent? Are such criteria factual or purely imputational?

INTENDING

DDE is predicated upon the belief that not all outcomes that are knowingly brought about are intended. This brings us directly to the heart of the philosophy of action and its central questions, "what is intention?" and "what is intentional action?" If the predicate distinction between intended and foreseen consequences does not hold, then DDE does not work as a test of the allowability of a proposed act.

One of the first things we find when exploring the concept of intention is that there is a fairly stark difference among philosophers of action and philosophers of law regarding when an act or an outcome is intended. Philosophers of law—and Anglophone law generally—follow the lead of the British Utilitarians who held that any outcome foreseen as liable to result from a contemplated action must be regarded as intended.[12] "There is a presumption in law," states Anthony Kenny, "that a man intends the natural consequences of his acts."[13]

Part of the divergence in the understandings of intention relates to the divergent purposes at work; the Utilitarians and philosophers of law were concerned with attributions of intent as they relate to the attribution of *responsibility*. By contrast, the philosophy of action is more concerned with conceptual clarity and logical precision. The law might say that a person who does *A* will be *considered* to intend all of the results of doing *A* (irrespective of their actual subjective mental states) if conditions C_1–C_n are met, while philosophy of action is concerned with the logical sufficiency of those conditions.

The Utilitarian / legal position can be traced to Jeremy Bentham's *Introduction to the Principles of Morals and Legislation*, in which he introduced two types of intention, direct and oblique.[14] As Alfred Miele and Steven Sverdlik explain, "Any 'direct' intention concerns a result of one's bodily movement such that 'the prospect of producing it constituted one of the links in the chain of causes by which the person was determined to the act.' An 'oblique' intention, in contrast, concerns a result that 'was in contemplation, and yet appeared likely to ensue in cases of the act's being performed, yet did not constitute a link in the aforesaid chain.'"[15] John Austin followed Bentham quite closely in Lecture XIX of his *Lectures on Jurisprudence*. The most important statement of the Utilitarian position is Henry Sidgwick's.[16] Sidgwick's argument is developed in two parts; in his discussion of Free Will and its relation to moral culpability he states: "The proper immediate objects of moral approval or disapproval would seem to be always the results of a man's volitions so far as they were intended—i.e. represented in thought as certain or probable consequences of his volitions. . . . It is most convenient to regard 'intention' as including not only such results of volition as the agent *desired* to realize, but also any that without desiring he foresaw as certain or probable."[17] He elaborated in the discussion of "Intuitionism": "For purposes of exact moral or jural discussion, it is best to include under the term 'intention' all the consequences of an act that are foreseen as certain or probable . . . undesired accompaniments of the desired results of our volitions are clearly chosen, or willed by us . . . while a man can resolve to aim at any end which he conceives as a possible result of his voluntary action, he cannot simultaneously resolve *not* to aim at any other end which he believes will be promoted by the same action."[18] Sidgwick's primary concern was with the attribution of responsibility: "We cannot evade responsibility for any foreseen consequences of our acts by the plea that we felt no desire for them, either for their own sake or as means to ulterior ends."[19]

Bruce Aune more recently articulated a similar view: "If at the time of action a man clearly, explicitly, and with certainty foresees that his intended act will have specifically describable consequences, which would not otherwise occur, then those consequences will be reflected in his practical reasoning and will be intended as a part of the total situation he decides to bring about."[20]

Although these Utilitarian formulations were made without reference to either DDE or its underlying Thomist understanding of intention, the Utilitarian view constitutes a direct challenge to those accounts. The Utilitarian formulations also provide the starting point for most contemporary discussions of intention; whether interested in defending DDE or not, there has been a concerted effort to rebut the Utilitarian equation of intention with foresight.

Responses to the Utilitarians have taken a number of forms, all of which are predicated on intention constituting a distinct mental phenomenon. Many efforts focus on identifying the components of intention; G. E. M. Anscombe and Donald Davidson emphasized desire and belief.[21] Anscombe rejected what she labeled the "Cartesian psychology" that regarded intentions as "interior act(s) of the mind which could be produced at will."[22] She rejected this understanding of intention both because it allowed too much and because as a result of allowing too much it opened the door to criticisms such as Sidgwick's. Borrowing from Wittgenstein, she took a "descriptivist" turn, in which an action is intended only under certain descriptions; hence the same physical act will be intended under one description and unintended under another. The source of that description is to be found in the agent's answer to the question why he or she is performing that act. If he or she is doing it *to* accomplish some end, then the act is intentional. If he or she is doing it unreflectively, or simply for its own sake, then the action is not intentional.

The two most influential positions on intention in debates over its role in DDE are those of Roderick Chisholm and Michael Bratman. Chisholm sets out a position intermediate to that of the Utilitarians and that of advocates for a strict I/F distinction. His starting point is the comparison of two principles governing intention, the "principle of nondivisiveness of intention" and the "principle of diffusion of intention." In the former, states Chisholm, "if (i) a man acts with the intention of bringing it about that p occurs and if (ii) he knows . . . that if p occurs then the conjunctive state of affairs, p and q, occurs, then (iii) he acts with the intention of bringing it about that the conjunctive state of affairs p and q, occurs."[23] In the latter principle: "from facts that (i) a man acts with the intention of bringing about a certain state of affairs and that (ii) he knows . . . that that state of affairs entails a certain other state of affairs, it does not follow that (iii) he acts with the intention of bringing about that other state of affairs."[24] Chisholm's conclusion is that although q is not per se intended, the conjunctive state of affairs is. Antony Duff, writing with specific concern for the role of intention in DDE, differs in a small but important way with Chisholm; rather than intending the conjunctive, Duff asserts that what the agent intends is to bring about p *despite q*; this, he insists, "gives a fuller picture of the practical reasoning which informs his action and thus of his action as the outcome or expression of that reasoning."[25]

Of all the investigations of intention, Bratman's account has perhaps been the most influential among those influencing discussion of DDE. For Bratman:

S intentionally A's if
(1) S wants to A and for that reason intends to try to A, and
(2) S A's in the course of executing his intention to try to A, and
(3) S A's in the way he was trying to A
. . . intention is a distinctive pro-attitude involved in intentionally A-ing"[26]

The conclusions Bratman draws seem to place him in the same camp as the Utilitarians. This is due to the distinction he works out between intention and intentional action. As Bratman articulates the distinction, we can intentionally do an act without the act being intended: "While to A intentionally I must intend to do something, I need not intend to do A."[27] This requires some clarification; an intentional act is an act with an intention behind it.

A is in the motivational potential of my intention to B, given my desires and beliefs, just in case it is possible for me intentionally to A in the course of executing my intention to B. If I actually intend to A then A will be in the motivational potential of my intention. But we need not suppose that if A is in the motivational potential of an intention of mine, then I intend to A. . . .

. . . The notion of motivational potential is intended to *mark* the fact that my intention to B may issue in my intentionally A-ing. . . .[28]

If S intends to B and S A's in the course of executing his intention to B . . . then S A's intentionally.[29]

Bratman offers a hypothetical that is easily transposable with our own Bomber scenario. In it, he intends to run a marathon; as he contemplates this action, he comes to realize that acting upon this intention will result in the wearing down of his shoes. It is not his intention to wear down his shoes. As evidence of the lack of intention, he states that there is no further reasoning or effort dedicated to the wearing down of his shoes. "My attitude towards wearing down my sneakers does not play the role in further ends–means reasoning that an intention to wear them down would normally play."[30] If he proceeds to run the marathon, and thus proceeds to wear down his shoes, Bratman holds that while he wears them down intentionally, he does so without an intention to do so. On its face, this seems to support the I/F distinction, and up to a point, it does; however, by retaining the intentionality of the action or outcome, Bratman maintains a way to acknowledge responsibility for unintended outcomes. Antony Duff reaches a very similar conclusion arguing that an agent can bring about an effect intentionally without intending to bring it about.[31]

Despite their differences (which are more significant than this brief survey indicates), these views share the conclusion that an intention must be something that the agent seeks. An *act* is intentional if the agent chooses to take it as a means to an end, and a *result* is intended if the agent seeks to bring it about. Shaw's recent treatment of intention nicely summarizes this view.[32]

Other interventions into this debate have come from authors specifically concerned with articulating a definition of intention that supports DDE. According to Joseph Boyle:

One intends one's ends, the states of affairs one aims to achieve in action, and one also intends one's means . . . Features of one's voluntary actions which are not one's ends or means are side effects. Side effects are consequences or other aspects of one's actions which are neither the goals one seeks in acting nor the precise states of affairs one is committed to realizing for the sake of these goals. They are properly regarded as outside one's intention in acting because their occurrence does not contribute to one's purposes; they are not part of what one wants to occur or of what, strictly, serves one's purposes.[33]

Rather than addressing any of the challenges to this sharp delineation of the bounds of what is intended, Boyle merely brushes them away. Alison Hills makes a very similar move: "An agent intends some state of affairs if she aims at it, tries to achieve it, chooses action on the basis of whether those actions contribute to achieving it, and monitors her success at achieving it. An agent merely foresees bringing about some state of affairs if she is aware that she will bring it about, but does not aim at it."[34]

THE MORAL SIGNIFICANCE OF INTENDING

> Think for a moment about the claim that the tactical bomber in dropping live bombs on the heads of civilians does not directly kill them![35]

In the previous section, we got some idea of the contours of the philosophical debates surrounding the theoretical tenability of the I/F distinction. In this section, we build on those questions as we turn from the tenability of the distinction to its moral significance. For Utilitarians the I/F distinction makes no moral difference; for defenders of DDE, of course, the distinction is paramount.[36] T. M. Scanlon makes one of the most aggressive challenges: "No one has ... come up with a satisfying theoretical explanation of why the fact of intention in the sense that is involved here—the difference between consequences that are intended and those that are merely foreseen—should make a moral difference."[37] The consequences here are the same as those of the previous section: if there is no moral difference in the I/F distinction, then DDE cannot perform the function for which it was designed.[38] The veracity and moral weight of the I/F distinction are not only philosophical points for defenders of DDE; they are articles of faith.[39]

In one respect, the debate over the moral significance of the I/F distinction is about competing notions of agency. In particular, we can again see a Utilitarian-Absolutist split. As R. A. Duff states:

> A Utilitarian regards outcomes or events, rather than actions, as of primary significance ... he is interested in human agents and their actions only secondarily, insofar as they can have an effect on what happens. ... [The individual] is the agent of, and responsible for, all of those effects which he does or can foresee and control. Distinctions between intention and foresight ... have no intrinsic moral significance ...[40]

> ... a consequentialist bases moral agency on knowledge and control.[41]

By contrast, Duff continues,

> [Defenders of DDE are] primarily concerned with the intentional actions of human agents rather than their consequences. What matters is not simply that an event occurs which I did, or could foresee and control, but the way in which I am related, as an agent, to that event: what matters is what I *do*; and 'what I do' is determined not just by what happens, but by the intentions revealed in my actions . . .[42]

It is a wholly agent-centered consideration.[43]

DDE's "roots lie in appraisal of character" rather than in the appraisal of action.[44]

Must we rely on the agent's own account of his or her intentions? Are there limits to what an agent can legitimately claim to intend or, perhaps more importantly, claim not to intend?[45] A recurrent question in the literature concerns the *characterization* of acts and intentions: May the agent in our hypothetical scenario claim only that she or he intends no more than the dropping of bombs on a specific building, or is there something insufficient or even disingenuous about that intention description? As Duff also states: "If we can describe what an agent does, as a means or as an end, without explicit reference to someone's death, then his action is not one of intentional killing . . . [but] there is a *logical* absurdity in suggesting that I can intend to decapitate, or cut into small pieces, or remove the heart of a living human being, without thereby intending his death . . . [there are] logical limits on what I can include in, or leave out of my descriptions of my intentional action."[46]

Defenders of DDE, following Anscombe, insist "there is not necessarily— indeed there is seldom if ever—one and only one correct description of a given act."[47] Although by characterizing intentions as answers to questions about why an agent acted thus, she opened the door to this sort of disingenuousness, Anscombe later insisted that the "Direction of Intention" was "an absurd device . . . you cannot just choose one [description] . . . and claim to have excluded others by that. Nor can you simply bring it about that you intend *this* and not *that* by an inner act."[48] Still, there are accounts of DDE that insist on the legitimacy of doing precisely this.[49]

Another important point is raised by Philippa Foot: the problem of "closeness." Related to the problem of redescription, this is an issue of one act being so empirically and conceptually close to another that they cannot be legitimately separated. Blowing up the spelunker in one famous example simply *is* killing him; crushing the head of the fetus simply is killing it.[50] According to Philip E. Devine, "Certain kinds of acts—the taking of human life for instance—are of such moral significance that terms denoting them may not be elided into terms denoting their consequences, which fail to reveal the morally significant character of the original act."[51] Hills, however, rejects closeness as a problem: "However 'close' X is to Y, even if X is *identical* with Y, it is possible for an agent to intend that X and not to intend that Y."[52]

Jonathan Bennett brings another problem to our attention. In challenging the moral significance of the I/F distinction, he introduces a third character to our hypothetical, the "Philosophically Sophisticated Terror Bomber" (PSTB). Starting with DDE supporters' use of Anscombe's view of intentions, PSTB chooses the site because noncombatants will be affected by the attack, and is motivated by the results of those noncombatants being bombed. However, PSTB asserts that he or she does not intend their *deaths*; indeed, their deaths are not necessary to the success of the plan. All that is needed according to PSTB, and all that he or she intends is the *appearance* of their deaths for the duration of the war.[53] "All that was intended by [PSTB], states Bennett, was that the people's bodies should be inoperative for long enough to cause a general belief that they were dead, this belief lasting long enough to speed the end of the war: there is nothing in that which requires a causally downstream inference that the inoperativeness be permanent; and so there is nothing requiring that the people actually become dead."[54] PSTB would claim that the act in question is "intentional as an apparent killing," but not "intentional as a killing. . . . 'The actual deaths can't be helped if I am to create the realistic appearance of death and destruction.'"[55] As further evidence that she or he does not intend their deaths, PSTB would be quite content to see a "reversal of change" in which the noncombatants went from being dead to returning to life. Bennett claims that supporters of DDE cannot answer PSTB; if, per Anscombe, it is up to the agent to characterize his or her intentions, then as far-fetched and indeed ridiculous as PSTB's intention claim, it remains philosophically tenable even in the full knowledge that "the people would become not merely inoperative for a while but downright dead."[56]

Warren S. Quinn tries to rescue DDE from Bennett by giving it a Kantian twist; what matters on his account is not intention, but "harmful agency" and using the noncombatants as "intentional objects." In Quinn's rendering, the difference between SB and TB should not be framed around whether the harm is intended, but should be focused on the fact that SB harms through "harmful indirect agency" and TB through "harmful direct agency".[57] "What seems specifically amiss in relations of direct harmful agency," states Quinn, "is the particular way in which victims enter into an agent's strategic thinking. . . . The agent of direct harm . . . has something in mind for his victims—he proposes to involve them in some circumstances that will be useful to him precisely because it involves them. He sees them as material to be strategically shaped or framed by his agency."[58]

Hills responds to Bennett's challenge (and, by extension, the problem of "closeness") by making the rather surprising claim that it *"must . . .* be possible for an agent to intend to blow someone up or to intend to make him seem dead without intending to kill him."[59] The latter part of her claim is certainly plausible, but the question is whether one can so intend when one uses bombing as the means to bring it about. She allows that if PSTB uses killing as the means to bring it about, then that would fail DDE, but she still maintains that this is only one plausible means to bring it about that the noncombatants are "merely inoperative."

Elsewhere she goes further in allowing that while harm may not be sought as an end in itself, it is legitimate for harm to be intended as an means to a good. "When an agent intends some harm as a means to a good end, she is committed to that harm. . . . But she is aiming at harm not for its own sake, but for the sake of the end for which the harm is a means. . . . Though it is bad to intend harm as an end, it need not be bad to intend harm as a means to some good."[60] This is a perplexing claim for a defender of DDE to make, given its Pauline foundation, and it seems quite plainly to violate the third rule of DDE.[61] In a move more perplexing still, Hills uses this reasoning to *defend* TB by asserting that as long as the end is good, then the proposed means of intentionally killing the noncombatants is morally acceptable.[62]

David K. Chan, in working out the moral difference between intended and foreseen killing, shifts explanatory (and axiological) emphasis from intending to *desiring*.[63] Building upon Bratman's account, Chan differs on one key point: it is not necessarily the case that "an agent who intends a side-effect must engage in means-end reasoning to solve a problem of how to bring about the side effect."[64] By removing this constraint, a secondary effect might be intended, and thus that leg of DDE falls, and by extension, so does one of the key distinctions between SB and TB. However, Chan is concerned to defend DDE, and for that reason, he turns from intention to desire. "Where [SB and TB] differ concerns not their beliefs but their attitudes towards killing. . . . For SB to choose a different kind of bombing from TB, they must disagree concerning the (*un*) *desirability* of the act of killing . . . in itself." He continues: "The moral distinction in double effect cases I am arguing for . . . is in terms of intrinsic desire, desiring something for its own sake . . . I will examine whether there is any difference between SB and TB in their desires regarding the act of killing . . . in itself prior to their connecting the killing with their respective goals."[65]

In this rendering, as long as killing noncombatants is not desired, but only tolerated, then the acts of SB are allowable under DDE. Perhaps the most important thing to take away from Chan's account is his separation of intention and desire. Contra some of the other defenders of DDE, one can intend a thing for which he or she feels no desire, thus SB does intend to kill the noncombatants but does not desire to, and thus this passes Chan's version of DDE.

RESPONSIBILITY

> The unintended evil effect, the bringing about of which is rendered licit by the [DDE], is clearly imputable to the agent: he knowingly and willingly brings it about.[66]

If, as it seems, there is a tenable philosophical-conceptual distinction between intending and foreseeing, and if this is furthermore a distinction with moral import, the question of responsibility remains. DDE is framed around the question of permissibility, but the issue of responsibility is not settled by declaring an act permissible. The philosophy of action as we have seen tends to support DDE's predicate position on the I/F distinction. However, with an eye toward Sidgwick, those accounts are emphatic in their conclusion that foreseen but unintended consequences nonetheless create responsibility for the agent: "*We can be held responsible for more than we intend.*"[67] Thomas Baldwin indicates that "an agent cannot avoid responsibility for the consequences foreseen . . . just by pleading that those consequences were not wanted by him, that he did not intend them."[68]

No matter the intention of the agent, she or he brought about the bad state of affairs E_2 and is thus responsible for its occurrence. As Miele and Sverdlik state, "Being morally responsible for *A*-ing requires neither that one *A*-ed intentionally nor that one intended to *A*."[69] The existence of responsibility is not predicated upon intention; Sidgwick therefore did not need to argue that all foreseen consequences are intended in order to make his larger claim about the responsibility of an agent for all consequences of an action.

Even the most strictly Thomist advocates of DDE are in agreement on this point.[70] DDE does not eliminate an agent's responsibility for the harms inflicted even if he or she judges those harms to be permissible. Intention and DDE speak only to permissibility, not to responsibility. Whether a harm is intended or unintended is not a factor in attributions of responsibility and the issues that arise from it. Even permissible injuries call for reparation.[71]

Notes

1. Cicero, *Pro Milone* IV.XI.

2. The Doctrine is sometimes referred to as a Principle or Act. When quoting I follow the author's usage; otherwise, I use "Doctrine," but I note Rovie's insistence that it does not qualify as a "doctrine" because "it is not taught as one by the Church." Eric Rovie, "Reevaluating the Historical Evolution of Double Effect: Anscombe, Aquinas, and the Principle of Side-Effects," *Studies in the History of Ethics* 2 (2006): 1n2.

3. Ralph Wedgwood, "Defending Double Effect," *Ratio* 24, no. 4 (2011).

4. Alison Hills, "Defending Doubling Effect," *Philosophical Studies* 116, no. 2 (2003): 133.

5. Aquinas, *Summa Theologiae*, II.II, Question LXIV, Article 7, Response. On the history of DDE, see Joseph T. Mangan, "An Historical Analysis of the Principle of Double Effect," *Theological Studies* 10, no. 1 (1949): 41–61; William Conway, "The Act of Two Effects," *Irish Theological Quarterly* 18, no. 1 (1951) 130–33; Peter Knauer, "The Hermeneutic Function of the Principle of Double Effect," *Natural Law Forum* 12 (1967); James F. Keenan, "The Function of the Principle of Double Effect," *Theological Studies* 54, no. 2 (1993)295–300; Rovie, "Reevaluating," 2–14; T. A. Cavanaugh, *Double-Effect Reasoning: Doing Good and Avoiding Evil* (Oxford: Oxford University Press, 2006): 1–72.

6. Daniel S. Zupan, *War, Morality, and Autonomy: An Investigation in Just War Theory* (Aldershot, Eng.: Ashgate, 2004). Passing reference is found in a number of EIR works.

7. Uniacke goes further and claims that the act needs to be "morally good." Suzanne Uniacke, "The Doctrine of Double Effect," *Bulletin of the Australian Society of Legal Philosophy* 16 (1980): 6.

8. In Grisez's account this is replaced by the criterion "The person acting must have a right intention." Germain Grisez, "Toward a Consistent Natural-Law Ethics of Killing," *American Journal of Jurisprudence* 15 (1970): 78.

9. Joseph Boyle, "Who Is Entitled to Double Effect?," *Journal of Medicine and Philosophy* 16, no. 5 (1991): 477–78; Philip E. Devine, "The Principle of Double Effect," *American Journal of Jurisprudence* 19, no. 1 (1974): 56.

10. Neil Francis Delaney, "A Note on Intention and the Doctrine of Double Effect," *Philosophical Studies* 134, no. 2 (2007): 103.

11. David McCarthy, "Intending Harm, Foreseeing Harm, and Failures of Will," *Noûs* 36, no. 4 (2002): 631.

12. Most notable in this regard is H. L. A. Hart, "Intention and Punishment," in Hart, *Punishment and Responsibility: Essays in the Philosophy of Law*, 2nd ed. (Oxford: Oxford University Press, 2008); H. L. A. Hart and Stuart Hampshire, "Decision, Intention and Certainty," *Mind*, n.s., 67, no. 265 (1958).

13. Anthony Kenny, "Intention and Purpose," *Journal of Philosophy* 63, no. 20 (1966): 642. Oberdiek goes further still, asserting "the law is justified in treating foreseen and intended consequences alike." Hans Oberdiek, "Intention and Foresight in Criminal Law," *Mind*, n.s., 81, no. 323 (1972): 389.

14. Joseph Shaw, "Intention in Ethics," *Canadian Journal of Philosophy* 36, no. 2 (2006): 189.

15. Alfred Miele and Steven Sverdlik, "Intention, Intentional Action, and Moral Responsibility," *Philosophical Studies* 82, no. 3 (1996): 265.

16. Anscombe mistakenly attributes the origin of this view to Sidgwick, but it was, of course, of older provenance. G. E. M. Anscombe, "Modern Moral Philosophy," *Philosophy* 33, no. 124 (1958): 11.

17. Henry Sidgwick, *The Method of Ethics*, 7th. ed. (1907; Indianapolis: Hackett, 1981), I.V.2. and fn. 1 (emphasis in original).

18. Ibid., III.I.2 (emphasis in original).

19. Ibid., III.I.

20. Bruce Aune, "Intention and Foresight," *Journal of Philosophy* 63, no. 20 (1966): 653.

21. G. E. M. Anscombe, *Intention* (Cambridge, Mass.: Harvard University Press, 1957); Donald Davidson, "Actions, Reasons, and Causes," and Davidson, "Intending," both in Donald Davidson, *Essays on Actions and Events* (Oxford: Oxford University Press, 1980).

22. G. E. M. Anscombe, "War and Murder," *Ethics, Religion, and Politics* (Minneapolis: University of Minnesota Press, 1981), 59.

23. Roderick Chisholm, "The Structure of Intention," *Journal of Philosophy* 67, no. 19 (1970): 633–47.

24. Ibid.

25. Antony Duff, "Intention, Responsibility and Double Effect," *Philosophical Quarterly* 32, no. 126 (1982): 3.

26. Michael Bratman, "The Two Faces of Intention," *Philosophical Review* 93, no. 3 (1984): 394–97.

27. Ibid., 378.

28. Ibid., 395–96.

29. Ibid., 396.

30. Ibid., 400.

31. Antony Duff, "Intention, Responsibility and Double Effect," 5.

32. Shaw, "Intention in Ethics," 205–12.

33. Boyle, "Who Is Entitled to Double Effect?," 479. Compare his earlier statement: Boyle, "Toward Understanding the Principle of Double Effect," *Ethics* 90, no. 4 (1980): 535–36. Masek relies upon a very similar formulation in his defense of DDE. Lawrence Masek, "Intentions, Motives and the Doctrine of Double Effect," *Philosophical Quarterly* 60 (2010): 3.

34. Hills, "Defending Double Effect," 134. She also presents the same view of intention in a later article: Alison Hills, "Intentions, Foreseen Consequences and the Doctrine of Double Effect," *Philosophical Studies* 133, no. 2 (2007): 257.

35. Jonathan Bennett, "Morality and Consequences," Tanner Lectures on Human Values, Brasenose College, Oxford University, May 1980, 96.

36. Justin Oakley and Dean Cocking, "Consequentialism, Moral Responsibility, and the Intention/Foresight Distinction," *Utilitas* 6, no. 2 (1994).

37. T. M. Scanlon, "Intention and Permissibility," supplement, *Proceedings of the Aristotelian Society* 74 (2000): 303.

38. James Hannik, "Some Light on Double Effect," *Theological Studies* 35, no. 5 (1975): 147.

39. Boyle, "Who Is Entitled to Double Effect?," 486; Joseph M. Boyle Jr., "Toward Understanding the Principle of Double Effect," *Ethics* 90, no. 4 (1980): 530.

40. R. A. Duff, "Absolute Principles and Double Effect," *Analysis* 36, no. 2 (1976): 73–74.

41. Ibid., 7.

42. Ibid., 74. Duff states, "an absolutist bases moral agency on intention: what is absolutely wrong is the *intended* killing of an innocent." Antony Duff, "Intention, Responsibility and Double Effect," 7.

43. Jeff McMahan, "Intention, Permissibility, Terrorism, and War," *Philosophical Perspectives* 23 (2009): 348.

44. Sophia Reibetanz, "A Problem for the Doctrine of Double Effect," *Proceedings of the Aristotelian Society* 98 (1998): 217.

45. Jeff McMahan, "Revising the Doctrine of Double Effect," *Journal of Applied Philosophy* 11, no. 2 (1994): 202.

46. R. A. Duff, "Intentionally Killing the Innocent," *Analysis* 34, no. 1 (1974): 17–18. The most egregious example of this practice is Geddes. Leonard Geddes, "On the Intrinsic Wrongness of Killing Innocent People," *Analysis* 33, no. 3 (1973).

47. Devine, "Principle of Double Effect," 48; Anscombe, *Intention*.

48. G. E. M. Anscombe, "Medalist's Address: Action, Intention and 'Double Effect,'" *Proceedings of the American Catholic Philosophical Association* 56 (1982): 23. Shaw recounts Anscombe's vacillation in detail. Shaw, "Intention in Ethics," 216–18.

49. Joseph M. Boyle Jr., "*Praeter Intentionem* in Aquinas," *Thomist* 42 (1978): 648–49.

50. Philippa Foot, "The Problem of Abortion and the Doctrine of Double Effect," in Woodward, ed., *The Doctrine of Double Effect: Philosophers Debate a Controversial Moral Principle*, ed. P. A.Woodward (Notre Dame, Ind.: University of Notre Dame Press, 2001), 143–55; Neil Francis Delaney, "Two Cheers for 'Closeness': Terror, Targeting, and Double Effect," *Philosophical Studies* 137, no. 3 (2008): 341–46; William J. Fitzpatrick, "The Intend/Foresee Distinction and the Problem of 'Closeness,'" *Philosophical Studies* 128, no. 3 (2006): 592–97; Alison McIntyre, "Doing Away with Double Effect," *Ethics* 111, no. 2 (2001): 242; Robert Hoffman, "Intention, Double Effect, and Single Result," *Philosophy and Phenomenological Research* 44, no. 3 (1984): 390; Cavanaugh, *Double-Effect Reasoning*, 82–91; Warren S. Quinn, "Actions, Intentions, and Consequences: The Doctrine of Double Effect," *Philosophy and Public Affairs* 18, no. 4 (1989): 339; Wedgwood, "Defending Double Effect," 7–9.

51. Devine, "Principle of Double Effect," 48.

52. Hills, "Intentions, Foreseen Consequences," 265.

53. Fitzpatrick, "Intend/Foresee Distinction," 589–91.

54. Bennett, "Morality and Consequences," 111.

55. Quinn, "Actions, Intentions, and Consequences," 341.

56. Bennett, "Morality and Consequences," 111. Predelli offers a number of similar counterfactual scenarios inspired by Bennett's original. Stefano Predelli, "Bombers: Some Comments on Double Effect and Harmful Involvement," *Journal of Military Ethics* 3, no. 1 (2004): 21–24.

57. Quinn, "Actions, Intentions, and Consequences," 342–43. Quinn's work has also engendered a number of responses. John Martin Fischer, Mark Ravizza, and David Copp, "Quinn on Double Effect: The Problem of 'Closeness,'" *Ethics* 103, no. 4 (1993): 707–25.

58. Quinn, "Actions, Intentions, and Consequences," 348–49.

59. Hills, "Intentions, Foreseen Consequences, 266.

60. Hills, "Defending Doubling Effect," 139. She continues in the same vein: "An agent who intends evil as an end has an inappropriate attitude toward evil, but an agent who intends evil merely as a means to a good end need not have a bad attitude toward evil." By Hills's account, it appears to be the case that it is perfectly licit to have a purely *instrumental* attitude toward evil and its infliction. Hill's position was in some respects anticipated by Frey. R. G. Frey, "Some Aspects to the Doctrine of Double Effect," *Canadian Journal of Philosophy* 5, no. 2 (1975): 259–83.

61. Romans 3:8. According to Boyle, "If the evil effect is brought about as a *means* to the good effect, then the evil effect must be intended, and the bringing about of the instrumental state of affairs is morally impermissible." Boyle, "Toward Understanding," 531.

62. Hills, "Defending Double Effect," 148.

63. Shaw argues against such a formulation, but without reference to Chan. Shaw, "Intention in Ethics," 195–97.

64. David K. Chan, "Intention and Responsibility in Double Effect Cases," *Ethical Theory and Moral Practice* 3, no. 4 (2000) 409–10.

65. Ibid., 415–16.

66. Boyle, "Toward Understanding the Principle of Double Effect," 529.

67. Kenny, "Intention and Purpose," 648–49 (emphasis in original).

68. Thomas Baldwin, "Foresight and Responsibility," *Philosophy* 54, no. 3 (1979): 351.

69. Miele and Sverdlik, "Intention, Intentional Action, and Moral Responsibility," 269, 272.

70. Uniacke, "Doctrine of Double Effect," 22–24.

71. Cavanaugh, *Double-Effect Reasoning*, 165–66.

CHAPTER NINE

Just War without Civilians

Laura Sjoberg

WHEN CRITICS OF U.S. PRESIDENT Barack Obama's inaction in Syria suggest that failing to intervene results in the tragedy that "innocent women and children end up in pools of their own blood" and mix a call to arms, based on the issue of women's rights, against the Syrian government with the language of just cause in the Just War tradition, the gendered nature of such justifications is not unique, coincidental, or aberrant to the tradition itself.[1] Quite the contrary, they echo recent declarations of President Bill Clinton on Kosovo and President George W. Bush on Afghanistan, advocating interventionist policy.[2]

These interventionist declarations on gender grounds may seem contradictory to many perceptions of the Just War tradition, but I argue that appearance is only surface level. This chapter contends that the Just War tradition has been constructed on, and is fundamentally tied to, the gender tropes that masculinize combatants as (male) "just warriors" and feminize civilians as (female) "beautiful souls," constituting men as by definition defenders of the innocent and women as by definition innocent and in need of defense.[3] I argue that the "noncombatant immunity principle" that identifies combatants and civilians and justifies fighting for civilians' protection is inseparable from gendered sex role stories about male just warriors and female beautiful souls that legitimate war, fantasize protection, and render actual protection impossible. The "noncombatant" or "civilian" immunity principle in *jus in bello* doctrine, and in particular its dependence on a gendered feminine notion of the "protected" in war(s), functions not to limit warfighting but to permit war making, in theory and in practice.

This chapter presents that argument and then explores what Just War theories might look like if wars were not fought "for" women, "over" women, attacking women, or "protecting" women. It proposes revising Just War theorizing by putting aside the gendered combatant/civilian dichotomy—that is, by delineating Just War "without civilians."

GENDER, PERFORMANCE, AND NONCOMBATANT IMMUNITY

The Just War tradition is performative; it is not a pregiven subject or the product of historical evolution, but a "reiterative and citational practice by which discourse produces the effect it names."[4] In this understanding, Just War theorizing cannot be reduced to or understood in its written evolution. Rather, Just War theorizing is expressive and constituted by utterances of Just War tenets. Just War theorizing is not something "out there" that is deployed in particular political situations; instead, it is "constituted by its employment, its deployment, and its manifestations in practice."[5] This approach makes it possible to understand war as a product of Just War narratives and Just War narratives as a coconstituted product of war(s).

Taking Just War theorizing as performative, this section focuses on a discussion of gendered performances of the noncombatant immunity principle. Looking through "gendered lenses" in order to "trace out the ways in which gender is central to understanding international processes," this chapter looks to uncover the assumptions about and perceived associations with gender that are necessary to make just war theorizing in its current constitution meaningful.[6]

Feminist work on the practice of gender in the noncombatant immunity principle has engaged in critically interrogating the gendered symbolic meanings of the combatant/civilian distinction. In this research program, feminists have inquired into the traits assigned to the ideal-typical "combatant" and his foil, the ideal-typical "civilian," in Just War narratives about combatants whose fighting serves to protect civilians. This work has identified the idea-typical combatant as a masculinized "just warrior,"[7] a figure who fights in wars not for a desire to engage in brutality but out of a responsibility to provide protection. That responsibility to provide protection is linked to the just warriors' masculinity, where provision of protection is linked to honor and full citizenship, but failure to provide protection results in shaming and emasculation.[8]

The just warrior's constitution as a provider of protection, however, requires the constitution of the ideal-typical civilian to be protected. If the just warrior's masculinity is affirmed and honor bestowed by providing protection, the question of who is being protected is key.[9] Feminist work has identified the idealized civilian as a feminized "beautiful soul,"[10] a figure whose defining characteristic is her innocence and need of protection from the evils of the enemy. Though the beautiful soul does not engage in warfighting, war cannot be fought without her, because her protection is required by the noncombatant immunity principle and is a key part of the state's ability to justify not only its war effort but also its existence.[11] This reaches into *jus ad bellum* Just War principles.

JUS AD BELLUM AND THE PERFORMANCE OF PROTECTION

The gendered "beautiful soul" reaches into *jus ad bellum* Just War principles because of the double role in which the gendered logic of the immunity principle casts her.[12] The "beautiful soul" is the civilian who needs to be separated from combatants and, once separated, granted immunity. That very need for distinction and immunity, however, also casts her as the just warrior's "other" who must be protected at all costs in order for a war to be just or justified. Whether that "beautiful soul" is Helen of Troy or Jessica Lynch, her innocence and need for protection or rescue serves as a rallying cry for fighting and winning wars.

The gendered ideal-typical civilian, then, legitimates not only particular warfighting tactics, but war making more generally. The war-justificatory logic in the role of the beautiful soul is both found in and fundamental to the Just War tradition's civilian immunity principle. The call to arms inherent in the need to protect the beautiful soul constitutes (and is constituted by) gendered notions of what a state or nation is and the gendered nationalisms that arise out of those conceptions of state or nation.

This is the case because women beautiful souls serve as reproducers of states or nations symbolically, culturally, and even biologically, both in the gendered noncombatant immunity principle and more generally.[13] This role of women in gendered nationalisms means that "women's bodies, relations, and roles become the battleground for different idealized versions of the past and constructions of the nationalist project for the future."[14]

As such, there is violence committed in the name of protecting the beautiful soul from violence, where "nationalism is naturalized, and legitimated, through gender discourses that naturalized the domination of one group over another through the disparagement of the feminine."[15] The noncombatant immunity principle, then, even though it seems like an optimal tool to protect its ideal-typical civilian "beautiful soul," not only legitimates fighting but also exposes the very object of its "protection" to vulnerability.[16] In fact, recent work has argued that there is a link between the logic of the noncombatant immunity principle and the harms of intentional civilian victimization.

GENDER AND INTENTIONAL CIVILIAN VICTIMIZATION

If the "beautiful soul" serves to motivate the ideal-typical combatant's benevolent service and to justify a state's war effort, adversarial parties in war are aware of the symbolic role that they play. The enemy's knowledge of the symbolic role of the beautiful soul affects which wars are fought and how warfighting is planned and executed. Since Carl von Clausewitz,[17] strategists have instructed that belligerents interested in victory should identify their enemy's "center of gravity" and destroy that. A "center of gravity" is a target with a combination of physical and symbolic value to a belligerent, where destroying it will handicap the opponent's ability to fight but do the most damage to the opponent's willingness to fight. In terms of the beautiful soul trope, therefore, "it follows that a group's desire to 'protect' their women motivates them to attack the women seen as belonging to the 'enemy.'"[18] In other words, "the principle of civilian immunity, then, paradoxically but still really, carried to its logical end, makes it strategically beneficial to attack (enemy) civilians intentionally and in large numbers."[19]

In fact, states that are militarily capable of mounting attacks on civilians do so in 35 percent of their interstate wars and more frequently in intrastate conflicts.[20] Recent feminist work has suggested that belligerents' engagement in intentional civilian victimization is actually attacking "civilians" as a proxy for the feminized "beautiful soul" trope, a motivation rooted in the noncombatant immunity principle.[21]

This realization is relatively recent. While feminist work has long explored the gendered dimensions of some attacks on civilians during war (such as rape), the idea that intentional civilian victimization writ large is gendered is still developing. Queues on how to theorize gendered intentional civilian victimization can be taken from feminist analysis of war rape, especially given that feminists have recognized war rape as a symbolic and communicative message of disparaging the enemy, where there is a "long history of associating actual women's rape with national, communal, and male dishonor."[22] Particularly, feminist work has framed the debate by characterizing raping women as attacking the "enemy" nation in two different ways. First, war rape attacks men's virility (and therefore their protective ability). Second, war rape attacks women as states' or nations' "center of gravity." My recent work argues that intentional civilian victimization as a whole functions along those same two axes, targeting the feminized, symbolic "beautiful soul" as a way to target the just warrior's willingness to fight. In this way, intentional civilian victimization can be seen as a gendered product of the gender tropes necessary to give the civilian immunity principle meaning.

THE GENDERED LOGIC OF THE IMMUNITY PRINCIPLE AS LEGITIMATING *WAR AD BELLUM*

This logic implies that belligerents attack the (women) civilians seen as belonging to their enemies for the same reasons that they protect the (women) civilians that they see as their own—because the noncombatant immunity principle serves to legitimate (apparently protective) violence in war(s). It at once licenses states to make war(s) given the protective mandate of *jus ad bellum* just cause logic and provides them with the logical path to total defeat of their enemies by depriving them of their *casus belli*, their own "beautiful souls."

I argue that this negative effect of the gendered noncombatant immunity principle has become a necessary part of contemporary performances of Just War theorizing, particularly to Just Cause claims. In this way, the noncombatant immunity principle can be seen to have three functions: first, it serves the traditionally understood function of limiting *in bello* conduct and behavior; second, and equally important, it serves as a permissive *ad bellum* to motivate violence in the name of protection; third, and least examined so far in the literature, it serves as a logic to motivate its direct violation. In other words, the noncombatant immunity principle is internally contradictory. It is crucial both to the protection of civilians and to attacks on civilians.

While all rules in some sense serve to tease "rebels" who see them as meant to be broken, the paradox of the noncombatant immunity principle is that the internal logic of the rule is key both to "good guy" justificatory logics of Just War but also to "bad guy" strategic logics of civilian victimization, where "civilian" is a proxy for "beautiful soul," much like "beautiful soul" is a proxy for "civilian" in first-order interpretations of the immunity principle.[23]

I argue that Just War theorizing's limiting and permissive functions then need to be weighed against each other, deontologically and practically. Deontologically, a principle that serves to motivate its own intentional violation is unsustainable. In practice, if the immunity principle's gendered tropes motivate not only *in bello* intentional civilian victimization but also *ad bellum* violent choices, the scales also tip against continuing to rely on a Just War approach that includes the civilian immunity principle (and its gendered performances). In this way, Just War theorizing can be seen as permissive, encouraging, supportive, and complicit in war(s).

The gendered intentional civilian victimization that the immunity principle motivates is effective because, according to V. Spike Peterson, "implicit in the patriarchal metaphor is a tacit agreement that men who cannot defend their woman/nation have lost their 'claim' to that body, to that land."[24] The attacks on (civilian) women work because they betray the failed masculinity of the "just warriors" tasked to protect the violated women, and belligerents wage such attacks (while defending their own women) in order to gain an edge vis-à-vis their opponents.

This incentive to attack civilians, and the resulting permissiveness of Just War theorizing, is reason for concern that Just War performances may be net harmful, especially given how salient Just War theorizing is in war-justificatory discourses in the policy world, especially among the policy elite in great powers. In other words, Just War theorizing is limiting *in bello* so much as it demands civilians be distinguished and protected, but it is permissive in that the protection of a belligerent's civilians serves to motivate belligerents to fight wars, and warfighting creates an incentive to attack opponents' civilians, given their (gendered) special place in Just War narratives and performances. The "beautiful soul" as a feminized, innocent other to the virile "just warrior" (and the resultant links between the ability to protect and virility) institutionalizes her protection as a "just cause" in performance if not in Just War's textually articulated standards. As such, while the civilian immunity principle is textually *in bello* limiting, it is performatively permissive both *ad bellum* and in *bello*.

THE INSEPARABILITY OF GENDER HIERARCHY AND THE JUST WAR TRADITION

I argue that the gendered tropes associated with the civilian immunity principle are not coincidental to or separable from its fundamental construction, layered on top of a gender-neutral, potentially effective immunity principle that is a part of a fixable Just War tradition. Instead, I argue, the permissiveness of the immunity principle (and therefore Just War theorizing) cannot be repaired within the existing boundaries of the Just War theorizing.

Just War performances currently are not just (or even mainly) the texts of Just War theorists. Instead, they are "as much manifested in pictures, images, and signifying words and phrases in the claims and speeches of political and military leaders" as in traditional just war texts.[25] Those pictures, images, and speeches feature prominently claims to protection of "the innocent," "the home-land," "our way of life," and even, explicitly, "women and children." Despite the apparent disappearance of other forms of gender inequality in war(s), the use of those tropes is increasingly prevalent, much like the intentional killing of civil-ian (women) in warfighting tactics. As I have argued before, "this is because just war narratives rely on the existence of a feminized Other, who plays the double role (and lives the double life) of 'protected' and *casus belli*. It is possible that this paradox is inherent in the idea of discriminating between combatants and non-combatants."[26]

This possibility would throw a wrench in feminist attempts to degender the Just War tradition and correct the gender stereotypes associated with the civil-ian immunity principle through reformulation. Feminist work to that end has looked to increase the recognition that men are often civilians and women are often combatants, arguing that evidence of those unexpected roles should com-plicate the just warrior/beautiful soul dichotomy.[27] Other feminist work has argued that masculinity should not be key to validation, and the ability to protect (by killing) should not be key to masculinity.[28] This work, which tries to decon-struct the immunity principle's gendered tropes of protection, is important but addresses the inefficiencies of the implementation of noncombatant immunity rather than the ways it is utilized as *in bello* and *ad bellum* permissiveness.

It also does not address the possibility that the gender tropes of just warrior and beautiful soul actually constitute the noncombatant immunity principle. Just War theorists have shown that it is often difficult to separate combatants and civilians in practice, even when there is ethical agreement on the need to do so.[29] Yet such a separation is essential to the noncombatant immunity prin-ciple, given that it cannot b implemented without knowledge of who to protect and who to target.[30]

The actual ability to distinguish between protector and protected in practice is then replaced with metaphors, shortcuts, visual identifications, and discur-sive cues. This makes the combatant/civilian dichotomy functional both among policymakers and among soldiers fighting wars.[31] The gendered tropes of just warrior and beautiful soul *are* those shortcuts that sustain the immunity principle, identifying "womenandchildren" as civilians in need of protection and burdening just warriors with their protection.[32] These tropes translate and simplify the noncombatant immunity principle, making it not only intelligible but functional in war practice, and therefore constituting it as an enduring principle of warfighting.[33]

To deal with that problem, my previous work has attempted to rescue the civilian immunity principle by introducing enforceable rules about who can be injured or killed *in bello* and who cannot. It has looked to formulate an *ad bellum* principle of "empathetic warfighting" or a "responsibility-for" approach,[34] supplementing the *ad bellum* proportionality principle. In short, my previous work has tried to limit both warfighting and targeting on the basis of responsibility, suggesting that "belligerents must attempt to understand the composition and political commitments of the people in the opposing society, [and] they must evaluate these commitments with an eye towards an empathetic understanding of opposing positions."[35] This "pays attention to the impacts of *in bello* decision-making on real people's lives, both short- and long-term."[36] Such an understanding addresses a segment of the issue. Rather than suggesting that avoiding civilians is the responsibility of those doing the targeting, it suggests that policymakers deciding whether or not to make a war are responsible to anticipate the result of targeting and makes protecting civilians primary to attacking combatants.

That corrective is insufficient, though. While it does prioritize the innocent over the guilty, it is still fundamentally reliant on the combatant/civilian dichotomy, which I argue is untenable. The alternative, then, becomes thinking about what Just War theorizing would look like without the combatant/civilian dichotomy.

Still, "just war without civilians" is difficult, if not impossible, to imagine, because "civilians *to protect from war* form part of the *authority of* just war discourses."[37] The *jus ad bellum* moral mandate of just cause relies on identifying some people as guilty of or complicit in the just cause that a belligerent has against its enemy. Without guilty people to target and innocent people to protect, war justification becomes much more difficult. In other words, without "civilians," there are no "combatants." Yet, ironically, with "civilians," there are no civilians. For these reasons, the task of either reformulating the civilian immunity principle or seeing Just War without civilians seems daunting, both in theory and in practice.

JUST WAR WITHOUT CIVILIANS

If the purpose of just war theorizing is to serve as a moderating influence in war making and warfighting, and despite that intent, it functions as a permissive force in war making and warfighting, then part or all of it needs to be supplanted to fulfill the intent of those who see the ethical importance of moderating the making and fighting of wars.

An easy answer might be turning to pacifism, but that rejects war rather than looking to moderate it. Such an answer suggests (I believe inappropriately) that there is no injustice more terrible than the least unjust war that could be imagined to combat the injustice. But imagining war without Just War seems equally, if not more, problematic. Clausewitz suggested discarding war ethics in favor of war making unrestricted by morality.[38] An amoral position on war does not recognize the need for moderation or justice, yet such a need seems clearly pressing in the face of the brutality of unmoderated war(s).

A harder answer, but one worth pursuing in my mind, is thinking about war ethics without the civilian/combatant dichotomy. If such an idea is workable, it would also eschew the us/them and public/private separations in war decision making, changing the ethical subjects and objects of Just War theorizing. Such an ethics of war would need to find a justification for fighting outside of the innocence of the beautiful soul and would need to motivate fighting outside of the masculine obligations of and honor sought by just warriors.

Instead, an ethics of war without civilians is one without us/them and public/private dichotomies, fundamentally altering the "us" that might decide, ontologically, to make wars and act to fight them. It is an ethics of war that needs an alternative justification for war than those who it cannot and will not be able to protect. Perhaps it starts at deconstructing dichotomous understandings of us/them as a way to deconstruct or a result of deconstructing the combatant/civilian dichotomy; "we" are inseparable from "them"—linked to, relationally dependent on, relationally constructed "with" "them," therefore targeting is not unidirectional. Such a war ethics might start at interdependence and intersubjectivity, basing its dictates on a communicative approach to war decision making. In this way, it might be possible to avoid or correct for the net public harm the Just War performances are or have become.[39]

After all, human rights and civilian protection discourses often "circumscribe women and men within their stylized gender roles" and "legitimate the use of force."[40] Often, discourses of civilian protection and civilian immunity go hand in hand to create and reinforce a "distinction between a civilized *us* and a barbaric enemy *other* [which] not only reenacts and reinforces racist colonial stereotypes but works to erase the violence . . . conducted in the name of [the] 'humanitarian.'"[41] As I have argued, this makes distinction between combatant and civilian ultimately untenable.[42]

If the distinction between combatant and civilian is ultimately untenable, what might a concept of Just War be like without that distinction? Feminist ontologies provide some hints for how to begin to reconstruct Just War theorizing. As Brooke Ackerly, Maria Stern, and Jacqui True explain: "Feminist ontologies that expand our notions of world politics to include the personal and previously invisible spheres, and that start from the perspective that subjects are relational (rather than autonomous) . . . demand self-reflexive methodologies."[43] There are two crucial elements here. First, an approach to world politics reliant on feminist ontologies will deconstruct the dichotomy between public and private (especially as it is inherent in the civilian immunity principle) and use self-reflexive methodologies to deconstruct (and then reconstruct) its subject (here, just war theorizing).

If subjects are relational (and therefore relationally autonomous),[44] the *jus in bello* content of Just War theorizing cannot be based on which individuals and which bodies can be targeted without the context of their relations and relationships with others. Instead, thinking about people as autonomous subjects ("the soldier" who attacks and protects "the civilian" who has no agency in that protection but is entitled to it or its performance) is a counterproductive direction for theorizing or planning warfighting. The current civilian immunity principle, and Just War's tenets that deal with the need to injure civilians (double effect and supreme emergency),[45] rely on figuring out which (discrete) individuals fit in which (discrete) categories, then assigning entitlements to them on that basis, then assigning responsibilities to combatants on the basis of civilians' entitlements.

Instead, a Just War without civilians would base the *jus in bello* treatment of *people* (relationally rather than individually) on the basis of their relationships—both to each other and to the cause for which the war is being fought. As Robin May Schott suggests, in times of war, "it would be better for a political community to critically examine its identity and the outsiders that its identity creates than to reassert the validity of its identity through force."[46] This suggests that the *jus in bello* content of a Just War theory without civilians would start with critical self-examination not only of the grievance or just cause but also of the people who are responsible for the just cause, and that Just War fighting would be based on the relationship of the targets to the targeters and the cause, taking account of complexity and context. Such an approach would make many more categorizations than "combatant" and "civilian" imaginable and would allow both theorists and practitioners to think about degrees of relationship and degrees of separation between not only belligerents but the people who constitute the states or ethnic groups "at war," with their constituent similarities and differences.

In addition to thinking about people differently, an account of Just War without civilians would need a new mechanism for recognizing participation and suffering in the making and fighting of wars and a new plan for accountability, accounting, and reevaluating *in bello* choices and results. In her evaluation of Just War theorizing, Schott offers such a mechanism, suggesting "witness" as a mechanism for recognizing the narrative nature of both strategic and tactical war-justificatory accounts.[47] She explains, citing Agamben, that "the word *witness* derives from the Greek word *martis*, the martyr, which derives itself from the verb meaning to remember."[48] According to Schott, "an ethical discourse of war that gives weight to witness . . . generates a discourse of war based on their experience of war, not abstracted from experience."[49] An experience-based account moves away from abstracting "civilians" to numbers, symbols,[50] and significations, and instead it conceptualizes victimhood in war(s) as lived experience—which forces humanization and corrects the artificial removal of emotion from ethical and strategic discussions of wartime targeting. As Schott explains, "the discourse of witness also make evident that there are many more complex positions in war than the position of warrior or the victim" and "gives *weight* to the pain of individuals and communities."[51] Witnesses—"soldiers," "civilians," "politicians," and "people"—in a multiplicity of positions, individually and collectively, vis-à-vis the just cause of the war and the fighting of the conflict, can *witness* an experiential account of not only the relational ethics of targeting but also the results of ethical calculations and decisions as relate to weaponry, chosen targets, level of force, and tactics used.

Such an experience-based notion of *jus in bello* ethics could (and should, in my opinion) build off of Christine Sylvester's analysis of sense and war.[52] Sylvester encourages us to think about "what security feels like and does not feel like" as a way to understand war experiences and their consequences.[53] Sylvester suggests that there is a "war sense" and a "security sense" that people experience as they make, fight, engage with, and respond to war(s).[54] I suggest that understanding witnesses' war senses, and their relationships, might be a more fruitful direction for *jus in bello* ethics and a foundation for Just War without civilians.

∽

If the noncombatant immunity principle is inescapably gendered, and its genderings a necessary element of both the principle itself and the Just War tradition that it anchors, then the Just War tradition as a whole is permissive and encourages violence. The permissive *ad bellum* and *in bello* implications of the gendered immunity principle serve to legitimate gendered war making and incentivize gendered intentional civilian victimization. If that is the case (and fundamental to contemporary Just War performances), then the Just War tradition itself is also a net negative until it is separated from the combatant/civilian dichotomy. This chapter suggests a rough outline of "Just War without civilians," based on relationships, experience, and witness.

Notes

1. See discussions in Laura Sjoberg, "The Gendered Realities of the Immunity Principle: Why Gender Analysis Needs Feminism," *International Studies Quarterly* 50, no. 4 (2006): 889–910; Laura Sjoberg, *Gender, Justice, and the Wars in Iraq* (New York: Lexington Books, 2006); and recent discussion of the parallels to the Obama Administration in Laura Sjoberg, "'Manning Up' and Making (the Libyan) War," March 23, 2011, blog post at the Duck of Minerva (http://duckofminerva.blogspot.com/2011/03/manning-up-and-making-libyan-war.html). The quote comes from Eric Golub's article in the *Washington Times*, "Syria, the Family Research Council, and Obama's Silence," August 16, 2012, at http://communities.washingtontimes.com/neighborhood/tygrrrr-express/2012/aug/15/syria-family-research-council-and-obamas-silence/ (accessed August 18, 2012).

2. Regarding Kosovo, see "Transcript: Clinton Justifies U.S. Involvement in Kosovo," *CNN*, May 13, 1999, http://www.cnn.com/ALLPOLITICS/stories/1999/05/13/clinton.kosovo/transcript.html (accessed August 18, 2012). Regarding Afghanistan, see George W. Bush's June 1, 2002, graduation speech at West Point Military academy, http://teachingamericanhistory.org/library/index.asp?document=916 (accessed August 18, 2012).

3. For the original articulation of this idea, see Jean Elshtain, "On Beautiful Souls, Just Warriors, and Feminist Consciousness," *Women's Studies International Forum* 5, no. 3–4 (1982): 341–48. For contemporary readings, see Kimberly Hutchings, "Feminist Ethics and Political Violence," *International Politics* 44, no. 1 (2007): 90–106; Helen M. Kinsella, "Gendering Grotius: Sex and Sex Difference in the Laws of War," *Political Theory* 34, no. 2 (2006): 161–91; Judith Gardam, "Gender and Non-combatant Immunity," *Trans-*

national Law and Contemporary Problems 3 (1993): 345–70; Sjoberg, *Gender, Justice, and the Wars in Iraq.*

4. See Judith Butler, *Excitable Speech: A Politics of the Performative* (New York: Psychology Press, 1997); as relates to international security law and ethics, see Laura J. Shepherd, *Gender, Violence, and Security: Discourse as Practice* (London: Zed Books, 2008). The quote comes from Judith Butler, "Contingent Foundations: Feminism and the Question of 'Postmodernism'" in Judith Butler and Joan W. Scott (eds.) *Feminists Theorize the Political* (London: Routledge, 1992). See also Cynthia Weber, "Performative States," *Millennium: Journal of International Studies* 27, no. 1: 77–95.

5. Laura Sjoberg, "The Inseparability of Gender Hierarchy, the Just War Tradition, and Authorizing War," in *Just War: A State of the Art*, ed. Cian O'Driscoll and Anthony Lange (Washington, D.C.: Georgetown University Press, forthcoming 2013). For other discussions of performative constitution in IR see Roxanne Lynn Doty, *Imperial Encounters: The Politics of Representation in North-South Relations* (Minneapolis: University of Minnesota Press, 1998); Laura Shepherd, *Gender, Violence, and Security*; Laura Shepherd, ed. *Gender Matters in Global Politics: A Feminist Introduction to International Relations* (London: Routledge, 2010); Cynthia Weber, *Simulating Sovereignty: Intervention, the State, and Symbolic Exchange* (Cambridge: Cambridge University Press, 1995); Jean Baudrillard, *The Gulf War Did Not Take Place* (Bloomington: Indiana University Press, 1995).

6. V. Spike Peterson and Anne Sisson Runyan, *Global Gender Issues* (Boulder, Colo.: Westview Press, 1992; 2nd ed., 1999). More recently, see Marysia Zalewski, "Feminist International Relations: Making Sense . . . ," in Shepherd, *Gender Matters in Global Politics*, 28. Lauren Wilcox, "Gendering the Cult of the Offensive," *Security Studies* 18, no. 2 (2009): 214–40 suggests that feminist analysis "ask what assumptions about gender (and race, class, nationality, and sexuality) are necessary to make particular statements, policies, and actions meaningful." This serves as methodological guidance for this chapter.

7. Elshtain, "Just Warriors, Beautiful Souls."

8. Nancy Huston, "Tales of War and Tears of Women," *Women's Studies International Forum* 5, no. 3–4 (1982): 271–82; Joshua Goldstein, *War and Gender* (Cambridge: Cambridge University Press, 2001). See also Judith Stiehm, ed., *Women and Men's Wars* (London: Pluto Press, 1983). R. W. Connell, *Masculinities* (London: Polity, 1995); Sjoberg, *Gender, Justice, and the Wars in Iraq.*

9. The feminist term for this has been the "protection racket," since masculine identity is based in protective ability and protective claims rather than actual protection. See Sue Rae Peterson, "Coercion and Rape: The State as a Male Protection Racket," in *Feminism and Philosophy*, ed. Mary Vetterling-Braggin, Frederick A. Elliston, and Jane English (Totowa, N.J.: Littlefield, Adams, 1977).

10. Elshtain, "Just Warriors, Beautiful Souls," using the Nietzchian "beautiful soul."

11. Brent Steele, *Ontological Security in International Relations: Self-Identity and the IR State* (London: Routledge, 2008). See also Jennifer Mitzen, "Ontological Security in World Politics: State Identity and the Security Dilemma," *European Journal of International Relations* 12, no. 3 (2006): 341–70.

12. See Laura Sjoberg and Jessica Peet, "A(nother) Dark Side of the Protection Racket," *International Feminist Journal of Politics* 13, no. 2 (2011): 162–81.

13. Nira Yuval-Davis, *Gender and Nation* (London: Sage, 1997), 2.

14. Jan Jindy Pettman, *Worlding Women: A Feminist International Politics* (St. Leonards, NSW, Australia: Allen & Unwin, 1996), 193. Ruth Seifert has described the effect as women's bodies becoming a "second front" for conflicts (see "The Second Front: The Logic of Sexual Violence in Wars," *Women's Studies International Forum* 19, no. 1/2 (1996): 35–43.

15. V. Spike Peterson, "Sexing Political Identity/Nationalism as Heterosexism," *International Feminist Journal of Politics* 1, no. 1 (1999): 34–65.

16. Cited in Cindy S. Snyder, Wesley J. Gabbard, J. Dean May, and Nihada Zulcic, "On the Battleground of Women's Bodies: Mass Rape in Bosnia Herzgovina," *Affilia* 21, no. 2 (2006): 190.

17. Carl von Clausewitz, *On War* (San Bernardino, Calif.: Brownstone Books, 2009; originally published in 1832 as *Vom Kriege*).

18. Sjoberg and Peet, "A(nother) Dark Side," 169.

19. Sjoberg, "Inseparability of Gender Hierarchy."

20. Alexander Downes, *Targeting Civilians in War* (Ithaca, N.Y.: Cornell University Press, 2008); Alexander Downes, "Desperate Times, Desperate Measures: The Causes of Civilian Victimization in War," *International Security* 30, no. 4 (2006): 152–95.

21. See Sjoberg and Peet, "A(nother) Dark Side," and Laura Sjoberg and Jessica Peet, "Targeting Women in Wars: Feminist Contributions," in *Feminism and International Relations: Conversations about the Past, Present, and Future*, ed. J. Ann Tickner and Laura Sjoberg (London: Routledge, 2011).

22. Pettman, *Worlding Women*, 191.

23. The "good guy" and "bad guy" logics here are references to Nancy Huston's "Tales of War and Tears of Women"

24. Peterson, "Sexing Political Identity/Nationalism," 48.

25. Sjoberg, "Inseparability of Gender Hierarchy."

26. Ibid.

27. See, e.g., Laura Sjoberg and Caron Gentry, *Mothers, Monsters, Whores: Women's Violence in Global Politics* (London: Zed Books, 2007) and other work on women's participation in combat, terrorism, and other forms of political violence. See, e.g., Annica Kronsell and Erika Svedberg, "The Duty to Protect: Gender in the Swedish Practice of Conscription," *Cooperation and Conflict* 36, no. 2 (2001): 153–76.

28. See, e.g., Joshua Goldstein, *War and Gender* (Cambridge: Cambridge University Press, 2001).

29. George R. Mavrodes, "Conventions and the Morality of War," *Philosophy and Public Affairs* 4, no. 2 (1975): 117–31 (121).

30. Richard Shelly Hartigan, *The Forgotten Victim: A History of the Civilian* (Chicago: Precedent, 1982), 7.

31. See, e.g., arguments made by George Lakoff and Mark Johnson, *Metaphors We Live By* (Chicago: University of Chicago Press, 1980), and Yuen Foong Khong, *Analogies at War: Korea, Munich, Dien Bien Phu, and the Vietnam Decisions of 1965* (Princeton: Princeton University Press, 1992). These books share the argument that people use particular (metaphorical, visual, or analogic) shorthands to make accessible complicated concepts and situations.

32. The term "womenandchildren" comes from Cynthia Enloe, "Womenandchildren: Making Feminist Sense of the Persian Gulf Crisis," *Village Voice*, September 25, 1990; discussed in detail in Helen Kinsella, *The Image before the Weapon: A Critical History of the Combatant and Civilian* (Ithaca, N.Y.: Cornell University Press, 2011). R. Charli Carpenter, *Innocent Women and Children: Gender, Norms and the Protection of Civilians* (Aldershot: Ashgate, 2006).

33. Kinsella, *Image before the Weapon*; Judith Gardam, "Gender and Non-combatant Immunity," *Transnational Law and Contemporary Problems* 3 (1993): 345–70.

34. See Sjoberg, *Gender, Justice*; and Sjoberg, "Gendered Realities."

35. Sjoberg, *Gender, Justice*, 102.

36. Ibid.

37. Sjoberg, "Inseparability of Gender Hierarchy."

38. See Clausewitz, *On War*.

39. Use here borrowed from Hayward R. Alker's *Rediscoveries and Reformulations: Humanistic Methodologies for International Studies* (Cambridge: Cambridge University Press, 2001) for a discussion of conflict as communication, borrowing heavily from Jürgen Habermas, *The Theory of Communicative Action* (Cambridge: Polity, 1981).

40. Margaret Denike, "The Human Rights of Others: Sovereignty, Legitimacy, and 'Just Causes' for the 'War on Terror,'" *Hypatia* 23, no. 2 (2008): 95–121; citing Anne Orford, *Reading Humanitarian Intervention: Human Rights and the Use of Force in International Law* (Cambridge: Cambridge University Press, 2003).

41. Denike, "Human Rights of Others."

42. Sjoberg, "Inseparability of Gender Hierarchy."

43. Brooke Ackerly, Maria Stern, and Jacqui True, eds. *Feminist Methodologies in International Relations* (Cambridge: Cambridge University Press, 2006), 7.

44. See, e.g., Nancy Hirschmann, "Freedom, Recognition, and Obligation: A Feminist Approach to Political Theory," *The American Political Science Review* 83, no. 4: 1227–44.

45. See, e.g., Walzer, *Just and Unjust Wars*.

46. Schott, "Just War and the Problem of Evil," 133.

47. Ibid.

48. Ibid., citing Giorgio Agamben, *Remnants of Auschwitz*, trans. Daniel Heller-Roazen (New York: Zone Books, 1999), 26–28.

49. Schott, "Just War and the Problem of Evil," 133.

50. For accounts abstracting to numbers see, e.g., Carol Cohn, "Sex and Death in the Rational World of Defense Intellectuals," *Signs: Journal of Women in Culture and Society* 12, no. 4 (1987): 687–718; Carol Cohn, "Wars, Wimps, and Women: Talking Gender and Thinking War," in *Gendering War Talk*, ed. Miriam Cooke and Angela Woollacott (Princeton: Princeton University Press, 1993). For accounts abstracting to symbols see, e.g., Iris Marion Young, "The Logic of Masculinist Protection: Reflections on the Current Security State," *Signs: Journal of Women in Culture and Society* 29, no. 1 (2003): 1–25; Sjoberg and Peet, "A(nother) Dark Side."

51. Schott, "Just War and the Problem of Evil," 133–34.

52. Christine Sylvester, "War, Sense, and Security," in *Gender and International Security: Feminist Perspectives*, ed. Laura Sjoberg (New York: Routledge, 2010).

53. Ibid., 26.

54. Ibid.

Jus post Bellum

CHAPTER TEN

Jus post Bellum

Justice in the Aftermath of War

Robert E. Williams Jr.

"FOR AS LONG AS MEN AND WOMEN have talked about war, they have talked about it in terms of right and wrong."[1] With this simple but important observation Michael Walzer begins his modern classic on Just War theory, *Just and Unjust Wars.* There is, as he reminds us, a language of justification associated with war that has been as persistent and as important as the language of strategy. And out of the many efforts to justify war and the way it is fought have come the principles of the Just War tradition.

However irrational war may seem, particular wars always have their reasons. But society's judgment of those reasons—the assessment of which are moral and which are not—has changed significantly over time. Consider the commands of Yahweh to the ancient Hebrews to take by force the territory of their neighbors and to annihilate the people they encountered in their wars of conquest.[2] Or consider the thirteenth-century slaughter of those deemed heretics in southern France in the Albigensian Crusade that Pope Innocent III authorized.[3] In both cases (and in many others that could be cited), genocidal wars were deemed not just moral but holy by those who embarked on them. Today, holy wars are no longer considered moral, at least outside of those groups that most of the world derides for being medieval in their outlook.

Just War theory may seem to be an island of stability in a tempestuous sea of moral reflection on war—the Golden Mean, perhaps, between pacifism and holy war—but it, too, has been subject to frequent and often quite significant change.[4] From a certain perspective that change may appear to be part of a long, slow, steady evolution, but on closer inspection its evolution may bear more similarity to the punctuated equilibrium postulated by paleontologists

Niles Eldredge and the late Stephen Jay Gould.[5] The theory of punctuated equilibrium suggests that, in the natural world, the evolution of species occurs in fits and starts, proceeding rapidly at some points and slowly at others. External factors—changes in the climate, the appearance of new predators, or volcanic eruptions, for example—create the conditions for the rapid evolutionary changes that yield new species.

It is not an enormous leap from evolutionary biology to the history of ideas. Socially constructed understandings, of which the complex of justifications known collectively as Just War theory is one, also adapt to meet the challenges that altered circumstances may present. It should not surprise us if the adaptations occur more rapidly in periods of cataclysmic change than in more sedate eras. To take, as an example, only the particular variety of Just War theory developed within Christianity, we know that the conversion of Constantine following the Battle of Milvian Bridge (312 C.E.) and the subsequent Edict of Milan (313 C.E.), which changed the status of Christianity in the Roman Empire, were important prods toward the development of Augustine's conception of Just War. Twelve centuries later, the often violent encounter of Europeans with the peoples of the New World led to a rethinking of certain fundamental principles of the Christian Just War tradition, particularly under the influence of religious thinkers such as Bartolomé de las Casas. It is worth noting, too, that Hugo Grotius's enormously influential *De Jure Belli ac Pacis* appeared in the middle of the Thirty Years' War.[6]

Just War theory, like ethical theory in general, develops where dilemmas are discerned. If the dominant culture perceives no problem with slavery, the subjection of women, or the rape of the environment, society is unlikely even to debate whether equality of persons or stewardship of nature are ethical imperatives. This, in fact, is one of the reasons that, until recently, little attention has been paid to the ethics of postwar settlements. Peace, after all, has not generally been problematized the way that war has been. A common assumption throughout history has been that the decision to go to war—a decision, that is, to set in motion the forces of death and destruction that accompany war—is one that imposes grave ethical responsibilities but that the decision to make peace—to stop the killing—makes no serious ethical demands. Consequently, Just War thinkers have elaborately theorized *jus ad bellum* without, until recently, giving much thought to *jus post bellum*. Thomas Hobbes famously compared war to stormy weather to make the point that there may be a proclivity to violence even when there is no actual fighting, but his meteorological metaphor can be put to a different purpose. Those who observe and ponder the ethics of war are like those who study the weather: storms excite great interest and diligent study, especially with respect to their causes. Not so with the calm that follows the storm, even if the causes of the next storm are to be found somewhere within it.

Although "just peace" has been a concern within the field of conflict resolution for many years,[7] and some antecedents of contemporary thought on *jus post bellum* can be found in the writings of Aristotle, Augustine, and Thomas Aquinas, among others, the idea that the principles of just peace might be developed as an extension of the Just War tradition is relatively new. The most obvious spur toward the articulation of *jus post bellum* principles was the troubled American occupation of Iraq. What George W. Bush desired was a reconceptualization of *jus ad bellum* principles that would sanction his belief in the need for preemptive (or, more accurately, preventive) war. What he got instead was a renewed commitment among most Just War theorists to the traditional understanding of self-defense (and its limitations) combined with a new awareness that *jus post bellum* merited serious attention.

The fact that the toppling of Saddam Hussein's brutal regime and George W. Bush's "Mission Accomplished" declaration aboard the uss *Abraham Lincoln* merely signaled the beginning rather than the end of the difficulties the United States would face in Iraq led both strategists and ethicists to reconsider the transition from war to peace and its difficult intermediate phase, occupation. It was apparent to many people that as cia director George Tenet later put it, "The war . . . went great, but peace was hell."[8] No one, however, should have been surprised to find that why and how the war was fought would have an impact on its aftermath. Although we have separate categories into which we can place prewar, wartime, and postwar moral considerations—*jus ad bellum*, *jus in bello*, and now *just post bellum*—it is in practice very difficult to pull on a single thread without unraveling the entire fabric of moral justification. This is well illustrated by one of the most widely debated of all wartime decisions, President Truman's decision to drop two atomic bombs on Japan at the end of World War II.

The circumstances that influenced Truman's deliberations are well known and can be recounted concisely.[9] The U.S. entry into World War II was justified as an act of self-defense with respect to Japan (on account of the Japanese surprise attack on Pearl Harbor) and as an act of collective self-defense with respect to Germany. The two principal Axis powers were, with good reason, regarded as militaristic regimes bent on regional, if not global, hegemony. For this reason, the objective of the war for the United States and its allies was not simply the defeat of the aggressors but an occupation that would facilitate regime change as well. This objective strongly influenced the way the war was fought. Rather than fight a limited war in an effort simply to defend parts of Europe, North Africa, and the Far East from aggression, the Allies proclaimed the objective of unconditional surrender and adopted the tactics of total war, including the terror bombing of German and Japanese cities.

Within weeks after he became president upon the death of Franklin D. Roosevelt on April 12, 1945, Harry Truman was pressed by Under Secretary of State Joseph C. Grew to consider modifying the demand that Japan surrender unconditionally. Grew, a former ambassador to Japan, was joined in his lobbying effort by Secretary of War Henry Stimson, Secretary of the Navy James Forrestal, and Admiral William Leahy.[10] The ferocity of the fighting as American forces island-hopped across the Pacific toward the Japanese home islands and the quasi-religious fervor with which not only the Japanese military but civilians as well seemed willing to defend Emperor Hirohito had convinced these four and others in the American government that unconditional surrender might be achieved only at the cost of vast numbers of both American and Japanese lives. Truman, who had served as an artillery officer in World War I, was sympathetic to these concerns and cognizant of the desirability of avoiding a costly invasion. But he also felt the necessity of honoring the commitment that FDR and America's allies had made to the aim of unconditional surrender as well as the sacrifices of tens of thousands of lives already toward that end. For weeks, Truman made no decision regarding a communication to the Japanese that would indicate U.S. willingness to permit the retention of the emperor following the Japanese surrender. In the end, Truman offered Japan this concession after Hiroshima and Nagasaki had been bombed. It was a decision that has given historians much fodder for debate, but what is noteworthy from the standpoint of Just War theory is the way American objectives framed at the beginning of the war with Japan affected decisions concerning the end of the war, including the portentous decision about how to bring the war to an end.

DEFINING AND DEFENDING *JUS POST BELLUM*

Jus post bellum—justice after war—is a set of principles to guide those making the transition from war to peace. Just as *jus ad bellum* principles exist to guide policymakers in the period before a war begins—posing questions about the ethics of resorting to war—and *jus in bello* principles exist to guide combatants in the conduct of war, so *jus post bellum* principles exist to offer moral guidance in the aftermath of war. *Jus post bellum* is not (or it should not be, at least) merely a list of directives concerning war crimes tribunals, reconstruction, peacekeeping, or even peacebuilding. If it is to be useful over the long term and consistent with the other parts of the Just War tradition, *jus post bellum* must offer principles akin to the last resort principle of *jus ad bellum* or the proportionality principle of *jus in bello*. It must provide moral principles to be weighed against other moral principles and strategic considerations rather than a list of rules and regulations.

Unfortunately, there is little consensus thus far even on how to approach the development of *jus post bellum* principles. Brian Orend, who has done as much as anyone to press the case for the inclusion of *jus post bellum* in Just War theory, has endeavored to articulate *jus post bellum* principles that closely follow in form those principles, such as right intention and discrimination, that are well established in the *jus ad bellum* and *jus in bello* parts of the Just War tradition. For example, in *War and International Justice: A Kantian Approach*, Orend includes among the principles of *jus post bellum* "just cause for termination," right intention, "public declaration and legitimate authority," discrimination, and proportionality, all of which are concepts generally found within standard lists of *jus ad bellum* and *jus in bello* principles.[11] In some cases, however, Orend's approach seems to be trying to fit a square peg into a round hole. Just as *jus in bello* requires a separate set of criteria from *jus ad bellum*, it is reasonable to suppose that *jus post bellum* will also require principles that are particular to the postwar context.

Before trying to find a set of norms that can gain widespread assent, it is important to determine what ends should be served by Just War theory in general and a conception of *jus post bellum* in particular. This, in turn, requires thinking about the foundations of the tradition.

Historically, Just War theory has been presented as an application of Christian dogma, natural law, Kantian ethics, and various other religious or philosophical positions. Today, however, it is best understood as a theory of human rights for wartime. In recognition of the dangers of an absolutist ethic—even one that emphasizes the protection of human life and dignity—Just War theory attempts to provide moral guidance for those situations when life and dignity can be protected only by war. It attempts to establish high barriers in order to limit the resort to war to those dilemmas that are truly solvable only by going to war. In fact, under modern international law, only self-defense, defense of others under a United Nations Security Council mandate, and humanitarian intervention appear to justify the resort to force in contravention of an otherwise absolute ban contained in Article 2(4) of the UN Charter. It also attempts to limit the inevitable violations of human rights caused by the use of force by restricting killing to combatants and requiring that the harms of war be proportional to the cause for which the war is fought.

It is important to note that Just War theory is not the same as human rights. Fighting even a Just War (and fighting it justly) involves what would constitute terrible human rights abuses in peacetime. That war is different is apparent in the provision of the International Covenant on Civil and Political Rights that permits states to derogate from many of their human rights obligations "in time of public emergency which threatens the life of the nation."[12] But, on the other hand, that the laws of war remain closely tied to human rights norms should be apparent from Common Article 3 in the four Geneva Conventions of 1949, which defines for all armed conflicts certain minimum standards of humanitarian law, including prohibitions against "violence to life and person," "cruel treatment and torture," and "outrages upon personal dignity."[13]

With this understanding of the relationship between Just War theory and human rights, *jus post bellum* can be regarded as a set of principles that facilitates the transition from war, in which human rights are restricted, to the more expansive peacetime human rights regime. This suggests that there are two basic states in international politics: war, in which human rights may be subordinated to the security of the state or the demands of an emerging responsibility to protect others, and peace, the normal condition in which the full range of human rights obligations exist.

Where does this leave us in our effort to formulate *jus post bellum* principles? It leaves us with a wide range of human rights obligations at the end of the transition from war to peace, but, unfortunately, it does not provide a simple checklist like the ones that *jus ad bellum* offers for judging the decision to go to war. There are, however, some conclusions in place of principles that can be offered.

From Aristotle to B. H. Liddell Hart and beyond, those who have seriously contemplated war have argued that peace is the proper objective of a just war.[14] Although pronouncements about this purpose of war may call to mind Woodrow Wilson's excessively hopeful description of World War I as "a war to end all wars," there is clearly an important truth in the belief that, as Liddell Hart wrote, "the object in war is a better state of peace."[15]

Until a lasting peace has been secured, there can be no restoration of human rights, which is the ultimate object of war. Setting aside the arguments regarding the justice of the U.S. rationale for the invasion of Iraq in 2003, serious *jus post bellum* concerns arose within months of the end of major combat operations primarily because of the obvious fact that the war had not, at least to that point, established anything close to a lasting peace within Iraq. Secretary of Defense Donald Rumsfeld argued that the violence occurring in Iraq after May 2003 represented the last gasps of a few "dead enders,"[16] but he was quickly proved wrong. The insurgency that developed in Iraq rapidly surpassed the regular war in the number of casualties produced, both military and civilian.

After peace has been secured, the human rights of all parties to the conflict must be restored. If the war was precipitated by an act of aggression or the commission of serious human rights abuses, those who have been victims must have their rights vindicated. If there are trials to be held and punishments to be meted out, the rights of the accused must be respected. And if the destruction wrought by the war has imperiled the economic security of people on either side, the right to a minimum level of subsistence must be ensured. This is hardly a comprehensive list of the victor's postwar requirements, but the basic idea is clear: when the fighting ends, the obligation to secure the human rights of all parties to the conflict begins.

However the obligations suggested by this rights-based theory are met, it is important that justice in the aftermath of war be given adequate attention. A well-developed and widely accepted concept of *jus post bellum* is important to correct both the complacency and the cynicism that often infect perceptions of what happens when a war has ended. Complacency is manifested in the common assumption that if the right side in a conflict prevails, justice will be assured. The victims of aggression and their defenders, it is thought, will inevitably be restrained in their treatment of their defeated foe; to do otherwise would be to forfeit the moral high ground that comes with standing up to an aggressor. And if, in victory, there is not perfect magnanimity displayed by those who were victims of aggression, this can be excused on the grounds that they are entitled to mete out punishment and seek reparations for the injuries they have suffered. The cynical view, on the other hand, is the one captured by Garry Wills's observation that "only the winners decide what were war crimes."[17] It assumes that in the aftermath of war, as in all other aspects of international politics, power is what matters, and thus it makes little sense to try to subject postwar conditions to moral scrutiny. Both perceptions are wrong—and dangerous.

PROBING *JUS POST BELLUM*

There is, clearly, an argument for *jus post bellum*, but this should not preclude taking a critical look at the concept. The mere fact that no one across nearly two millennia of Just War thinking considered it necessary to articulate *jus post bellum* principles should give us pause. At the very least, it may require that we look to matters beyond the occupation of Iraq to explain why *jus post bellum* principles seem now to be filling a need that was not generally recognized by Just War theorists earlier. After all, the first wave of *jus post bellum* scholarship predated the invasion of Iraq in 2003.[18]

If there are deeper reasons for the turn toward *jus post bellum* than a poorly planned war in Iraq and its impact on Just War theory, they are likely to be found in the significant changes that have occurred in the nature of warfare and in the milieu within which wars are fought. Put simply, it is becoming more difficult to make peace even as more is being expected from peace settlements.

Two related changes in the international system that, although impossible to quantify, appear significant nonetheless are the development of the idea that justice is essential to the creation and sustenance of peace and the rise of a global humanitarian ethos, one that includes widespread acceptance of international human rights norms. The consequences of the punitive peace that followed World War I ensured that peace would be approached differently after World War II. The Allies were willing to assign guilt following World War II—in fact, it seemed imperative to do so given the atrocities that had occurred during the war—but they did so individually, and on the basis of judicial proceedings, rather than collectively and in summary fashion. Since then, the idea of war guilt clauses in peace agreements has become repugnant to most while postconflict tribunals and truth commissions have become more common as both the parties to conflict and the international community as a whole seek justice, whether retributive or restorative. These changes naturally demand that some attention be paid to the principles relevant to postwar justice, which is another way of saying *jus post bellum* principles.

The rise of international human rights and a global humanitarian ethos is not solely a post–World War II phenomenon—international humanitarian law dates back at least to the 1864 Geneva Convention for the Amelioration of the Condition of the Wounded and Sick in Armed Forces in the Field—but the emphasis of the United Nations Charter on human rights and, in the years immediately following World War II, the Nuremberg war crimes trials, the adoption of the Genocide Convention and the Universal Declaration of Human Rights (both in 1948), and the formulation of the 1949 Geneva Conventions were decisive in moving the world in a new direction. This change in the international system, characterized by Ruti G. Teitel as a shift toward "the law of humanity,"[19] has meant, among other things, that victors are now widely regarded as having obligations toward the vanquished, or at least toward the people of the losing side who may themselves be considered victims of war. The post–World War II experience looms large in this regard. If Germany and Japan could be spared general retribution and actually be rehabilitated after the war, then it must be that all have a right to decent postconflict treatment in the absence of personal responsibility for crimes. World War II established a model of sorts for postconflict justice, but it proved difficult to apply in Korea, Vietnam, Iraq, and elsewhere in the years following World War II. The global humanitarian ethos came without clear instructions for its implementation. The effort to develop *jus post bellum* principles has been one response.

There are a number of problems that confront the effort to articulate a useful framework for evaluating justice in the aftermath of war. Most are common to all aspects of the Just War tradition, but some are unique to *jus post bellum*.

As noted earlier, the division of the Just War tradition is based on the intuitive view that there are distinct phases in warfare. Simply put, there are separate before, during, and after phases that correspond to the Latin prepositions *ad*, *in*, and *post*. There have always been problems with this understanding. Many societies throughout history have been confronted with a state of war that precedes the onset of hostilities and sometimes follows their conclusion. This, in fact, is the condition that Thomas Hobbes compared to stormy weather in *Leviathan*. There are, arguably, even more ways that the lines between war and peace, whether of the prewar or postwar type, can be blurred today than there were in Hobbes's day. The various forms of low-intensity conflict, as with sporadic military operations conducted by the Burmese military against ethnic minorities in Burma, blur the distinction, often deliberately, between peace and war. Rather than looking for certain characteristics of conflict that would allow for an "objective" determination of when peace passes into war and back again, contemporary theorists are more inclined to acknowledge that the categories are socially constructed and thus more subject to the vagaries of political discourse than to the more rigid categories of ethical and legal analysis. Thus a terrorist attack is an act of war—unless it's not, in which case it may be a criminal act.

If acts of terrorism and the various possibilities for responding to them illustrate the difficulties in distinguishing peace from the onset of war, the Iraq and Afghanistan wars have become the principal exhibits illustrating the difficulties inherent in separating war from whatever follows it. In Iraq, regular military forces were routed and the government of Saddam Hussein was driven from Baghdad in a matter of weeks. But four years later, the United States was forced to initiate a "surge," increasing the number of troops in Iraq in an effort to conclude a war that clearly had not ended with what had been described in May 2003 as "the end of major combat operations." In Afghanistan, the removal of the Taliban regime within weeks of the war's initiation in October 2001 has been followed by over a decade of counterinsurgency warfare aimed at establishing enough stability in Afghanistan to allow coalition forces to depart without ensuring a complete reversal of the war's gains.

A second problem besetting the concept of *jus post bellum*, shared with other aspects of the Just War tradition, is its state-centric character. As articulated thus far, *jus post bellum* principles generally assume that the war being terminated is an interstate conflict in spite of the fact that, since World War II, the number of interstate wars has declined dramatically. At least ninety of the conflicts that have occurred since 1945 are classifiable as civil wars.[20] Very few recent conflicts have been interstate in character, although the attention given to the U.S. wars in Afghanistan and Iraq tends to obscure this fact.

Along with the rise of intrastate war comes the rise of nonstate actors as combatants. While most are rebel forces fighting civil wars, there are also terrorists fighting asymmetric wars. On the state side, private military contractors are playing a larger role than ever before, with impacts on Just War theory that are just beginning to be explored.

Efforts to develop a coherent account of *jus post bellum* confront a third problem that arises from the asymmetries that commonly exist at the end of a war. The rules that dictate whether it is just to go to war and those that specify how war ought to be fought are the same for all parties (or potential parties) in a conflict. (There is a significant exception if the validity of Michael Walzer's concept of supreme emergency is granted.) The same, however, cannot be true for the rules that pertain to the postwar environment, at least not where the outcome has been decisive. The imbalance of power that exists between victor and vanquished at the end of a war necessitates that the two sides be held to different ethical standards, with most of the restraints that might be associated with *jus post bellum* being imposed on the victor. The victor, after all, is in the unique position of being able to punish war crimes, impose changes on the government or society, and set terms for reparations. For this reason, most efforts to date to formulate a list of principles underlying *jus post bellum* have focused on the victor's duties even though this may mean the concept is incomplete.

THE WAY FORWARD

If *jus post bellum* represents a reasonable response to changes in the nature of warfare and the development of a new law of humanity—if, in other words, it is a worthwhile addition to Just War theory—then how are these problems to be overcome? A human rights foundation for *jus post bellum* principles is the key.

In a world where intrastate wars far outnumber interstate wars, it is important to base Just War principles on something other than a largely outmoded idea of absolute sovereignty. It may well be that nonstate actors should be discouraged in most circumstances from waging war; however, denying them any consideration in Just War theory or international humanitarian law is not the way to do so. Witness the global censure of U.S. treatment of enemy combatants in the so-called War on Terror. Respect for basic human rights, even in the case of terrorism suspects, is a better policy and one that could undergird a Just War theory for an age of intrastate war. It is also completely consistent with state sovereignty exercised in the interest of human security.

Because states have a right to derogate from most of their international human rights obligations when the existence of the state is threatened, and because intrastate war often poses an existential threat, international human rights law alone cannot ensure the protection of basic rights in time of war. Nor should we expect it to. Just War theory—and international humanitarian law—serve this purpose by offering human rights–based norms adapted to the circumstances of war.

Tying *jus post bellum* principles to human rights can also help Just War theory rationalize the asymmetry that arises at the end of war by acknowledging that power and authority are in fact morally relevant qualities in war as in peace. Human rights obligations generally fall on the state in its dealings with those who live under its authority. This is no different from the situation at the end of a war when most *jus post bellum* obligations fall on the winning side. All are enjoined to respect life and human dignity; not all are in a position to violate the injunction.

The problems that arise from the difficulty of separating the various phases of war are less easily addressed by an insistence on making human rights the foundation of Just War theory in general and *jus post bellum* in particular. Nevertheless, a rights-based conception of *jus post bellum* can generate a more positive blurring of lines by facilitating the transition between war, in which many human rights are held in abeyance, and peace, when the full range of rights is restored. And if Just War theory can blur the line between war and peace along a spectrum of rights rather than a spectrum of violence, it will have helped to strengthen the global humanitarian ethos that has emerged since 1945.

Notes

1. Michael Walzer, *Just and Unjust Wars: A Moral Argument with Historical Illustrations* (New York: Basic Books, 1977), 3.

2. See, for example, Deuteronomy 20:10–18 and Joshua 6:1–21.

3. See Jonathan Sumption, *The Albigensian Crusade* (New York: Faber and Faber, 2000).

4. See James Turner Johnson, *Just War Tradition and the Restraint of War: A Moral and Historical Inquiry* (Princeton, N.J.: Princeton University Press, 1981); and James Turner Johnson, *Ideology, Reason, and the Limitation of War: Religious and Secular Concepts, 1200–1740* (Princeton, N.J.: Princeton University Press, 1975).

5. The theory has undergone significant refinements over the past forty years, but for the original version see Niles Eldredge and Stephen Jay Gould, "Punctuated Equilibria: An Alternative to Phyletic Gradualism," in *Models in Paleobiology*, ed. T. J. M. Schopf (San Francisco: Freeman Cooper, 1972), 82–115.

6. Hugo Grotius, *The Law of War and Peace (De Jure Belli ac Pacis)*, trans. Louise R. Loomis (New York: Walter J. Black, 1949).

7. See, for example, Glenn Stassen, *Just Peacemaking* (Louisville, Ky.: Westminster/ John Knox Press, 1992); John Paul Lederach, *Building Peace: Sustainable Reconciliation in Divided Societies* (Washington, D.C.: United States Institute of Peace, 1998); and John Paul Lederach, *The Moral Imagination: The Art and Soul of Building Peace* (New York: Oxford University Press, 2010).

8. Quoted in Dan Caldwell, *Vortex of Conflict: U.S. Policy toward Afghanistan, Pakistan, and Iraq* (Stanford, Calif.: Stanford University Press, 2011), 163.

9. For a good recent account, see Campbell Craig and Sergey Radchenko, *The Atomic Bomb and the Origins of the Cold War* (New Haven, Conn.: Yale University Press, 2008), 65–73.

10. Martin J. Sherwin, *A World Destroyed: The Atomic Bomb and the Grand Alliance* (New York: Alfred A. Knopf, 1975), 225.

11. Brian Orend, *War and International Justice: A Kantian Perspective* (Waterloo, Ont.: Wilfred Laurier University Press, 2002), 269–70. See also Brian Orend, *The Morality of War* (Peterborough, Ont.: Broadview Press, 2006), 160–89.

12. See the International Covenant on Civil and Political Rights, 999 U.N.T.S. 771, *entered into force* March 23, 1976, Art. 4 (1).

13. See, inter alia, Geneva Convention for the Amelioration of the Condition of the Wounded and Sick in Armed Forces in the Field, 75 U.N.T.S. 31, *entered into force* October 21, 1950, Art. 3 (1).

14. See Robert E. Williams Jr., "A More Perfect Peace: *Jus Post Bellum* and the Quest for Stable Peace," in *Ethics beyond War's End*, ed. Eric Patterson (Washington, D.C.: Georgetown University Press, 2012).

15. B. H. Liddell Hart, *Strategy*, 2nd ed. (New York: Praeger, 1974), 339.

16. Caldwell, *Vortex of Conflict*, 168.

17. Garry Wills, "The First Casualty," *New York Times* (Book Review), September 14, 1975, 2.

18. See Orend, *War and International Justice*; Brian Orend, "*Jus Post Bellum*," *Journal of Social Philosophy* 31, no. 1 (Spring 2000): 117–37; Brian Orend, "Justice after War," *Ethics and International Affairs* 16 (2002): 43–56; and Davida E. Kellogg, "Jus Post Bellum: The Importance of War Crimes Trials," *Parameters* 32 (2002): 87–98.

19. Ruti G. Teitel, *Humanity's Law* (New York: Oxford University Press, 2011), 4.

20. Dan Caldwell and Robert E. Williams Jr., *Seeking Security in an Insecure World*, 2nd ed. (Lanham, Md.: Rowman & Littlefield, 2011), 195.

CONTRIBUTORS

AMY E. ECKERT is associate professor of political science at the Metropolitan State University of Denver. Her work has appeared in *International Studies Quarterly, Journal of Global Ethics, International Political Theory*, and the *Denver Journal of International Law and Policy*. She is the coeditor, with Laura Sjoberg, of *Rethinking the Twenty-First Century: New Problems, Old Solutions* and author of a forthcoming textbook on ethics and international relations. She is program chair of the 2013 International Studies Association–West meeting and secretary of ISA's International Ethics section.

CARON E. GENTRY is lecturer in the School of International Relations at the University of St. Andrews. Her research interests include feminism and gender studies, terrorism, and political theology. She is the author of *Offering Hospitality: Questioning Christian Approaches to War* (University of Notre Dame, 2013). She coauthored *Mothers, Monsters, Whores: Women's Violence in Global Politics* (Zed, 2007) and coedited *Women, Gender, and Terrorism* (University of Georgia Press, 2011) with Laura Sjoberg. She is published in *International Feminist Journal of Politics, International Relations, Terrorism and Political Violence*, and *Critical Studies in Terrorism*.

LUKE GLANVILLE is a fellow in the Department of International Relations at the Australian National University. He has a forthcoming book titled *Sovereignty and the Responsibility to Protect* and has published articles in journals including *International Studies Quarterly, European Journal of International Relations*, and *Human Rights Law Review*.

HARRY D. GOULD is associate professor in the Department of Politics and International Relations at Florida International University. He is the author of *The Legacy of Punishment in International Law*, as well as numerous articles and book chapters on topics in normative international political theory, constructivist international relations theory, and international legal theory. He is currently completing a book on the concept of prudence and is coediting a volume on political judgment in international relations.

ERIC A. HEINZE is associate professor of political science and international studies at the University of Oklahoma. He is the author of *Waging Humanitarian War: The Ethics, Law and Politics of Humanitarian Intervention* (SUNY, 2009), editor (with Brent Steele) of *Ethics, Authority, and War: Non-state Actors and the Just War Tradition* (Palgrave, 2010), and editor of *Justice, Sustainability, and Security: Global Ethics for the 21st Century* (forthcoming, Palgrave, 2013). He has published numerous scholarly journal articles and book chapters, with research most recently appearing in the *Review of International Studies, Global Governance, Political Science Quarterly*, and the *Journal of International Political Theory*. He is currently writing a book on the ethics of global violence. He teaches courses on international relations, human rights, Just War theory, international law, international organizations, and international relations theory.

DAN HENK retired in 2012 after forty years of government service. At the time, he was serving as a social anthropologist on the faculty of Air University and simultaneously as the director of the U.S. Air Force Culture and Language Center. Since 2005 he also served as director of African studies at the U.S. Army War College and as chair, Department of Security Strategy, (DoD) Africa Center for Strategic Studies. He researched and lectured widely in Europe and Africa. He holds a B.A. in history from The Citadel and an M.A. and PhD in anthropology from the University of Florida. His later publications explore defense budgeting in African countries, evolving military roles and missions, and emerging new definitions of "security," with a focus on environmental security.

KIMBERLY A. HUDSON is assistant professor of international security at the Air War College, Montgomery, Alabama. She received her PhD in 2008 from the Political Science Department at Brown University. Her research and teaching interests include Just War theory and conflict resolution/negotiation. She is the author of *Justice, Intervention, and Force: Re-assessing Just War Theory in the Twenty-First Century* (Routledge, 2009), which focuses on moral arguments surrounding the resort to war, with particular emphasis on armed humanitarian intervention.

SEBASTIAN KAEMPF is lecturer in peace and conflict studies at the School of Political Science and International Studies at the University of Queensland. His research interests lie in the moral and legal questions surrounding the use of force, historical and contemporary asymmetric conflicts, and the role of war in a transforming global media landscape. His research has been published—among other sources—in *Third World Quarterly*, *Review of International Studies*, *International Relations*, and *Small Wars and Insurgencies*. He also co-runs a new website dedicated to media, war, and peace called TheVisionMachine, at www.thevisionmachine.com.

ALEXA ROYDEN is an associate professor and the director of international studies at Queens University of Charlotte in Charlotte, North Carolina. She teaches courses in international relations and political theory. Her research interests include global governance, international security, human rights, and the ethics of warfare. A former defense consultant, she continues to explore emerging military technologies, their effect on the battlefield, and the legal and ethical implications associated with contemporary and future forms of warfare.

LAURA SJOBERG is associate professor of political science at the University of Florida. Her research on gender and international security has been published in dozens of scholarly journals and eight authored or edited books, including, most recently, *Gendering Global Conflict: Toward a Feminist Theory of War* (Columbia University Press, 2013). She is homebase editor of the *International Feminist Journal of Politics*.

BRENT J. STEELE is an associate professor of political science and international relation, and the director of faculty programs for the Office of International Programs at the University of Kansas. His research interests include U.S. foreign policy, Just War theory, torture, and accountability in global politics. He is the author of three books and also the coeditor of two volumes. His research has been published in a number of international studies journals, with articles appearing most recently in *Critical Studies on Security*, *Millennium*, *International Studies Review*, *Journal of International Political Theory*, and *Review of International Studies*. He teaches courses on international relations theory, international ethics, United States foreign policy, and critical security studies.

ROBERT E. WILLIAMS JR. is professor of political science at Pepperdine University, where he teaches courses on international ethics and international organization and law. He is the author, with Dan Caldwell, of *Seeking Security in an Insecure World* (2nd ed., 2012) and the editor, with Paul Viotti, of the two-volume *Arms Control: History, Theory, and Policy* (2012). He also writes on international human rights.

INDEX

Abidjan Peace Accord, 69–70
accidents (friendly fire), 83–84, 102, 106
accountability, 31, 33–34, 41, 105, 158
Ackerly, Brooke, 157
Aegis Combat System, and Iran Air Flight
    655, 104
Afghanistan: as asymmetrical challenge for
    United States, 80, 102, 122; HRW report
    on casualties in, 122; and interventionist
    declarations, 148; and *jus post bellum*, 176;
    and Taliban, 176; and UAVs in AfPak region,
    102; U.S. casualties in, 83, 84t
African Union (AU), and Constitutive Act to
    protect, 56
Agamben, Giorgio, 158
AirLand Battle doctrine, 86
airstrikes, target discrimination and planning
    of, 122
al Qaeda, and territoriality, 102
ambiguity, and moral agency, 107–10
America. *See* United States
Anscombe, G. E. M., 135, 139–40
Aquinas. *See* Thomas Aquinas, Saint
Aristotle, 17–19, 169, 172
armies. *See* military roles
Arms to Africa scandal, 69
assassination, 104–11
asymmetrical risk-free warfare: and Just War
    tradition, 80–90, 92–93, 102, 105, 118–23;
    theoretical challenges to, 79–82, 93
AU (African Union), and Constitutive Act to
    protect, 56
Augustine, Saint, 19–20, 33–34, 168–69
Aune, Bruce, 135
Austin, John, 134
authority: political, 17–29; procedural, 18, 22–
    23. *See also* legitimacy / legitimate authority

Bacevich, Andrew J., 88
Bagnoli, Carla, 60n26
Baldwin, Thomas, 142
Battle of Omdurman, 90–91

Baumann, Zygmunt, 85–86
beautiful soul trope, 12, 148–56
Beck, Ulrich, 85
Bellamy, Alex J., 4, 18, 20, 25, 62–63
Bellum Civile / Bellum Romanum, and
    reciprocity principle, 91
Bennett, Jonathan, 140–41
Bentham, Jeremy, 134
bias, as epistemic, 7, 17–21, 24
Bin Laden, Osama, 102, 112–13n21, 120
bombers, 89–90, 132–33, 140–41
Bosnia casualties, 84t
Boyle, Joseph, 137–38
Branch Energy, and EO, 68–69
Bratman, Michael, 135–37, 141
British Imperial Army, 90
Brown, Christopher, 4
Burma conflict, 175
Bush, George H. W., 87
Bush, George W., 54–55, 121, 148, 169
Bush Doctrine, and Just War tradition, 2, 20

Canada, on human security, 31
casualties: attitude toward, in Vietnam war,
    79; in Battle of Omdurman, 90; correlation
    of planning and noncombatant, 122; and
    Doctrine of Double Effect, 117; U.S. military
    (1861–2011), 83–84, 84t
casualty aversion, and rethinking Just War
    tradition, 3, 9–10, 79–80, 83, 86–87
Catholic Church, 3, 19–21, 130
Central Intelligence Agency (CIA), 83, 105, 169
Chan, David K., 141
Chisholm, Roderick, 135–36
Christianity, and development of Just War
    theory, 168
Christian theology, on legitimate authority, 19
Churchill, Winston S., 90
CIA (Central Intelligence Agency), 83, 105, 169
Cicero, 49–50, 52–53, 56
civilian contractors. *See* private military
    companies (PMCs)

civilians: and beautiful soul trope, 148–56; and ethics of just war theorizing, 156–59; gendered victimization of, 151–53. *See also* noncombatants

civil wars, 55, 63, 176

Clarke, Victoria, 113n21

Clausewitz, Carl von, 65, 151, 156

Clinton, Bill, 55, 120, 148

closeness, and DDE, 139–41

COIN (counterinsurgency field manual), 40

Cold War, as deterrence strategy, 36, 119–21

collateral damage, 105–6, 109–10, 117, 123

colonialism, 19–20, 35, 90–91, 157

communication, and cross-cultural competency, 42

community living, 23, 26, 41–42

conflict management, 42, 168–69

Constantine, and Christian Just War tradition, 168

Conventional Prompt Global Strike (CPGS), 115–16, 118–23, 127

cosmopolitanism, and R2P, 53

counterinsurgency field manual (COIN), 40, 92–93

Counter-Terrorist Center, 105

CPGS (Conventional Prompt Global Strike), 115–16, 118–23, 127

crimes against humanity, 41, 56. *See also* war crimes

cross-cultural competencies, 41–42

Darfur crisis, and AU intervention, 56

DARPA (Defense Advanced Research Projects Agency), 121

Davidson, Donald, 135

decision making, 104–5, 124–25, 155–56

Defense Advanced Research Projects Agency (DARPA), 121

democracy / democratic states, 4, 18, 20, 26

democratic peace, and human security, 31

deprivation, and R2P, 52

Der Derian, James, 89

Desert Shield, as casualty averse, 79

Desert Storm, as casualty averse, 79, 84t, 87

deterrence concept, 36, 118–21

Devine, Philip E., 140

diplomacy, as Cold War strategy, 36

discrimination principle: and CPGS, 115–16, 118–23; and *jus in bello*, 116–18

Doctrine of Double Effect (DDE): and diagram of standard reasoning, 132; ethics of, 11–12, 131–33; and harm as means to good, 141,

143; and I/F distinction, 131–33, 136–42; and noncombatant casualties, 102, 117, 131–33 (*see also* intent); Pauline foundation of, 141

Doe, Samuel, 68

drones, 89, 103. *See also* unmanned aerial vehicles (UAVs); weapons / weapons systems

duality, of authority and legitimacy, 18–21

Duff, Antony, 136–37

Duff, R. A., 138–39

duty to protect, 48–50, 52–58. *See also* Responsibility to Protect (R2P) doctrine

ECOMOG (Economic Community of West African States Monitoring Group), 69

Economic Community of West African States Monitoring Group (ECOMOG), 69

education of military, 40–41

EIR (Ethics and International Relations), and DDE, 12, 131

Eldredge, Niles, 167–68

Elshtain, Jean Bethke, 2–4

Enlightenment era, and social contract, 33

environmental security, 33

EO (Executive Outcomes), 63–64, 67–73

ethical conduct: and civilian/combatant dichotomy, 156–59; as high bar for security sector agencies, 37–38; and *jus ad bellum* principle, 177; and *jus post bellum* restraints, 176–77; as new knowledge for military members, 41; and nuclear retaliation, 119–20; and prudential criteria, 62–63; theoretical roots of, 33–34; and UAVs, 98–99; and witness accounts, 158

Ethics and International Relations (EIR), and DDE, 12, 131

ethnic cleansing, 24, 51

European Security Strategy, 39

European Union (EU), on human security, 31, 39–40

Executive Outcomes (EO), 63–64, 67–73

feminism, and reconstruction of Just War theorizing, 17, 149, 151–52, 154–55

Finland, 36

food security, 33

Foot, Philippa, 139–40

foreign language skills, as expectation for military education, 40

Forrestal, James, 170

freedom, notions of, 26, 32–33, 45, 52

Fricker, Miranda, 18, 21–22, 26

friendly fire, 83–84, 102, 106

Gaddafi, Muammar, 24
gender: and intentional civilian victimization, 151–52; and noncombatant immunity, 149–50, 152–53
Geneva Conventions: and Amelioration of the Condition of the Wounded, 174; and humanitarian law, 80–82, 91–92, 172; 1949 formulation of, 172, 175; and 1977 expansion of legitimate authority, 19, 24
genocide, 24, 51, 55–56, 71, 167
Genocide Convention, 175
Gentili, Alberico, 3, 50–51
Giddens, Anthony, 85
Global War on Terrorism, 10, 20, 98, 108–11, 120–21, 126, 177. See also warfare
Gould, Stephen Jay, 168
Gray, Chris H., 79
Greek warriors, as heroic, 88
Grew, Joseph C., 170
Gross, Michael, 4
Grotius, Hugo, 34, 50, 168
Gulf War, 79–80, 87–90

Hanson, Victor D., 88–89
Hauerwas, Stanley, 2
health security, 33
Held, Virginia, 4, 18, 25
Herring, George, 87
Herz, John H., 99–100, 102–3, 109
Hills, Alison, 137–38, 140–41
Hobbes, Thomas, 168, 175
Holy Roman Empire, 19
holy war tradition, 19, 167
hostile intent, 122
HRW (Human Rights Watch), 122
humanitarian intervention: assigning obligation to, 53–57; in Cicero's On Duties, 49; as duty, 8, 33, 48–49, 60n26; and individual soldiers, 61n46; as morally obligatory, 48, 50–53, 57–58; and R2P doctrine, 48, 51–52; UN adoption of, 19, 33
humanity: and Bellum Civile / Bellum Romanum, 91; crimes against, 41, 56; and intervention, 48–49, 51; postmodern context of, 104
human relations, 38, 40–41
human rights: and duty to protect, 8, 33, 48–49, 51–52; and jus post bellum principles, 172–74, 177–78; Just War tradition of, 171; protection of, as moral duty, 57; subordinated in wartime, 172–73; and UN Charter, 174–75

Human Rights Watch (HRW), 122
human security, 31–34, 39, 43, 177. See also security
Human Security Response Force, 39
Human Terrain System (U.S.), 40

ICC (International Criminal Court), 32
ICISS (International Commission on Intervention and State Sovereignty), 32–33, 48, 52
identity power, as subspecies of social power, 22–24
ideology, as secular religion, 85–86
I/F (intention/foresight) distinction, 131–33, 136–43, 146n60
IHL (International Humanitarian Law), 80–82, 91–92. See also Geneva Conventions
immunity principle, 9, 12, 98, 116–17, 149–50, 152–57, 159
income security, 33
India, peacekeeping role of, 36
Indochina (Vietnam) War, 79, 82–90, 84t
injustice, 21–26
institutionalization, and duty to protect, 55–58
intent: and DDE, 133–38; direct versus oblique, 134–38; governing principles of, 135–36; hostile, 122; moral significance of, 138–42; philosophical views of, 133–38; vis-à-vis desiring, 141
intention/foresight (I/F) distinction, 131–33, 136–43, 146n60
International Commission on Intervention and State Sovereignty (ICISS), 32–33, 48, 52
international community, and human security paradigm, 31, 34
International Court of Justice, and nuclear weapons debate, 118–19
International Covenant on Civil and Political Rights, 172
International Criminal Court (ICC), 32
International Humanitarian Law (IHL), 80–82, 91–92. See also Geneva Conventions
International Relations (IR), 12, 21–22, 24–26, 131
intervention. See humanitarian intervention; military intervention
IR (International Relations), 12, 21–22, 24–26, 131
Iran, threat-assessment for airstrikes against, 123
Iran Air Flight 655, 104
Iraq War, 23, 80, 84t, 169, 173, 176

Isaacs, Arnold R., 85
Islam, radical, and Western democracies, 20

Japan, on human security, 31
Johnson, James Turner, 65
jus ad bellum principle: and assessment
of adversary's strengths, 63, 71–73; and
dual nature of authority/legitimacy, 18–
21; and human security paradigm, 31; and
moral agency, 98–99; and performance of
protection, 150–51; and PMCs, 8–9, 62–73;
and reasonable chance of success criterion,
62, 64–66, 71–73; and territoriality, 98–99;
and transition to *jus post bellum*, 169
jus in bello principle: and challenge of
risk-free warfare, 79–97; and DDE, 133;
and discrimination principle, 115–18; and
experience-based theorizing, 158; and
moral agency, 98–99; and PMCs, 72;
and proportionality principle, 115–18; and
relational subjects, 157–58; and territoriality,
98–99
jus post bellum principle: critique of, 174–
77; definition and defense of, 170–73;
development of, 168–70; and intrastate/
nonstate actors, 176; and just peace, 12;
and Just War tradition, 177–78; and moral
agency, 98–99; as post–Iraq War, 169; and
territoriality, 98–99; transition to, from
jus ad bellum, 169; and World War II
rehabilitation, 175
Just and Unjust Wars (Walzer), 4, 167
just cause, 32, 63–66, 71, 152–53
justice, and human rights, 52, 173–75
just peace tradition, 169
just warrior tradition, 149–50
Just War theory/tradition: and aggressor-
defender paradigm, 35; and Bellum Civile /
Bellum Romanum, 91; and Catholic moral
theology, 130; and changes in security
sector, 30; and civilian immunity principle,
149–50, 152–56; as without civilians,
156–59; and conflation of sovereignty, 6;
criteria for, 19, 48–50; and DDE criteria,
131–33; development of, 167–69, 171–
72; and epistemic injustice, 21; and
gender hierarchy tradition, 153–55; and
humanitarian intervention principles,
48; and human rights, 172; and human
security, 33–34; and IHL, 80; and *jus
post bellum*, 177–78; and killing in war,
80–90; marginalization of, 3–6, 72–73,

82–90; and moral agency, 49–50, 81,
98–99; and nuclear strategies, 118–23;
peace as objective of, 172; as performative,
149; postmodern challenges to, 108–11;
as predating Westphalian system, 73; and
prudential principle, 62–63; and reasonable
chance of success, 62–63, 71–72; and
reciprocity threshold, 92–93; and relational
subjects, 157–58; and right intention
principle, 101–2; and rise of PMCs, 72–73;
and technological superiority, 82–90; and
territoriality, 98–99; three parts of, 171;
universalization of, 91; U.S. paradox of,
91–92; and Western superiority, 4

Kaag, John, 107
Kaldor, Mary, 39
Kant, Immanuel, 140
Kaufman, Whitley, 107
Kenny, Anthony, 134
killing in war, 80–82, 104–11
Killion, Thomas, 89
Kissinger, Henry, 79
Kitchener, Horatio, 90
Kochi, Tarik, 4, 18, 25–26
Korean War, 36, 84t
Kosovo, 36–37, 51, 80–81, 83, 84t, 148

Law, Charles, 89
Laws of War, 80, 88, 91–92, 133
Leahy, William, 170
Lebanon, 4, 84t
legitimacy / legitimate authority: defined,
18–19; dual nature of, 18–21; and epistemic
bias, 7, 17–29; expansions of, 19–20; moral
versus legal, 22–23; and nonstate actors,
17–29; as resting on righteousness and piety
(Augustine), 20; as secular (Luther), 21; as
sovereign (Augustine / Thomas Aquinas),
19–21; and territoriality, 99; Walzer's view
of, 20
liberal hermeneutic, critique of, 20
Liberia, U.S. special relationship with, 54–55
Libya, 24, 89
Liddell-Hart, B. H., 172
livelihood capacity, 42
local populations, 41
Lockean thought, and 1977 Additional
Protocols, 24
London School of Economics, 39
Luther, Martin, 21
Luttwak, Edward N., 86

Mahdi Militia (Iraq), 108
Mandela, Nelson, 24
Manichean vision, and liberal hermeneutic, 20
Maritain, Jacques, 59n19
Maronite Christians, of Lebanon, 4
masculinity, and just warrior tradition, 149–50, 153–55
Mayer, Jane, 105
McCaffrey, Barry, 87
mercenary forces. *See* private military companies (PMCS)
Miele, Alfred, 134, 142
military contractors. *See* private military companies (PMCS)
military education, and cross-cultural competence, 40–41
military intervention: and cross-cultural considerations, 42–43; as just response of last resort, 52; and R2P, 48; and sovereignty, 102
military organizations, 35–43
military roles, 8, 30, 34–35
Miller, David, 53
mineral exploitation (mining), and PMC contracts, 68–69
moral agency: ambiguity of, 106–8; and asymmetrical warfare, 82–90; components of, 100–101; confounded in perpetual warfare, 104–11; and DDE Utilitarian-Absolutist split, 138–39; individual and collective, 101; and intention, 106–7; and Just War tradition, 98–102; postmodern challenges to, 108–11; and prudential criteria for *jus ad bellum*, 62–64; and responsibility, 142–43
moral legitimacy, 17–18, 21–22, 80
moral philosophy, on intentionality, 133–38
Morgenthau, Hans, 103
mutuality, 3–4, 6–7
mutual risk, and reciprocity principle, 81

nationalism, 86, 99, 150
nationality, moral relevancy of, 53
National Patriotic Front of Liberia, 68
NATO (North Atlantic Treaty Organization), airstrike criteria for, 122
natural law, and legitimate authority, 19
netcentric warfare. *See* Vietnam War
New World, and intervention theories, 50
Nickel, James, 52
Nixon, Richard, 85
non-aggression, codified in international law, 19

non-aligned countries, as peacekeepers, 36
noncombatants: and asymmetrical warfare, 79, 81, 105, 118–23; and DDE, 130–33; and gender immunity, 149–50; HRW report on Afghanistan casualties, 122; and immunity principle, 12, 116–17; as intentional objects, 140–41
non-intervention, codified in international law, 19, 50–51
nonstate actors, 25, 52, 176
North Atlantic Treaty Organization (NATO), airstrike criteria for, 122
North Korea, 123
nuclear weapons, and *jus in bello* criteria, 10–11, 118–23
Nuremberg war crimes trials, 175
Nussbaum, Martha, 53

Obama, Barack, 51, 102, 105, 115–16, 121, 148
obligation to intervene. *See* humanitarian intervention
occupation, as intermediate phase of warfare, 169
oil exploration, by PMCS, 68
Okros, Al, 45–46n20
On Duties (Cicero), 49–50, 52–53, 56
O'Neill, Onora, 53–55
Operation Desert Storm, 79, 84t, 87
Operation Geronimo, 102
Orend, Brian, 171

Pakistan, 89, 102
Paul, Saint, and DDE, 141
peace, 172, 174
peace agreements, 69–70, 174
peacekeeping, as role for non-aligned countries, 36
Peace of Westphalia, 21. *See also* Westphalian system
Peet, Jessica, 12
Persian armies, 88–89
personality / social pathology, as military education subjects, 41
personal security, 33
perspective taking, and cross-cultural competence, 42
Peterson, V. Spike, 153
philosophers of law, on intention, 134
Philosophically Sophisticated Terror Bomber (PSTB), 140–41
Plato, on legitimate authority, 17–19
PMCS. *See* private military companies (PMCS)

political authority, and epistemic bias, 17–29.
See also legitimacy / legitimate authority

political violence, and hermeneutical injustice, 24–26

postcolonial era, and 1977 Protocol Additional Geneva Conventions, 19

posthuman warfare, and postmodern military, 89–90

postmodern America, and risk aversion, 86, 88

power concept, and assessment of adversary's capabilities, 63, 71–72

private military companies (PMCs): and aftermath of contract work, 69; and assessment of power/success, 63–66, 70–73; development of market for, 66–68; Executive Outcomes (EO), 63–64, 67–68; as freelance contractors, 72–73; and reasonable chance of success, 8–9, 62–75; and related mining/mineral companies, 68–69; Sandline, 69–70; services provided by, 67, 71; Singer's typology of, 66–67; spear analogy of, 66–67

procedural authority: defined, 18; and moral credibility, 22–23. *See also* legitimacy / legitimate authority

Project on Defense Alternatives, 122

proportionality principle: and CPGS, 115–16, 122–23; and DDE, 131–33; and *jus in bello*, 116–18

Protocol Additional Geneva Conventions (1977), 19

prudential principle, as *jus ad bellum* criterion, 62–64

PSTB (Philosophically Sophisticated Terror Bomber), 140–41

Qaeda, al, and territoriality, 102

Quadrennial Defense Review (U.S.), 40, 89–90, 115–16, 121

Quinn, Warren S., 140–41

rape, as associated with male dishonor, 151–52

Reagan, Ronald, and countercontrol nuclear strategy, 120

reasonable chance of success criterion: continuous assessment of, 71–73; future of, and privatized conflicts, 69–73; as moral principle, 64; and PMCs, 64–66, 70–73; as prudential consideration, 64; and Sierra Leone, 70–73

reciprocity (mutual risk) principle: in age of colonialism / European empire, 91; and

asymmetrical warfare, 80–82; post–Vietnam War, 82–90

relationship building, and cross-cultural competence, 42

religion, embedding of, in American psyche, 85–86

remote weapons. *See* unmanned aerial vehicles (UAVs); weapons / weapons systems

Rengger, Nicholas, 2, 5

responsibility, and intention, 134–35, 142–43

Responsibility to Protect (R2P) doctrine, 8; and allocation of duty to intervene, 53–57; and expansion of legitimate authority, 19; focus of, on prevention of crises, 58; and humanitarian intervention, 48; and human security, 31; limits to costs of, 56–57; and new vision of security, 32–33; and sovereignty, 6

Revolutionary United Front (RUF), and Sierra Leone's civil war, 63, 66, 68–73

risk aversion: and asymmetrical warfare, 80–90, 92–93, 102, 105, 118–23; of European colonial powers, 90–92; of postmodern America, 86, 88–90

robots. *See* unmanned aerial vehicles (UAVs)

Roman Catholic Church. *See* Catholic Church

Roosevelt, Franklin D., 170

R2P. *See* Responsibility to Protect (R2P) doctrine

RUF (Revolutionary United Front), and Sierra Leone's civil war, 63, 66, 68–73

Rumsfeld, Donald, 173

Rwanda: civil war in, 55; genocide in, and Just War criteria, 50–51

Sandline (PMC): and EO, 69; and Sierra Leone countercoup, 69–70

Sankoh, Foday, 68

Scanlon, T. M., 138

scholarship, on human security, 31

Schott, Robin May, 157–58

security: and conceptual change, 30–34; defined, 32–33, 37–38; environmental, 33; in EU, 31, 39–40; European Security Strategy, 39; health, 33; human, 31–34, 43; humanitarian, 35; income, 33; and *jus in bello* ethics, 158–59; and legacy ideas, 43; personal, 33; and R2P principle, 32; shifts in understanding of, 34–35; threats to, 33–34

security sector agencies, 37–43

self-defense, as states' procedural authority, 19

self-preservation, and Grotius's view of
intervention, 50
September 11, 2001, and arguments for
intervention, 51
Sharkey, Noel, 107
Shaw, Martin, 137
Shearer, David, 69
Shue, Henry, 52, 54–55, 57
Sidgwick, Henry, 134–35, 142
Sierra Leone, use of PMCs, 63–64, 66–73
Singer, Peter W., 5, 66–67, 109
sobels (epithet), 68
social contract concept, 33
social organization, as cross-cultural
consideration, 42
social power, and epistemic injustice, 22
Somalia, 36, 84t, 89
South African apartheid, 24
sovereign states: and *jus post bellum* principle,
176; and legitimate authority, 18–21, 35;
and mutuality, 6; as privileged actors, 23;
as secular, 21; as security actors, 34;
versus substate actors, 21; as Westphalian
insiders, 17
sovereignty: and legitimacy, 26; as outmoded
for Just War principles, 177; and
responsibility, 45n15; and technology, 100;
and territoriality, 99–100; Thomas Aquinas's
view of, 20–21
Soviet Union, and Cold War strategies, 119–20
Sri Lanka, 24
statehood, conflation of, 4–6
states: autonomous, 20, 22, 100–101, 104; as
gendered, 15; as key security actors, 34;
priority of duties to protect, 52–53, 55;
right of non-intervention versus intervention,
51–52
Stern, Maria, 17
Stimson, Henry, 170
Strasser, Valentine, 68–69
Strategic Bomber (SB), and DDE, 132–33,
140–41
Strategic Resource Corporation, and EO, 68
substate actors, 17–18, 20–21, 23–26
success of just war, and principle of last resort,
64–66
Sverdlik, Steven, 134, 142
Sweden, peacekeeping role of, 36
Sylvester, Christine, 158
symmetry of combatants, and Just War
tradition, 81–82
Syria, 148

Taliban, 102, 176
Tamilese, versus Sri Lankan state, 24
Tan, Kok-Chor, 54
targeted killing, 104–11
Taylor, Charles, 68
technology: and asymmetrical warfare, 82–85,
88–90; and transformation of power centers,
99–100; weapons, and moral agency, 104–11
Teitel, Ruti G., 175
Tenet, George, 169
territoriality, 99–100, 102–4, 108–11, 112n12
Terror Bomber (TB), and DDE, 132–33, 140–41
terrorism: defined, 25; difficulty in defining,
176; and epistemic bias, 24; and facial
recognition of UAVs, 103; as subjective term,
24–25. *See also* Global War on Terrorism
Thirty Years War, and Peace of Westphalia, 21
Thomas Aquinas, Saint: and DDE, 131, 143; on
jus post bellum, 169; on legitimate authority,
19–21, 34; on self-defense, 131; and social
contract principle, 33–34
Thomism. *See* Thomas Aquinas, Saint
threat assessment, and proportionality, 123
Tilly, Charles, 34–35
Total Force policy, of U.S. military, 86
True, Jacqui, 17
Truman, Harry S., 169–70

UAVs (unmanned aerial vehicles), 10, 89, 98–
99, 102–4
United Nations (UN): Blue Helmets as
legitimate authority, 19; codifies Westphalian
norms, 19; Genocide Convention, 175; on
human security concepts, 31; ICC, 32; 1998
Rome Statute, 32; 1977 Protocol Additional
Geneva Conventions, 19; peacekeeping
forces, Chapter VI mandates, 36; R2P
doctrine, 19; 2005 World Summit document,
32–33; Universal Declaration of Human
Rights, 51, 175
United Nations Charter on human rights,
174–75
United Nations Security Council (UNSC), 19,
56, 171–72
United States: as confounding moral agency,
104–8; effects of Vietnam War on, 85;
hot pursuit agreement of, with Pakistan,
102; military casualty figures of, 84t;
military mission/role of, 40–41; and moral
justification for risk-free war, 79–97; as
postheroic, 86; as privileged actors, 23; rise
of postmodern society of, 86

universal freedom from want/fear, 32–33
unmanned aerial vehicles (UAVS), 10, 89, 98–99, 102–4
UNSC (United Nations Security Council), 19, 56, 171–72
U.S. Civil War, casualties, 84t
U.S. Defense Department, Quadrennial Defense Review, 40, 89, 115–16, 121
U.S. military: and Air Force technology, 89–90, 115–16, 121; airstrike criteria for, 122; Army/Marine COIN of, 40, 73, 92–93; Global Strike Concept of, 115–16, 121; Human Terrain System of, 40; as postmodern/postheroic, 88–90; post-1973 reforms of, 86–87; and UAV pilot stress, 103
Utilitarians, 134–35, 138

Vattel, Emer de, 50
Vietnam Syndrome, and Weinberger Doctrine, 87–88
Vietnam War, 79, 82–90, 84t
violence: and conceptual shifts of security sector, 30; monopoly on, challenged by substates, 25; varieties of, 25–26

Walzer, Michael: on definition of success, 65; on identity prejudice, 23; *Just and Unjust Wars*, 4, 167; on legitimacy/authority, 18; on moral agency, 101; on noncombatants, 105; on obligation to intervene, 53; on sovereign state authority, 20; supreme emergency concept of, 176; on UAV pilot stress, 103
war crimes: and asymmetrical warfare, 81; and collateral damage, 105–6; as defined by winners, 173; global attention to, 41; against humanity, 41, 56; Nuremberg trials for, 175; postmodern challenges to identification of, 110–11
warfare: asymmetrical risk-free challenge of, 80–90, 102, 105, 118–23; evolution of, 11, 88, 90, 99–100; offensive versus defensive, 35; as perpetual, 102–4; phases of, 169, 175–76;

as postheroic/postmodern, 88–90; push-button (Morgenthau), 102; and territoriality, 99–100. *See also* Global War on Terrorism
War on Terrorism, 10, 20, 98, 108–11, 120–21, 126, 177
weapons / weapons systems: Aegis Combat System, 104; ancient, 88; ArcLight missile system, 121; autonomous/unmanned, 88–90, 98–99, 104–8; ballistic missiles, 115–16; conventional versus nuclear, 11; CPGS, 115–16, 118–23; Davy Crockett missile, 121; hypersonic conventional missiles, 115, 123–26, 128n16; as legacy items, 43; Maxim machine gun, 90; nuclear, 115–16; and postmodern moral agency, 104–11; predator drones, 89; and sliding scale of autonomy, 104; Trident missiles, 121, 128n14. *See also* unmanned aerial vehicles (UAVS)
Weinberger Doctrine, 86–88
Westphalian system: critique of, 4; and epistemological injustice, 17, 21–24; and global war on terrorism, 108–11; and hegemony of, 25–26; and legitimate authority, 19, 21; maintained by privilege and power, 23; national military model of, 71; and social power, 22; and substate groups, 24–25
Wilcox, Lauren, 103
Williams, John, 99, 108–9
Wills, Garry, 173
Wilson, Woodrow, 172
women, as civilian beautiful souls, 150–51
World Trade Organization (WTO), and U.S. financial interests, 23
World War I, U.S. casualties in, 84t
World War II: and *jus post bellum* principle, 175; U.S. casualties in, 84t; and U.S. Just War theorizing, 170
WTO (World Trade Organization), and U.S. financial interests, 23

Yemen, posthuman weapons against, 89